COLLABORATIVE AI

Artificial Intelligence, Expertise, and Pedagogy in English Language Teaching

Joshua M. Paiz

Collaborative AI offers a timely and practical roadmap for educators navigating the challenges and opportunities of teaching in an AI-rich world. Grounded in the principles of ethical integration and human-centered pedagogy, this book introduces the concept of "Collaborative AI" – a framework that emphasizes the productive partnership between human educators and AI systems. Rather than replacing teachers, AI is positioned here as a tool to enhance language instruction, streamline assessment, and personalize learning while safeguarding professional autonomy and student agency.

Written for TESOL professionals, applied linguists, teacher educators, and instructional designers, this book blends accessible explanations of AI technologies – generative AI, natural language processing, machine learning – with real-world examples, pedagogical strategies, and policy guidance. Joshua M. Paiz covers key issues such as digital equity, data ethics, academic integrity, and professional development, offering concrete suggestions for classroom use and institutional planning.

Across nine chapters, *Collaborative AI* guides readers through the history, potential, and pitfalls of AI in English language teaching, concluding with an optimistic yet critical call for educators to lead the way in shaping responsible and inclusive AI practices. This is a must-read resource for anyone seeking to integrate emerging technologies into language education while keeping pedagogy, ethics, and learner well-being at the center.

JOSHUA M. PAIZ is assistant dean for technology, trades, business, and hospitality at Frederick Community College, and has 15 years of classroom experience in English language teaching and teacher education.

JOSHUA M. PAIZ

Collaborative AI

Artificial Intelligence, Expertise, and Pedagogy in English Language Teaching

UNIVERSITY OF TORONTO PRESS
Toronto Buffalo London

Toronto Buffalo London
utppublishing.com
Printed in Canada

ISBN 978-1-0498-0025-7 (paper)
ISBN 978-1-0498-0027-1 (EPUB)
ISBN 978-1-0498-0026-4 (UPDF)

Library and Archives Canada Cataloguing in Publication

Title: Collaborative AI : artificial intelligence, expertise, and pedagogy in English language teaching / Joshua M. Paiz.
Names: Paiz, Joshua M., author
Description: Includes bibliographical references and index.
Identifiers: Canadiana (print) 20250266032 | Canadiana (ebook) 20250266067 | ISBN 9781049800257 (paper) | ISBN 9781049800264 (PDF) | ISBN 9781049800271 (EPUB)
Subjects: LCSH: English language – Computer-assisted instruction for foreign speakers. | LCSH: English language – Study and teaching – Technological innovations. | LCSH: Artificial intelligence – Educational applications. | CSH: English language – Computer-assisted instruction for second language learners.
Classification: LCC PE1128.3 .P35 2026 | DDC 428.0078/563—dc23

Cover design: Greg Jorss

The manufacturer's authorised representative in the EU for product safety is Mare Nostrum Group B.V., Mauritskade 21D, 1091 GC Amsterdam, The Netherlands. Email: gpsr@mare-nostrum.co.uk.

We wish to acknowledge the land on which the University of Toronto Press operates. This land is the traditional territory of the Wendat, the Anishnaabeg, the Haudenosaunee, the Métis, and the Mississaugas of the Credit First Nation.

University of Toronto Press acknowledges the financial support of the Government of Canada, the Canada Council for the Arts, and the Ontario Arts Council, an agency of the Government of Ontario, for its publishing activities.

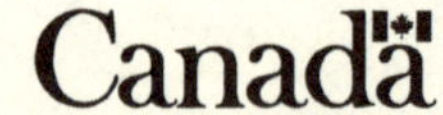

Contents

Preface: AI Transparency Statement

A common worry that I hear in training workshops, interdepartmental meetings, and professional blogs – and, make no mistake, I feel it is an entirely justified one – is that with the advent of generative AI, we're entering uncharted ethical territory. How are we, as human readers, to decide what information we encounter is worth our time? If we read to engage with the ideas of our (human) peers, how can we decide that a text is derived from human cognition and not simply the (semi-)automated output of an AI agent? If you prefer a more optimistic reading of these discourses, we could ask ourselves what the professional ethics should be around using this new cognitive and compositional affordance. This transparency statement is, therefore, my attempt at transparency and modeling. Table P.1 below shows the AI agents that I used during the composition of this manuscript and a summary of how they were deployed.

Table P.1 Deployed AI Agents and Compositional Uses

AI Agent	Use in the Composition Process
Chat GPT-4	Chat GPT-4 is a generative AI and was used to receive preliminary feedback on style/clarity, generate possible outlines for chapters, and to help revise/clarify certain passages.
Google Gemini	Google Bard is a generative AI and was used to receive preliminary feedback on style/clarity and to generate possible outlines for chapters.
Perplexity.ai	Perplexity.ai is a generative AI that was used during research and planning to help with resource discovery.
Grammarly Pro	Grammarly Pro, an assistive AI, was used during editing and revision to improve clarity and grammaticality, as well as to improve tone and style.

List of Abbreviations

AES	Automated essay scorer
AI	Artificial intelligence
AIED	AI in education
AGI	Artificial general intelligence
EAL	English as an additional language
EAP	English for academic purposes
EFL	English as a foreign language
ELL	English language learner
ELT	English language teaching
ESL	English as a second language
ESP	English for specific purposes
GPT	Generative pre-trained transformer
IEP	Intensive English program
ITS	Intelligent tutoring system
L2	Second language
LLM	Large language model
LMS	Learning management system
ML	Machine learning
NLP	Natural language processing
SLA	Second language acquisition
TESOL	Teaching English to Speakers of other languages, also TESOL International Association

COLLABORATIVE AI

1

An Introduction to AI: A General Guide for Human Educators

In late November 2022, generative artificial intelligence (AI) blasted into the public consciousness (Lock, 2022) when OpenAI made a beta (or testing) version of their soon-to-be popular ChatGPT to the general public across the majority of the globe (OpenAI, 2023a). Almost immediately, the social – and, soon after, traditional – media were aflame, running story after story on positive and negative topics. In the early days, stories ranged from asking if generative AI would replace you at work (Devlin, 2023), how to incorporate AI into workflows ethically (Chen, 2022), what generative AI means for how we build and maintain trust (Haven, 2022), whether or not schools should ban generative AI for students, teachers, or both (Roose, 2023), questioning just how smart (or dumb) generative AI agents *really* are (Bogost, 2022), pondering how culturally and linguistically inclusive generative AI could be(come) (Walker Rettberg, 2022), to a whole slew of other topics both pedestrian and domain-specific. And I will not deny the exigence for all this media attention. For the first time in recent memory, a tech innovation that seemed immensely powerful and paradigm-shifting landed in the public's lap with relatively little fan fair or build-up. However radical generative AI agents like ChatGPT may feel, they are part of a long lineage of incremental research and development, and many of the topics that were bubbling to popular attention in the winter of 2022/2023 have been talked about in computer and data sciences since at least the 1940s (see Crawford, 2021; Mitchell, 2019; Pasquale, 2020). What had once been a niche topic for AI, machine learning (ML), and natural language processing (NLP) researchers suddenly became a very real public matter.

And, speaking honestly, that is the reason for this book. Not only as a species but as a discipline, we have come face-to-face with a tool that could have profound implications for what we do as professionals of research and practice. And, unlike our colleagues in AI, ML, and NLP, we find ourselves having to have very serious conversations about this disruptive force *in situ* – while the force is present in our daily lives and not while it is just a set of wire diagrams on a whiteboard in some engineering development lab in Silicon Valley. In this first chapter, I aim to demystify AI for you, as even a basic understanding of the underlying technology will be helpful as we conceptualize what its advent means for use as English language teaching (ELT) practitioners, teacher educators, and action researchers.

Artificial Intelligence: A (Quick) Primer

This current section emerges from the recognition that there is a need to "catch up" with the rapid advancement of AI. Before we explore our central query – "How can/will AI impact what we do in ELT?" – laying down some groundwork is crucial. This involves understanding what AI is, how it functions (rest assured, we'll keep the technical jargon to a bare minimum) and identifying two overarching categories to classify different AI systems. My purpose is to arm you with fundamental knowledge (albeit basic compared to computer engineers and data scientists) that will enable you to engage in AI discussions confidently and competently. Moreover, it is intended to assist you in becoming a critical participant in these oral or written conversations.

To put it differently, the capacity to interact with AI systems and engage in critical discourse about them is likely to become an essential social literacy skill. That is, I maintain that this skill may come to be required to participate effectively in broader disciplinary and societal dialogues in the not-too-distant future (Alexander, 2008; Gee, 2015). Furthermore, by providing this foundational knowledge, I will attempt to typify one of the key principles we'll promote when we discuss AI's pedagogical and professional implications in ELT – transparency.

Generally, artificial intelligence is the capability of a machine or a computer algorithm to learn through its experiences, respond to new stimuli, and generate unique outputs, performing tasks that were previously considered a domain solely belonging to human intelligence (see Mitchell, 2019). For instance, assessing whether a given piece of text carries a predominantly positive or negative sentiment was once deemed an ability exclusive to humans. Yet, with the advent of sentiment analysis, we can now train machines to do exactly this. Combined with collaborative and content filtering technologies, this capability has been used to create recommendation systems in platforms like Amazon and Netflix (Liu, 2020).

While the present form of AI might appear revolutionary and potentially intimidating, it is important to note that the aspiration to create machines of this nature has been embedded in computer science and engineering for a considerable duration. Early visionaries such as Charles Babbage – who envisioned modern computers – and Ada Lovelace – brilliant mathematician and contemporary of Babbage who would come to be known as the 'mother' of programming – dreamt of machines performing elaborate tasks, manipulating symbols, and even "thinking" in ways that mirror how humans use language to carry out complex actions and discover new knowledge (Vardi, 2016). Nevertheless, our contemporary understanding of AI is a relatively recent conceptualization.

Addressing the minute intricacies of AI's inner workings is beyond my capabilities as an applied linguist and emerging NLP specialist and developer, but also beyond the needs of this book and its audience of ELT practitioners – for the curious, however, Mitchell's (2019) *Artificial Intelligence: A Guide for Thinking Humans* is very accessible (and thorough). For our purposes, part of what makes discussing AI's workings difficult is that the response varies, heavily contingent on the specific AI model under discussion. Still, it is important to underscore that the workings of present-day AI rely on a combination of several fundamental technologies: machine learning (ML), an AI discipline focused on the capability to learn and progress from experiences without direct programming; neural networks, which replicate the operations of the human brain to decode and manage data; and NLP, enabling AI to handle, interpret, generate, and communicate in human language (Crawford, 2021 Mitchell, 2019). These essential components provide the building blocks for most AI systems today, even though their utilization and application differ across diverse AI models.

Machine learning is a subset of AI that offers the remarkable capability for a computer system to learn from experience, much like human beings do. While traditional programming involves a set of explicit instructions to perform a task, machine learning is different. It is as though the computer becomes a student itself, learning patterns from data it receives, and gradually improving its performance in tasks over time without a human needing to write new code for each new problem it encounters (see Mitchell, 2019; Shalev-Shwartz & Ben-David, 2014). Picture it this way: instead of meticulously writing out step-by-step instructions for a computer to follow, we give the computer a goal and a set of examples of how to reach that goal. It is akin to teaching a child to differentiate between different animals, not by providing a list of explicit characteristics for each animal, but by showing them many pictures of different animals and letting them work out the distinctions themselves.

Just like humans learn from experience, ML algorithms use mathematical models to find patterns in data and learn from them. The more data they encounter, the more they "understand," refining their models and improving their accuracy over time. This automated "learning" process is the essence of machine learning. It gives AI the ability to handle complex tasks that adapt to new situations. It may depend on varying amounts of human intervention and direction (i.e., supervised, unsupervised, and reinforcement learning methods (see Mnih et al., 2015). So, whether it is a language learning app adjusting to a student's proficiency level, or flashy generative AI agent that produces novel output, machine learning is the engine that powers these seemingly 'intelligent' behaviors.

Following our exploration of machine learning, we explore a specific type of machine learning model known as a neural network. This term likely conjures up images of the brain, and rightfully so! Neural networks are designed to imitate the human brain's structure and function, hence the term "neural." Just as our brains consist of interconnected neurons transmitting and processing information, neural networks consist of artificial neurons, or "nodes," that process and pass on information similarly. It may help to imagine the neurons in our brains as a team working together to solve a complex puzzle. Each team member takes a different piece of the puzzle and examines it. They then share their findings with the rest of the team. As each member receives information about other pieces, they can adjust their understanding of their own piece and how it fits into the bigger picture. A neural network operates in much the same way, but with data instead of puzzle pieces.

Neural networks take an input (like an image, a sentence, or any other kind of data), and pass it through a series of hidden layers, each composed of multiple nodes. Every node applies a mathematical function to the information it receives, altering it slightly, before passing it on. By the time the information reaches the output layer, it has been transformed into something meaningful – whether that is recognizing a face in a photo, understanding a spoken command, or any other task the network was designed for (see Mitchell, 2019; Shalev-Shwartz & Ben-David, 2014; Wang et al., 2018). While this might seem complicated, the beauty of neural networks is their adaptability. They learn from errors and adjust their "thinking." For example, suppose a neural network is trained to identify images of cats, and it incorrectly identifies a dog as a cat. In that case, the error will lead to adjustments in the network, making it more accurate in future identifications.

For you as an educator, understanding neural networks is crucial because they form the backbone of many AI tools you might use in your classroom, such as voice recognition, personalized learning tools, certain educational games, and more germane to our discussion here, AI agents that you and your students may choose to deploy to aid in the learning process. By understanding the basics of how they operate, you can better appreciate their capabilities and limitations.

This brings us to the emergence of AI systems such as ChatGPT and Google Bard, which denote a pivotal progression in AI, as they harness the power of large language models (LLMs). LLMs belong to a subset of AI models trained on enormous quantities of textual data sourced mostly from the internet's publicly accessible resources, as well as a substantial collection of specialized documents available in the public domain (Zhao et al., 2023). The revolutionary aspect of these AI models lies in their capacity to factor in the context of a much larger text and assimilate this context – and the relationships between words and phrases – into their comprehension, paving the way for accurate predictions of word sequences to yield coherent outputs, largely in alignment with the Gricean Maxims. It is exactly this ability that separates modern AI from older, older NLP paradigms would have struggled with this because they could not focus their attention on these relationships when encoding the data passed to them. This would lead older models like Bag of Words (BoW) to consider both "live to work" and "work to live" as being functionally the same because they would be vectorized – turned into numbers – to the same value (Vaswani et al., 2017).

For example, ChatGPT leverages the Generative Pre-trained Transformer (GPT), a sophisticated version of neural networks designed to discern relationships between words in sentences and employ this understanding to generate original outputs. A neural network can be envisioned as a web of deeply interconnected nodes, commencing with an input and traversing through multiple hidden layers where calculations based on specific weights and biases lead to an output (Mitchell, 2019). Its goal is to function much like the biological neurons that exist in your brain. If trained properly, neural networks can deliver remarkably accurate outputs for novel inputs. In a metaphorical sense, neural networks can be likened to a river system for data. The river system, or the neural network, provides the path and direction for the data. Transformer models like GPT for ChatGPT and PaLM2 for Google Bard act as the water molecules flowing through this system. They begin their journey from the source (input) and travel across the vast landscape of the neural network (river system), undergoing transformations (processing) along the way and ultimately reaching the destination (output), carrying with them the impact of the journey. This journey through the neural network helps to generate the final, meaningful output. Another aspect that marks GPT and PaLM2 as groundbreaking is their extensive training on hundreds of billions of tokens (Ghahramani, 2023; Zhao et al., 2023).

A Taxonomy of AI Agents

A wide array of different AI agents exists, each with considerable respective scope of capabilities. So, developing a taxonomy allows us to classify AI agents to make decisions about how and when to deploy them during teaching and learning interventions. Here, I will classify AI agents into three possible categories – generative, constructive, and assistive. Below, I will provide a more detailed description of each category, its capabilities, and general use cases. I will also provide examples of some more popular AI agents that would fit into that category. I will end this section by summarizing that information in a more easily accessible tabular form (see also Appendix A for a listing of AI agents organized by use case).

Generative AI

Generative AI are a class of AI agents that create novel outputs based on input from the user. Said another way, generative AI create something new that didn't exist before being prompted by the user. It is important to note that most generative AI agents are highly specialized to produce only a single kind of output – e.g., text, music, video, images, etc. This is because of how generative AI are created and trained. Most generative AI must be highly specialized because of the labor and resources that go into creating and training the underlying models that make them work (Mitchell, 2019; Woolridge, 2021). Take something like the ChatGPT from OpenAI, the generative AI agent perhaps most responsible for rocketing AI from a Sci-Fi plot device to a key component of public discourse. ChatGPT can generate text, and that is about it. For the moment, we will ignore the simple line drawings it can produce, as even these are made solely of text elements called characters or chars in some programming languages, a primitive data type from which more complex ones are created (see Kalb, 2022; Loy et al., 2020). Consider the text you are reading in this e-book. Each word is actually a sequence of individual characters. In computing, each of these characters is stored as a primitive data type, aptly named "characters," or "chars." Now, when these characters are grouped together, they form what we know as a word.

In computing terminology, this grouping is called a "String," a derived data type. And in many computing systems, a String is seen as an array (an ordered series) of characters. This arrangement provides us with the capability to manipulate this String. Much like how we would locate a word on a page in a book, in computing, we can identify and manipulate parts of the String by knowing the location of individual characters within it. This ability to manage and work with groups of characters is a key aspect of how computers handle and understand text.

But processing a text, never mind understanding some aspect of that text, is far from simple. For a generative AI to work, it must be able to do a few things. It must be able to take input from the user, understand the meaning of that input, figure out the user's intention behind providing that input, and then it can finally generate meaningful output that addresses the user's original input. To understand the input from the user, the generative AI agent will need to have been trained on a massive set of data so that it can understand that natural language input. And, to produce meaningful output, it would likewise need to be trained on a massive set of examples to learn how to create that novel output. So, a system like ChatGPT has been trained on some 410 billion tokens (Brown et al., 2020). This means ChatGPT, as an example, has learned to be very adroit at creating text because that is what was used to train it. Since it wasn't trained using images, it cannot produce images. It is almost like it doesn't know that they exist except in some more abstract manner that it may have encountered in texts. So, if we ask a text-based generative AI to produce a picture of a dog, it may be able to provide a compelling text-based description. Still, it will not spontaneously produce a picture of a dog that has never existed before. To produce images, we would need to specially train the AI model on a massive set of images, which is exactly what happened with DALL-E, OpenAI's image-based generative AI. DALL-E was trained on some 12 million images to be able to produce novel images (OpenAI, 2023b). And, to get any one model to be able to do both of these tasks is exceptionally resource intensive when it comes to training and operating the model. If we were to add another output mode, like speech or image generation, it would significantly increase the complexity of the model. The AI would need additional training on relevant data (audio data for speech, image data for images), and the model's architecture might need to be modified to handle the generation of these new types of outputs. Furthermore, interpreting and evaluating the quality of the output in multiple modes can be challenging. We can apply various metrics for text output to evaluate its quality, such as its relevance, fluency, and coherence. For outputs like images or audio, different evaluation methods are needed. And, for each new input/output type we wanted to the AI to be able to parse and create, we would have to create an ever more complicated model, and our training, storage, and compute demands would likewise increase (see Crawford, 2021; Mitchell, 2019). While not insurmountable, and indeed the goal of Artificial General Intelligence (AGI) researchers, it is beyond AI agents' abilities (Roitblot, 2020).

So, no single generative AI agent can do everything. Instead, integrating AI into one's workflows requires us to be aware of these limitations and to deploy tools that meet the demands of the task in which we are engaged. Because of this, it is helpful to further compartmentalize generative AI based on what it can actually produce. One of the most salient sub-categories then will be text-based generative AI, or generative AI, whose primary mode of output is novel text. We can include agents like OpenAI's ChatGPT, Google's Bard, and Perplexity AI in this category. Each of these AI agents will take input from the user and create novel text that had not existed previously. Indeed, because of the random element in generation, providing the same AI with the same prompt doesn't guarantee that the same output will be produced each time. What differentiates these different AI agents is the kind of texts they will produce. ChatGPT and Bard can best be seen as highly flexible models capable of producing output in a wide array of genres. Perplexity, on the other hand, tends to produce more academic texts in the form of summaries and syntheses of other scholarly texts. Meanwhile, something like Salesforce's CTRL is more suited to generating sales emails and product descriptions (Socher, 2019).

Image generation is another sub-category that has received much attention lately (see Diaz, 2023; Weatherbed, 2023). OpenAI's DALLE-2, for example, can take text input from the user to create novel images that range from the whimsical to the hyper-real. Something like Stable Diffusion from Stability AI can do something very similar. Meanwhile, Firefly from Adobe can touch up images, add in missing elements, or even touch up "imperfections," large and small, based on input from the user (Adobe, 2023). There are also AI agents specialized in creating clip-art and stock-art style images (e.g., StockImg AI). Remarkably, AI technology has also been used to create incredibly realistic human faces. Nvidia's ThisPersonDoesNotExist, for instance, utilizes generative adversarial networks (GANs) to generate hyper-realistic faces of non-existent people, a technology that NVidia plans on using to help create new world and gaming experiences (Gadney, 2022; Paez, 2019). While these generated images can be used for a variety of benign purposes such as creating avatars for online games or populating virtual environments, the technology also presents ethical challenges, especially regarding identity and privacy. Even fashion and design is feeling the impacts of image-based generative AI. IBM Research's DRESSformer uses a conditional variational autoencoder (CVAE) to produce fashion design sketches based on text prompts (Harreis et al., 2023), which can be as specific as "a summer dress with floral patterns." This kind of technology has the potential to revolutionize industries, allowing designers to quickly visualize new concepts and opening up new opportunities for personalization and customization.

When it comes to video creation, we're nearing a troubling time with the emergence of AI Deepfakes. We'll revisit this ethical sticking point later, but for now, let us briefly explore what video AI are capable of as a sub-category of generative AI, which has come to impact the video industry significantly, providing novel ways to generate and edit content. Systems like EleutherAI's VQGAN-CLIP have been instrumental in creating AI-generated videos from text prompts, revolutionizing how we think about video production (Crowson et al., 2022). Similarly, platforms like Synthesis AI offer ways to generate hyper-realistic human characters and animations for films, games, and virtual reality environments (Synthesis AI, 2023). These advancements automate tedious editing tasks and offer exciting possibilities for creating new types of visual narratives.

And finally, music was once held as the final bastions of purely human expression, even by AI researchers (see Mitchell, 2019; Pasquale, 2020). However, even the music industry is seeing rapid creation and deployment of generative AI agents. OpenAI's MuseNet, for instance, can compose original pieces in various genres and styles, demonstrating the AI's capacity for creativity and versatility (OpenAI, 2023c). Meanwhile, services like Jukebox, also from OpenAI, generate custom soundtracks by considering factors such as mood, tempo, and genre and can even create "simple singing" (OpenAI, 2023d). More recently, Sony's AI, Flow Machines, has made headlines by producing entire albums and collaborating with artists to create new compositions, potentially transforming how music is created (Sony, 2023). These developments can potentially democratize music production, giving artists new tools to explore and pushing the boundaries of what is musically possible. But, as in art, advancement in this area must be measured against the costs it took to train these AI agents, which often involved petabytes of data, much of it "public" data, where the creators did not have the option to offer consent for their materials to be used as part of AI's training set (Millman, 2023).

Constructive AI

The second class in our taxonomy is comprised of constructive AIs. A constructive AI agent takes input from the user and modifies that input to render some improvement over the original. Here, AI has been part of the correction, revision, and editorial processes for many of us for far longer than generative AI has been stealing headlines, and it may be operating below the level of conscious awareness for the end user. For example, if you've used any Microsoft Office product since about 2016, AI has provided you with feedback on your writing (Lopez, 2016; Toncic, 2020). Or, if you've ever clicked the magic wand icon in your phone's photo app, AI has been used to adjust colors, brightness, and more (Manovich, 2017). So, the key difference between constructive and generative AI is that constructive AI will not necessarily create something wholly new. Instead, it modifies and attempts to approve the input provided by the user to meet some specific goal – better grammaticality and readability, better image composition, cleaner sound quality, etc.

Creating a list of constructive AI agents can be difficult for the above reasons. They are often directly integrated into an existing product that we have already deeply integrated into our workflows – e.g., Microsoft Word, Google Docs – or into our daily lives – e.g., our mobile phones and the panoply of system apps that come preloaded onto them directly from the manufacturer. But stand-alone examples do exist. So, as before, I will now seek to offer you an overview of some of the more popular constructive AI agents that exist at the time of writing by considering their use cases across the same major categories of text, video/image, and sound.

Assistive AI

Assistive AI refers to a special class of AI agents that have either been purpose-built, adapted, or otherwise repurposed to aid individuals with some form of temporary or permanent disability (de Freitas et al., 2022; Hussain Shah et al., 2021). Assistive AI may include commercial solutions, such as Google's *Live Transcribe* service, to help convert speech into text in real time for hard-of-hearing individuals. Or it may rely heavily on machine learning and computer vision to help provide blind individuals the ability to navigate in a sighted world more safely (Yadav et al., 2020). Assistive AI are often paired with specialty medical and assistive devices to provide additional functionality for its users, and as such, tends to represent a significant investment of time and money for the user to obtain (Lenker et al., 2013). This brief definition will suffice for our purposes here because Assistive AI represents a very niche use case and one to which the typical ELT practitioner will have limited exposure. Should you encounter Assistive AI as a regular part of your practice, I would encourage you to partner with your learner or their parent(s), guardian(s), or carer(s) to better understand their Assistive AI and if/how it might interface with your classroom practices.

A General Framework for Collaborative AI

Now that we have our taxonomy of AI agents well in hand, I would now turn our attention (and joint cognition) to a general framework that we can apply to various aspects of ELT practice that we'll discuss throughout the rest of this book. This framework, from which this book takes part of its title, is one grounded in cooperation and joint action and will be referred to as *collaborative AI* (see also Paiz & Yamazaki, 2023). As we venture into the realm of "Collaborative AI," we grapple with the idea of human agents – students, teachers, researchers, parents, among others – not just using, but actively partnering with AI systems. Here, I would encourage you to envision a model, firmly rooted in the humanity of the user, that leverages the power of AI to extend our capabilities, facilitating meaningful, balanced, and transparent interactions between humans and machines. This partnership is guided by eight integral principles: Human-in-the-Loop, Complementarity, Transparency, Algorithmic Fairness, Empowerment, Student-centeredness, Trust, and a Human-first approach. Admittedly, these eight principles will manifest differently as we move through the different contexts and applications upon which we will focus in later chapters; however, I will here offer a base definition of each around which we can begin to organize our cognition as it applies to AI agents and their use in ELT context.

Human-in-the-Loop

Human-in-the-Loop means that a human agent must always be part of the process when deploying AI agents and systems in educational contexts (Office of Educational Technology, 2023) Here, I would echo the researcher at the US Department of Education in advocating for the essential role of the human agent in steering the course of AI-informed decision-making processes. Said another way, human users are not mere passengers on this journey, but active navigators, ensuring that the AI systems that we use do not find themselves operating in an isolating, acontextual vacuum of computation and algorithms or making decisions that are to the detriment of the humans that are on the receiving end. Rather, it is our human judgment, our wealth of experience and insight, that serves as a guiding beacon, grounding the AI's operations in the realities of our shared world. Remember, while modern AI systems may appear quite capable, they are, in essence, tools designed to augment our abilities. Their power lies not in autonomy, but in their capacity to support our actions and decisions with the vast computational abilities at their disposal. Therefore, as we proceed to harness the potential of these AI systems, we must always remember the intrinsic value of human judgment in shaping the direction of AI.

Complementarity

As we probe deeper into exploring the Collaborative AI framework, let us focus on an imperative principle: *Complementarity*. As intriguing as the notions of AI may be, we must keep in mind a cardinal rule – AI is a collaborator, not a substitute (Pasquale, 2020; Kostka & Toncelli, 2023; Paiz & Kostka, 2023). The principle of Complementarity invites us to envision AI as a (semi-)reliable companion as we seek to craft educational encounters that support student learning and success. They exist solely to amplify human skill and expertise and should never been viewed (or worse used) as an autonomous entity to replace it. In essence, AI's role is to augment our inherent capabilities and assist in achieving our pedagogical and classroom goals more effectively and efficiently. In the world of English language teaching (ELT), this means AI systems are not intended to usurp the invaluable role of educators. Instead, they serve as intelligent allies, providing personalized assistance, augmenting learning processes, and freeing educators to focus more on tasks requiring human touch and judgment. Remember that technology is merely a tool; its effectiveness is determined by the hand that wields it. As such, the principle of Complementarity underscores that AI's power lies in its ability to supplement and augment human effort, not replace it. As we proceed through this book, we'll explore how this principle illuminates our understanding of AI and informs its use in an ELT context.

Transparency (Explainable AI)

Continuing on to principle three, let us draw our attention to another crucial principle that lights our way: *Transparency and Explainability*. The AI systems that we deploy in our classrooms and our professional practice should not be enigmatic black boxes but rather should be as a clear crystal cube, each of its actions, decisions, and processes being as lucid as the material it is made of. The significance of *transparency* in AI goes beyond merely understanding the machinery (Lepri et al., 2018; Burrell, 2016); it is about cultivating an environment where AI systems can be interrogated and understood, where their operations are accessible and their decisions comprehensible (Office of Educational Technology, 2023; Pasquale, 2020). Said more simply, transparency is not about understanding the algorithms and models that make an AI "tick"; instead, it is about openness and accessibility as it applies to how AI systems have been trained and how they go about applying that training to decision-making.

Now, consider explainability as the detailed tour guide to our crystal cube. It involves the ability of our AI system to elucidate its actions in a manner that makes sense to us, the thinking humans making use of the AI agent (Khosravi et al., 2021; Mitchell, 2019). When an AI system makes a choice, offers a suggestion, or corrects an error, it should be capable of providing a rationale that you or I could understand. Picture a language-learning AI tool, for instance. It is not enough for it to merely correct a grammatical error made by a student. Ideally, it should explain the reason behind the correction, fostering a learning opportunity for the student or an on-ramp for the human educator to short-circuit the AI feedback loop and override its feedback with something more fitting to the student's needs, abilities, and learning preferences. As we venture deeper into the world of Collaborative AI, we'll continue to unwrap the importance of these principles, exploring how transparency and explainability contribute to making AI not just a tool, but a potential partner in our ELT practice.

Algorithmic Fairness

Turning now to the fourth pillar of our Collaborative AI framework, we explore the thorny issue of *Algorithmic Fairness*. This principle speaks to the idea that our AI collaborators should always strive to make decisions that are unbiased and equitable, untouched by factors such as race, gender, or any other protected characteristics unless they are explicitly relevant and ethically justified (Barocas & Selbst, 2016; Hardt, 2014; Wallach, 2018). In essence, fairness in AI is more than just a desirable attribute; it is a fundamental requirement for any system that aspires to assist in decision-making processes, particularly in the highly personal, human context of English language teaching (see also Akgun & Greenhow, 2022; Office of Educational Technology, 2023).

Why, you may ask, is this so crucial? Well, AI systems, as we have discussed, learn from the real world. And unfortunately, the real world is riddled with biases. Without careful oversight and diligent management, these biases can seep into our AI tools, tainting their outputs and perpetuating unfairness (O'Neil, 2016; Barocas et al., 2013). Therefore, we must be ever vigilant to the risks and remain active in our efforts to ensure our AI collaborators operate in a manner that is just and unbiased. Akin to our previous principles, this notion of Algorithmic Fairness is not simply a technical challenge; it is an ethical one that asks of us as educators, researchers, and practitioners to advocate for fairness and justice in our AI partners. As we wade further into the world of Collaborative AI, we'll further unpack the intricacies of this principle, examining how it can help mold AI from a mere tool to an equitable partner in our ELT endeavors.

Empowerment

Empowerment is a central tenet when we think about the use of AI in any setting, but it is particularly critical in an educational context, where it refers to approaching AI agents and tools as a means of equipping both educators and students with the tools, information, and capabilities to make effective decisions and take actions that benefit their learning or teaching journey (see MLA-CCCC, 2023; Office of Educational, 2023). AI systems, when designed and utilized appropriately, can significantly contribute to this sense of empowerment. They can offer personalized insights and recommendations, facilitate access to resources, automate repetitive tasks, and foster a learning environment that caters to individual needs and preferences. However, it is important to note that this means creators of AI systems must purposefully create them in a way that does not contribute to overriding human agency; rather, it is about providing augmentative support that enables educators and students to exercise their agency more effectively. It means creating systems that respect, and indeed are designed around, the autonomy of the human users. AI should enhance and support human decision-making rather than dictate or limit it.

It is also crucial that the implementation of AI systems does not result in over-reliance on the technology, which could potentially undermine human motivation, creativity, and critical thinking skills. Because of this, I argue that we will increasingly see AI agents and tools become key parts of our sociocognitive apparatus (see Atkinson, 2002), but this does not mean that this emerging cognitive affordance should completely replace that of the user. Key to this, especially when we connect it back to education, is the emergent need for educators to consider how they will purposefully (dis)engage with AI systems in ways that support learners critical (tech) literacy (Orsini-Jones et al., 2021).

Student-Centeredness/Student-First

Student-Centeredness or a *Student-First approach* is a fundamental principle when discussing the use of AI in an educational context. This concept shifts the focus from teaching to learning, placing the student at the heart of educational experiences. In the context of AI, every output, decision, or action arrived at either by AI or through AI tools should be driven by the primary goal of facilitating and enhancing student learning and success. Every element of the AI system – its design, operation, feedback, and even the data it utilizes for learning – should all be geared towards the needs, abilities, goals, and preferences of the student (see also Office of Educational Technology, 2023; Pasquale, 2020). AI systems should not only adapt to each student's unique learning style, but they should also contribute to creating an environment that encourages self-directed learning and fosters intellectual curiosity. The ultimate goal is not just to teach, but to inspire students to become lifelong learners. This doesn't mean that AI should replace the role of human educators. Quite the contrary, the role of educators becomes even more essential in a student-centered model, as they guide students in their learning journey, using AI as a tool to better cater to individual student needs. By maintaining a student-centered approach in our utilization of AI, we can ensure that technology serves us in crafting more enriching, personalized, and effective learning experiences. As we continue to explore the world of Collaborative AI, we should bear in mind the paramount importance of putting our students first.

Trust(, but Verify)

As we journey further into our exploration of Collaborative AI, we find ourselves at the seventh pillar of our framework, the principle of *Trust but Verify*. This principle echoes an age-old wisdom, reminding us that while our AI collaborators can offer novel and insightful output, they can also occasionally fall into the trap of fabricating information or producing misinformation. It is therefore critical that we never take AI-produced information at face value (Kohnke et al., 2023; Rudolph et al., 2023). While modern AI systems, especially generative AI built on massive LLMs, are surprisingly powerful – and can give the appearance of being rather knowledgeable – they are also well known to occasionally make up information in an attempt to fulfill a user request. To call this lying would be to attribute intentionality to a machine system that lacks consciousness, which is perhaps problematic (Evans et al., 2021; Zhou et al., 2023). As unlike humans, AI doesn't possess innate common sense or deeply contextual understanding. It merely simulates these qualities based on the data it is been trained on. So, while it might convincingly generate content that seems accurate, it has no inherent understanding of truth or falsehood. It merely generates what it has learned to generate.

This leads us to the core tenet of this principle – the importance of critical literacy. The ability to critically analyze and evaluate information is paramount when interacting with AI (Kohnke et al., 2023; Kostka & Toncelli, 2023). We must be ever-vigilant, continually questioning and scrutinizing the information that AI systems present to us. Indeed, this critical AI literacy may well come to form the foundation of a new form of technological literacy that will be required of all of us as we inhabit an increasingly AI-rich world (see Pasquale, 2020; Crawford, 2021). So in the grand tapestry of Collaborative AI, the principle of "Trust but Verify" emerges not as a cautionary note but as a beacon, guiding us towards meaningful, productive, and, above all, conscious engagement with AI systems in our teaching practice. As we traverse further into this AI-enriched terrain, we'll see how this principle shapes our understanding of AI and defines its role in our ELT endeavors.

Human-First Approach

Our eighth, and final, guiding principle is that when utilizing AI agents and tools, we must strive for a *Human-first Approach to AI*. As we inch our way into an increasingly AI-infused reality, it is paramount that we keep this principle at the forefront of our minds. As educators, everything that we do should be focused first, and foremost, on our learners and their needs. And, as educational administrators, I would argue that all of our decision-making should be centered around the human stakeholders that populate our institutions. Said more simply, we must always put people – their needs, expertise, experiences, and perspectives – first, even if it means removing (however temporarily) AI systems from the equation. So, what does it mean to be Human-first in the context of AI?

In essence, the Human-first principle holds that AI should serve as an enabler and enhancer of human capabilities, not as a substitute (Pasquale, 2020; Crawford, 2021). The core goal of AI, especially in the context of education, should be to amplify human potential, enrich learning experiences, and support educators and learners in their shared journey of knowledge exploration. This perspective emphasizes the role of AI as a tool in service to humanity, rather than viewing humans as servants to technology. It is all too easy to become entranced by the seemingly magical capabilities of modern AI, to see it as a silver bullet that can solve all educational challenges. But the Human-first principle nudges us back to reality, reminding us that AI, despite its impressive advancements, is not the teacher – we are. It encourages us to value and leverage human expertise, intuition, creativity, and empathy – attributes that, for now, remain distinctly human and are beyond the reach of AI (Evans et al., 2021; Zhou et al., 2023).

Furthermore, this principle cautions against the dehumanization that can come with overreliance on technology. It underscores the need for human oversight, accountability, and critical thinking in the deployment and use of AI systems, especially in a learning environment where the stakes are high, and the impact is profound. This principle, in many ways, serves as a compass, ensuring that as we venture further into the world of Collaborative AI, we remain oriented towards our true north – that is, placing the humanity of learners and educators at the heart of the AI integration process. As we continue to unravel the intricacies of Collaborative AI, we will probe deeper into how this Human-first principle can guide us in creating meaningful, engaging, and truly human learning experiences. In the end, as we navigate this thrilling yet daunting terrain of AI, let us remember, we are not alone. We are collectively, educators, learners, and administrators, stepping into a future where AI stands not as our master, but as our tool – a tool that we wield with the firm grip of human values, ethics, and wisdom.

What to Expect in *Collaborative AI*

With some important background knowledge to help you better understand AI firmly in hand, as well as a taxonomy of AI agents around which to organize our thinking firmly in hand, I would now turn our attention to what you can expect in the upcoming chapters of this book. My goal in providing this overview is to help you, the reader, make an informed decision about how you will engage with this book. Certainly, it would be great if you could read it from cover to cover, but in this busy world, finding the time to do so can be challenging at the very best of times – never mind the significant time crunch that exists for so many ELT practitioners.

In chapter 2, we will explore the role of AI in education, with a focus on English language teaching. The chapter offers a brief history of AI in education, discussing key milestones and developments. This chapter will first focus on the subtle rise of AI for assessment and classroom management before discussing the gradual growth of support AI, like Grammarly, and the advent of powerful generative models like ChatGPT and Dall-e, which are posed to kickstart a revolution for the workplace and private life. It also introduces various AI-driven tools and applications specifically designed for ELT, examining their benefits and limitations. By exploring the emergence of AI in the educational landscape, this chapter sets the foundation for understanding AI's potential to enhance ELT practices and learning experiences. This conversation will be extended in chapter 3, which will explore the practical applications of AI in language learning and teaching, focusing on English language teaching. The chapter discusses how AI-enhanced tools, such as Duolingo for personalized language learning and Grammarly for grammar and writing assistance, can improve discreet language skills like vocabulary acquisition and grammatical competence. It also addresses how to adapt AI tools to accommodate diverse learner needs and preferences, ensuring inclusivity and effectiveness in language learning, helping learners to acquire more complex skills like intercultural competence and critical metacognition. By providing specific examples, the chapter illustrates the potential of AI to transform the ELT landscape and create engaging, differentiated learning experiences.

In chapter 4, our attention will turn more explicitly to pedagogy. It will outline pedagogical approaches for effectively integrating AI into English Language Teaching. It emphasizes the importance of combining human expertise with AI support, ensuring a student-centered learning experience. For instance, the chapter explores the use of the flipped classroom model, where AI tools like Quizlet can be employed for pre-class vocabulary learning while in-class time is dedicated to interactive, collaborative activities led by the teacher. This chapter will demonstrate how pedagogically sound AI integration can enhance teaching practices and improve student outcomes in various ELT contexts. Chapter 5, meanwhile, will move from the day-to-day pedagogical concerns of the practitioner to that of assessment. It focuses on the role of AI in assessment and feedback within the English language teaching context. It highlights AI-driven assessment tools and techniques, such as automated essay scoring systems and adaptive quizzes, that can provide timely, personalized feedback to students. The chapter also explores how AI can enhance the traditional feedback process by assisting teachers in identifying areas for improvement, enabling more targeted and practical guidance, and helping to manage teacher workloads in humane ways that support teacher well-being and student learning. By leveraging AI in assessment and feedback, educators can better support student learning and progress throughout the language acquisition journey.

In chapter 6, we will begin to address the ethical and inclusive considerations of implementing AI in English language teaching. It highlights data privacy and security concerns, exemplified by the need to protect students' personal information when using AI-driven tools. The chapter also emphasizes the importance of promoting digital equity and inclusivity, discussing strategies like incorporating accessible AI technologies for learners with disabilities, and ensuring that AI tools are culturally sensitive and unbiased. This chapter will conclude by discussing AI-related issues in academic integrity as they relate to student success. By tackling these concerns, educators can create a responsible and inclusive learning environment that harnesses the benefits of AI without compromising ethical standards or student learning, and in ways that acknowledge the real threat to academic integrity posed by the unethical, uncritical deployment of AI assistance by learners. This will lead to our discussion on institutional and classroom policy in chapter 7. It provides guidelines for responsible and effective AI integration, considering factors such as privacy, ethical considerations, and pedagogical best practices. The chapter also addresses professional anxieties and concerns that may arise during AI adoption, offering practical advice and strategies for managing the transition. By establishing clear policies and guidelines, educators and administrators can ensure that AI technologies are effectively and responsibly integrated into ELT practices, fostering a collaborative and supportive learning environment.

From here, we will begin to look further ahead to consider both how we prepare future educators and what the near future may hold for ELT and AI. In chapter 8, we will focus on the importance of teacher professional development in the context of AI integration in English language teaching. It outlines strategies for building AI literacy and competence among educators, such as participating in workshops, webinars, and online courses. The chapter also emphasizes the need for continuous professional growth, as the AI landscape evolves rapidly, and encourages educators to stay up to date with the latest advancements and best practices. By prioritizing professional development, teachers can effectively leverage AI tools in the classroom, ensuring that their teaching practices remain relevant and aligned with current educational trends. Chapter 9 concludes by discussing emerging trends and technologies, such as advanced NLP and immersive virtual reality environments, and their potential impact on ELT. For example, increasingly powerful NLP applications could lead to AI-powered chatbots that tailor their communicative style to the ongoing inputs of the learner, tailoring both response content, tone, and style to their needs, further contributing to efforts to provide differentiated instruction. This chapter also highlights the enduring importance of human expertise and emphasizes the need for a collaborative approach, where educators and AI work together to create meaningful learning experiences. By envisioning a future where AI and human expertise complement each other, the chapter concludes with an optimistic outlook on the potential of AI to transform and enhance the field of ELT.

Again, given the seemingly meteoric rise of certain types of AI – Generative AI specifically – it can feel rather daunting to consider the implications of this rapidly changing world and its implications for our work as educational practitioners and language teachers. However, as AI is here – and likely here to stay – there really is no time like the present to dive in and skill-up, two ends that this book will strive to help you achieve.

2

Building an AI-Rich World: AI and Education

Introduction

The rapid advancements in AI, particularly in the form of Generative AI, have catapulted us into uncharted territory, where AI agents such as OpenAI's ChatGPT, Google's Bard, and Anthropic's Claude2 have rocketed into our collective attention and, for some, become an integral part of workflows and professional practice (Luxton, 2014; McKinsey & Company, 2023; Song, 2019). Yet, this AI-rich world is not just about novel tools; it is about the profound potential to redefine educational experiences and empower both educators and learners if properly leveraged by professionals, managed by AI tech companies, and deployed by educational institutions.

In this chapter, we will explore AI's historical presence in education, tracing its roots from early experiments like ELIZA and PARRY to the present-day landscape of AI-driven assessment, classroom management, and support tools (Holmes & Tuomi, 2022; Roll & Wylie, 2016; Woolf, 1991). This investigation will continue by advocating for a critical AI literacy, because of the increasingly AI-rich personal and professional spheres that they will inhabit once they leave our classrooms (McKinsey & Company, 2023). From there, we will turn our attention to the proliferation of increasingly capable language-based AI that fulfills a wide array of roles and uses before discussing the advent of generative AI – the likely impetus for many of you to pick up this volume in the first place. Along the way, this chapter will make connections to ELT classroom practice and educational objectives, underscoring the myriad ways that AI was already always in the background, hovering just outside of the conscious awareness of most practitioners. Understanding the history and development of AI in education generally, and in ELT more specifically, helps us to understand that this is not some radical, unexpected moment in which we currently find ourselves. Instead, it has been slowly creeping up on us. And, many of us, the ed tech gurus aside, have been caught somewhat unawares. With this knowledge in hand, we will be better positioned to make meaningful and informed decisions as practitioners, researchers, and administrators. More immediately, this understanding will help us better consider how our key principles from chapter 1 will translate into pedagogical and professional practice when we explore those topics in later chapters. So, without further ado, let us take a look at the surprisingly long history of AI in Education.

A Brief History of AI in Education

AI has a surprisingly long history in the field of education, spanning back to shortly after the inception of the AI as a subfield of the computer sciences in the 1950s (see McCarthy et al., 1955/2006; Mitchell, 2019). Almost immediately, AI entered higher education first as a site of research, as with ELIZA (Weizenbaum, 1966, 1976) and PARRY (Colby, 1975). Both of these AI systems were designed to have a protracted conversation with the user, with ELIZA being programmed to attempt to redirect conversations that strayed beyond its bank of pre-programmed responses. And the interactions were convincing facsimiles of actual conversation to many users, at least up to a certain number of conversational turns and assuming the user stayed within the realm of mostly banal small talk (Natale, 2019). These two early AI would come to heavily influence the human-machine interaction pattern we now recognize as the modern chatbot, where a user enters natural language prompts, and the machine produces a text-based output (Bassett, 2019; Switzky, 2020). A pattern still used today by AI tools like ChatGPT and Claude2.

Moreover, these early experiments also laid the groundwork for the development of AI in education, demonstrating the potential of AI to engage with users in a meaningful way. This led to, in 1970, the first AI system purpose-built to help support education was brought online as part of Jaime Carbonell's doctoral research at the Massachusetts Institute of Technology (MIT). Seeking to highlight the potential of computer-assisted instruction (CAI) systems, Carbonell created SCHOLAR, an AI designed to help students learn geometry (Carbonell, 1970; Woolf, 1991). SCHOLAR, and many of its contemporaries (e.g., MYCIN, DENDRAL, etc.) were examples of *expert systems* (see McFarland & Parker, 1990; Mitchell, 2019). Expert systems are a class of AI programs designed to replicate the decision-making and problem-solving capabilities of human experts in specific domains. They achieve this by using a knowledge base comprised of rules, facts, and heuristics, which is created through the expertise of human specialists in the particular field (Buchanan & Shortliffe, 1984; Mitchell, 2019). These knowledge bases encompass a wide range of domain-specific information, such as rules of thumb, logical deductions, and cause-effect relationships, which are carefully encoded to enable the expert system to reason through complex problems and provide informed solutions. The operation of an expert system typically involves the following key components:

- Knowledge Base: This repository holds the domain-specific information in the form of rules and facts. These rules are created by human experts who provide insights into how problems in the domain can be approached and solved.
- Inference Engine: The inference engine is the core reasoning component of the expert system. It uses the rules and facts from the knowledge base to draw conclusions and make decisions based on the input it receives.
- User Interface: Expert systems are designed to interact with users, typically through a user-friendly interface. Users can input queries or problem descriptions, and the system responds with relevant recommendations or solutions.
- Explanation Mechanism: A crucial aspect of expert systems is their ability to explain their reasoning. This explanation mechanism allows the system to provide justifications for its decisions, enhancing user understanding and trust in the system's outputs.

Moreover, many of these expert systems were examples of what is known as *symbolic AI*, a class of AI somewhat dissimilar to more modern systems as they were often programmed with explicit knowledge bases and rules about "the world" that were used to guide their decision making and the feedback that they provided to the user (see Flasiński, 2016; Mitchell, 2019). In the case of expert systems, the knowledge base, which contains domain-specific information and rules, is represented using symbols, and the inference engine manipulates these symbols to draw conclusions and make decisions. The reasoning process in expert systems follows symbolic logic, allowing the system to simulate human expertise in a particular domain through symbolic representation and reasoning. Symbolic AI has, to a certain extent, fallen out of favor in many AI applications because of the costly nature of creating a knowledge base and the symbolic logic that human beings must explicitly program before the system can come online (see Boden, 2018; Flasiński, 2016).

The next significant advancement of AI into the field of education came in the 1980s as researchers began to integrate explicit pedagogical knowledge and cognitive modeling into computing systems. This shift, coupled with advancements in computing power, algorithmic capabilities, cognitive modeling, and human-computer interaction, led to the emergence of intelligent tutoring systems (ITS), designed to provide learners with personalized feedback and guidance without human intervention (see Roll & Wylie, 2016; Woolf, 1991). These systems use various AI techniques to mimic the behavior of human tutors, attempting to provide students with tailored feedback and guidance based on an understanding of the student's individual needs, responses, and misconceptions (Wenger, 1987; Koedinger & Corbett, 2006).

An early example of one such system is Johnson and Soloway's (1984) PROUST system, designed to help students understand errors in computer programs they had written. A few features made this system revolutionary. For example, PROUST could offer feedback on errors, or bugs in computer science parlance, that was not just connected to syntactic errors in the actual code the student wrote. It could also provide feedback on logical errors via complex modeling of goals and learner intentionality. Said another way, PROUST wasn't just a "grammar checker" for code catching missing curly braces ({ . . . }, used in languages like C and Java to denote blocks of related code) or the use of programming language specific reserved words, such as "int" or "const," as names for variables. It could offer feedback on logical faults in the code, such as when a control loop is written so that the code inside is unreachable and will never execute (see also Woolf, 1991). Another feature that made PROUST so groundbreaking was that it incorporated cognitive models of the learner and tutoring best practices to guide its decision-making algorithms that governed what feedback to give learners and when to provide it, if at all (see Soloway et al., 1987). Despite these advancements, PROUST wasn't without issue, with some students reporting the feedback as obtuse and unhelpful. However, this spurred further attempts to innovate ITS by incorporating additional cognitive, pedagogical, and communicative models to facilitate student learning and feedback uptake (Anderson et al., 1995; VanLehn, 2006; Woolf, 2009).

ITS remains relevant today and can be found in a variety of applications. One such example is Carnegie Speech, an Intelligent Tutoring System designed to help with English language learning. Utilizing speech recognition and artificial intelligence technologies, Carnegie Speech provides personalized, real-time feedback on learners' pronunciation and fluency. This system reflects the broader trend in education where ITS are being harnessed to provide tailored, individualized learning experiences. Indeed, the past 20 years of development have also witnessed the rise of highly specialized language ITS platforms, such as the Tactical Language and Culture System (see Johnson, 2007; Johnson & Valente, 2009). Developed to train defense personnel, the Tactical Language and Culture System combines linguistic training for "boots-on-the-ground" communicative needs with detailed cultural training to facilitate collaboration during international military exercises (Johnson & Valente, 2009). Its linguistic training focuses on communicative task-based learning with feedback provided to the learner based on the inputs that they provide to the system, with divergent pathways and reinforcement activities being provided to the learner as appropriate (Johnson, 2007. Whether for language acquisition, mathematics, or other subjects, modern ITS continue to innovate and adapt, offering new tools and strategies to meet the diverse needs of learners across the globe (Eskenazi, 2009; Pelton & Carnegie Speech, 2012).

The Rise of AI for Assessment and Classroom Management

While the integration of AI in the form of intelligent tutoring systems (ITS) marked a significant evolution in personalized learning, the innovation did not stop there. The succeeding wave of advancements began to explore areas beyond instruction, reaching into the intricate domains of student assessment and classroom management. This new chapter, initiated in parallel with the continual refinement of ITS, sought to leverage AI to redefine how educators evaluate, organize, and manage their classrooms. The very developments in algorithms and computational power that had allowed ITS to create a working facsimile of human tutoring were now being employed to automate administrative tasks, develop precise metrics for student evaluation, and even predict educational outcomes (see DiCerbo, 2020; Shute & Rahimi, 2017). This burgeoning field, rich in potential and complexity, not only extends the reach of AI in education more generally and English language teaching more specifically, but it also adds a new dimension to how technology can be harnessed to facilitate both teaching and learning. In the following section, we will explore the arrival of AI and AI-based solutions to the questions of assessment and classroom management, digging into both its potential for transformative, student-centered impact and the inherent challenges presented by automating the human-centric labor that is teaching and learning.

AI and Assessment of Learning/Teaching

The assessment landscape in modern education has undergone a profound transformation with the advent of artificial intelligence (AI). Whereas traditional assessment methods rely on human judgment and labor-intensive processes, AI brings automation, perceived precision, and expanded personalized analysis to the forefront of educational evaluation. AI-driven assessments are not bound by the limitations of manual marking and are capable of providing near instant, and some would claim unbiased, evaluations that align with predefined criteria (see González-Calatayud et al., 2021; Shute & Rahimi, 2017; Swiecki et al., 2022). Moreover, AI's potential extends beyond simple grading systems, encompassing complex areas like cognitive modeling, pattern recognition, and predictive analytics to gauge student understanding and learning progress (Office of Educational Technology, 2023; Roll & Wylie, 2016). This technological shift has not only helped to streamline certain assessment processes but has also enriched them with insights that were previously difficult to obtain or highly time-consuming to derive (see Celik et al., 2022; Swiecki et al., 2022). In the following sections, the application and impact of AI in assessing student performance within the context of ESL/EFL will be explored, shedding light on how this innovative technology impacts professional practice in language education.

In the realm of language assessment, AI has paved the way for innovative techniques that have had an array of impacts on evaluating learners' proficiency in ESL/EFL contexts. Rather than relying on standardized, one-size-fits-all testing, AI-enabled assessment systems can dynamically adapt to individual learners, providing precise diagnostics that reflect their unique abilities and areas for growth (Borrego, 2023; Keerthiwansha, 2018). Such approaches may encompass not merely the assessment of grammatical and syntactical knowledge but may also extend to complex facets like pronunciation, intonation, and cultural understanding (Kim, 2023; Swiecki et al., 2022). Before continuing, I should note that using assessments that utilize either AI or its underlying technologies (e.g., NLP and ML) assessments is far from a recent innovation (see Chapelle & Chung, 2010); indeed, AI and its underlying technologies have been part of the assessment landscape since the 1990s. What has changed more recently is how accessible AI-based assessment tools are, which has seen their deployment in settings divorced from their original context of large-scale assessment and becoming a larger part of regular classroom assessments.

One area where there has been considerable growth in the use of AI-powered assessment has been in assessing speaking, pronunciation, and conversation (Chapelle & Chung, 2010; Borrego, 2023; Kim, 2023). This has been greatly facilitated by the development of NLP and speech recognition tools, allowing AI-powered assessments to offer real-time assessments and feedback of student learning as it relates to L2/FL pronunciation and prosody in a manner that has been designed to facilitate long-term learning and success (e.g., Kim, 2023). Often, these tools are incorporated into classroom learning management systems (LMSs) or into ITAs like Duolingo, providing learners with timely feedback without the delay caused by assessment bottlenecks that often occur in language classes that typically have little instructional support outside of the instructor of record, who teaches between 3–6 sections of language classes on average – representing a rather heavy workload under the best of conditions. One should note that this feedback has been shown to have a net-positive impact on student learning, who typically view the AI-generated feedback as increasing their perceived satisfaction with classroom instruction and, more importantly, found the feedback to be effective in guiding the learning journeys (Borrego, 2023, pp. 81–1). Additionally, these assessments often provide important analytics to the instructor to help guide classroom instruction in ways that better meet the needs of the learners that they are working with, further empowering assessments – regardless of their original design – to serve a formative function that drives student learning and success (Shum & Luckin, 2019).

AI-supported assessments have also increasingly been deployed in assessing student writing through the use of automated essay scoring (AES) systems, such as ETS' *e*-rater and Pearson's *WriteToLearn*. *e-rater*, for example, employs a combination of machine learning algorithms and natural language processing to evaluate essays on various dimensions, including syntactic and lexical analysis, content relevance, grammatical accuracy, and discourse structure. Utilizing a scoring rubric aligned with human grading, *e-rater* generates a numerical score that often complements human scorers for greater reliability and validity, and this alignment with human scores is a feature that appears to improve as the underlying technologies do (c.f., Lee, 2016; Lee et al., 2008; Powers et al., 2001). Similarly, Pearson's *WriteToLearn* not only offers automated scoring but also provides formative feedback aimed at improving student writing skills. Both systems highlight the evolving role of AI in education, offering timely and consistent evaluations while also enabling educators to focus more on in-depth instruction and personalized learning. However, it is crucial to remember that while these systems offer many advantages, they are not without limitations, such as the inability to fully understand nuances in human language and potential biases towards certain writing styles or structures

(Lee, 2016; Powers et al., 2001). Therefore, they are often best used in conjunction with human assessments for a more comprehensive evaluation of student writing.

The budding need for AI-driven assessment tools in ESL/EFL is further accentuated by the challenges of a globalized world, where English language proficiency can often be considered a prerequisite for academic and professional success. With a diverse range of learners and ever-expanding educational settings, manual assessments may struggle to keep pace with the growing demand for efficiency and fairness (Huggins-Manley et al., 2022). Herein lies the potential power of AI, with its ability to assess with consistency and granularity, bridging the gap between what traditional methods can offer and what the dynamic landscape of ESL/EFL education requires (see Borrego, 2023; Keerthiwansha, 2018; Kim, 2023).

Turning our attention to the other side of the learning/teaching dialogic, we find ourselves at a very nascent moment. There has, so far, been relatively little use of AI in assessing the work of teachers. And, perhaps, this is where we need to proverbially knock on wood. It is likely due to both the complexity of assessing professional teachers as well as understandable push back from professional organizations and teachers' unions. Take a moment to reflect on the last time that you observed another teacher – either in an administrative capacity or as a peer. There is considerable disciplinary and contextual knowledge that must be synthesized to not only make sense of what is being observed, but also to provide meaningful feedback to the educator being observed. Said another way, to understand why a teacher chose a particular pedagogical approach for a specific lesson requires me, as an observer, to understand not only a diverse panoply of teaching methods but also the training background of the teacher, their teaching philosophy, the lesson being taught, and the needs of the learners. It is a highly contextual act, and this is one area where AI simply cannot compete with human observers. At least not yet. That being said, I would not be surprised to see ed tech companies try to "meet consumer need". Indeed, we can probably see the proverbial writing on the wall as AI comes to be used to assess interviewees in industry through platforms like *MyInterview* and *Curious Thing* (see Arakawa & Yakura, 2022).

AI-Assisted Classroom Management

I would now turn our attention to the realm of classroom management, which we will understand here as the complex, emergent, and (occasionally) contested set(s) of practices, strategies, and skills employed by educators to create and maintain a structured learning environment, ensuring that students are actively engaged, disruptions are minimized, and educational objectives are achieved (see Doyle, 2013; Oliver et al., 2011). And, it is here where the dissenting voices against AI-integration into education can, justifiably, get quite loud. In part because of the dangers or routinizing the assessment and judgment of human beings, their abilities, and their potential without a human-in-the-loop (see Pasquale, 2020) – a clear and present danger that has been well discussed in criminal justice where algorithmic unfairness can doom people of color to longer sentences and higher bail rates (c.f. Shi, 2022; Villasenor & Foggo, 2020). And, partly because of the gross potential for privacy violations and the stripping away of students' (and teachers') rights to a private life in the classroom free from constant categorization, analysis, and assessment (Huang, 2023; Weinberg, 2020). A popular refrain in the popular press is that the widespread adoption of AI-enabled classroom management systems heralds the arrival of a draconian, malevolent Big Brother, hell-bent on vacuuming up every ounce of personal data for the purposes of minute social control and exploitation. And, while I agree that such abuses happen and will happen again if AI systems are not adequately regulated and integrated into our professional discourses, practices, and training, I find the framing of these arguments to be occasionally made in bad faith.

Indeed, there are what Westerners might consider quite disconcerting examples. Of the use of AI for classroom management – although we must acknowledge that this comes with, perhaps more than, its fair share of surveillance of students and teachers. Take, for example, some of the reports on AI being used to aid teachers with classroom management in China. In one case, a mix of high-definition cameras, headbands, and AI-powered classroom management and sentiment analysis software has been used to monitor student engagement in learning and direct teachers' remediation efforts for students who (temporarily) disengage from classroom learning (Hao, 2019; Lee, 2018). Over-surveillance aside, such minute regulation of students' bodies and lives is a serious threat to the underlife in the classroom, which has been shown to facilitate learning and engagement even if it manifests as a temporary *disengagement* from sanctioned activities (Brooke, 1987; Mueller, 2009). However, these uses are relatively restricted in their global scope at present and, more importantly, would face significant regulatory and professional hurdles in places like the United States and the European Union (see Office of Educational Technology, 2023; Pasquale, 2020).

Now, if this is the first you have heard of such initiatives, it can be a shock to the system. However, it is important to remember that even in classroom management, AI has already been part of educational practices to varying degrees since the early 2000s. And, with the recent generative AI boom, it is unlikely to disappear from classroom management for the foreseeable future. So, here, I will instead turn our attention to some of the uses of AI for classroom management that may feel more familiar (and perhaps acceptable).

Administrative Task Automation

Perhaps the most benign use of AI for classroom management is using AI-powered tools and platforms to assist in automating certain administrative tasks – a considerable time sink for many educators who are already facing considerable demands on their time between lesson planning, curriculum design, assessment, and student needs intervention. Indeed, a recent report from McKinsey and Company suggests that educators spend some 50 hours a week on work-related tasks, and of that, some 13 hours are on repetitive, rote tasks that could be automated. By automating such tasks, we would stand to free up educators' time and cognitive resources to deploy their expertise in more meaningful ways that support student learning and success or that otherwise support the institutional mission and values (Bryant et al., 2020; see also Office of Educational Technology, 2023). And, in this regard, there are already a slew of potential AI-powered tools to support educators, many of which may already be familiar to them if they are not already deployed in the institutions in which they work.

Two common platforms that can help in automating administrative tasks are *Canvas* from Instructure and *Behavior Support* (formerly *Kickboard*) from PowerSchool. *Canvas*, which incorporates other functionalities to support teaching and learning typical to learning management systems (LMSs), uses AI and NLP to aid educators in designing and rolling out assignments by parsing announcements and assignment sheets to compile a course calendar and flag potential conflicts for educator review and revision. Moreover, using AI-powered educational analytics, *Canvas'* gradebook can help ID grading errors, suggest curves, and track student progress through smart reports and intelligent dashboards (Instructure, 2023). Meanwhile, PowerSchool's *Behavior* product utilizes AI and NLP to track student behavior and attendance to power a predictive analytics platform that can generate reports and recommend interventions to educators to help support at-risk students and provide documentation for institutional or regulatory needs (PowerSchool, 2022).

Admittedly, there are concerns about the pervasive surveilling and datafication of students (see Gulson et al., 2022; Marachi & Quill, 2020). And, here, we must return to the question of algorithmic fairness. While

PowerSchool's own reporting (ibid.) suggests that its platforms can help reduce student behavioral issues from interrupting formal schooling, one must question the underlying algorithms and whether or not they have inherited – or worse, learned – any bias against students from marginalized backgrounds (see Fedders, 2019; Regan & Jesse, 2019). Indeed, given AI's troubled racial past and outcries from AI ethicists that temporarily capture national headlines, it is not difficult to see how such systems can introduce considerable problems that could continue to marginalize and restrict access for at-risk students and students from marginalized communities.

Virtual Assistants

Virtual assistants, like Apple's Siri and Amazon's Alexa, have slowly become an ever-present and (moderately helpful) companion for many, given their increasing integration with personal tech like smartphones, smartwatches, and connected cars. That being said, their integration into education, and ELT more specifically, remains relatively mild. However, virtual assistants that leverage AI and NLP to parse students' questions and find contextually appropriate answers have emerged over the past decade and a half. But they tend to be purpose-built by institutions to address a specific need or incorporated on the backend, behind the scenes, and out of conscious awareness for all except the most ardent consumer of edtech news (Reyes et al., 2019). That being said, they do represent a use case for AI and its underlying technologies to help meet students' needs while respecting instructors' time constraints.

Take Georgia Tech University's Jill Watson, hailed as one of the first "virtual TAs" (Georgia Tech, 2016). Jill Watson was a purpose-built virtual assistant to aid in addressing students' questions that came up in a forum. Jill Watson, built upon IBM's Watson platform, was designed by Goel and his graduate students to interact with students in the forum of his Knowledge-based AI undergraduate course, utilizing its awareness of the forum and course content to address student concerns in a timely manner, while allowing the instructor of record to focus on more intensive student needs and more robust course planning and implementation (Goel & Polepeddi, 2018). Other companies have sought to also bring virtual assistants into their e-learning platforms, with Pearson also partnering with IBM to bring Watson to their e-learning portfolios to offer a similar real-time, language powered assistance to students and instructors that use Pearson's courseware (Pearson, 2018).

Early research suggests that using virtual assistants positively impacts student learning and motivation in part by fostering agency and ownership over the learning process. González et al. (2022), for example, examined students' use of an AI-powered virtual assistant in a software engineering course. They found that the virtual assistant in the course, alongside other edtech and instructional interventions, greatly facilitated student learning and completion of capstone projects that aligned with their emerging professional interests. Others looking to the adoption of virtual assistants in business and hospitality have noted that it is likely that chatbots will emerge as a dominant AI-integration paradigm in higher education to support students, faculty, and staff (Skrebeca et al., 2021).

Predictive Analytics

Here, we return to an idea that has impacted multiple of the preceding sections of this chapter. Whether we are focused on classroom and learning management systems (CMS/LMS), automating administrative tasks, or personalizing learning, predictive analytics has been hovering in the background. *Predictive analytics* refers to the use of statistical and machine learning techniques in AI-backed educational technology systems that analyze current and historical data to make predictions about future learner outcomes and student behaviors (see Ashrafimoghari, 2022; Rienties et al., 2018; Siemens & Baker, 2012). Generally, this may include demographic information about the student, historical course performance and behavior reports, test scores, and engagement metrics (e.g., days absent, number of tardies, number of disciplinary referrals, time on an IEP, etc.). In the language learning context, the body of data used for predictive analytics may expand to include writing and speaking samples from the student, quiz scores, reading comprehension scores, and other longitudinal data pertinent to language learning (see Ashrafimoghari, 2022; Siemens & Baker, 2012).

Historically, predictive analytics have been used for a variety of tasks, chief among them is identifying at-risk students. Here, the data fed into the system from teachers, administrators, councilors, and CMS/LMS sources is used to identify students who may benefit from either additional support or early intervention (Wolff et al., 2013). This aims to prevent students from falling behind their peers academically and contribute to long-term student learning and success. Beyond this use, predictive analytics are also used to help inform the adaptive learning systems that were discussed earlier in this chapter. In this use case, predictive analytics will use the data collected about the student to tailor content delivery, reinforcement activities, and even assessments to the individual learners' level and needs. Doing so allows an adaptive learning platform, like Duolingo, to proactively sequence future lessons and select learning activities most likely to contribute to student engagement and success. More recently, predictive analytics have been used to help educators with curriculum planning and delivery by utilizing the data mined from CMS and LMS platforms to offer data-driven insights into the instructional approaches that resonate most with their learners (see Li et al., 2014; Quirk & Chumley, 2018). This, ideally, allows educators to make informed decisions that will facilitate learning and student success while also decreasing the amount of time that the educator has to spend wading through the data – allowing the educator to focus more time and energy on what really matters, classroom instruction, and student support.

That being said, predictive analytics is not without its potential issues. And many of them will be familiar at this point – namely, there are potential issues of data privacy, algorithmic bias, and errors in interpreting the data due to faulty underlying models. Data privacy concerns, for example, necessitate a careful consideration of data privacy. This is made even more salient when we pause to realize that the acquisition and utilization of student information are no longer confined to classroom walls; they extend to various digital platforms that collect data points ranging from student engagement levels to proficiency rates while the student is at school, home, the library, or anywhere they may be accessing the CMS or LMS platforms their teachers/schools deploy in support of their instruction. Therefore, compliance with data protection laws, such as the Family Educational Rights and Privacy Act (FERPA) in the United States or the General Data Protection Regulation (GDPR) in Europe, becomes paramount. As such, ELT practitioners must be vigilant in selecting AI tools that adhere to local, national, and international data privacy laws. Moreover, there should be a transparent mechanism for students and guardians to understand what data are being collected and for what specific pedagogical goals.

Turning our attention to the issue of algorithmic bias, we encounter another critical issue with ethical ramifications. When the data used to train AI algorithms contain biases, be they related to ethnicity, social background, gender, or linguistic diversity, these biases become an integral part of the predictive outcomes. In the context of ELT, this can result in teaching strategies or interventions that disproportionately impact marginalized or underrepresented communities. The risk is that these AI-powered tools may inadvertently perpetuate or even exacerbate existing inequalities in educational settings. It behooves those involved in the development and application of AI in ELT to scrutinize data sets for potential biases rigorously and continually update AI models to correct any detected skewing of results.

Finally, the efficacy of AI in ELT is significantly impacted by how well educators can interpret and apply the predictive data generated. An algorithm is only as useful as the human actions that follow its predictions. Therefore, there is a growing need for professional development programs that equip language teachers with the skills to understand data analytics. Misinterpreting data can lead to ill-advised educational interventions, such as misallocating resources or employing ineffective teaching strategies. The translation of raw data into actionable pedagogical steps requires not just an understanding of the technology but also a nuanced grasp of the broader educational context in which this technology is deployed. Educators, thus, need to be trained in both technical and interpretive skills to use AI-based insights responsibly and effectively.

While we have probed into the potential pitfalls and challenges posed by predictive analytics – and, by extension, to a certain extent, AI – in ELT, it is crucial to recognize that we are swiftly moving towards an era that seems likely to be dominated by AI. This is a fact that is readily spoken to by the explosion of publicly available AI tools that operate off of a variety of economic models – free, freemium, and subscription/fee-based. Moreover, we have seen an explosion in fortunes for companies connected to AI and seen pivots from tech giants, well established in their respective fields to AI, (e.g., NVIDIA's move from graphics cards to AI chips, Meta's move from social media to AI, etc.). Indeed, AI has even become a matter of national security and defense and not just mere scientific/industrial pride (see Crawford, 2021; Pasquale, 2020). Regardless of these challenges, our students will inevitably inhabit an AI-rich world. And, it will likely be one that is even more explicitly so than the one we ourselves grew up in – where AI moved from books and movies to a background process running on smart devices in our homes and pockets.

Given this reality, ELT practitioners must move beyond merely teaching languages and culture. It becomes our responsibility to contribute to institutional efforts to equip students with the knowledge and skills they will need in this evolving landscape. Here, I will acknowledge the seeming "role creep" inherent in this statement, having language educators take on more responsibility when many of them exist in part-time and contingent roles. However, we have had to take on similar responsibilities when we have helped students acquire basic computer literacy skills in computer-mediated classes (see Davie & Wells, 1991; Lupo & Erlich, 2001). Said another way, students must be prepared not only to interact with AI but also to understand its nuances, capabilities, and limitations.

The rise of AI is not limited to assessment, classroom management, intelligent tutoring systems, and predictive analytics. The following sections will explore the propagation of constructive and generative AI systems, providing the reader with a working knowledge of these systems' potential implications for ELT. These innovations are likely to have profound impacts on teaching and learning, more generally, will likely also greatly influence the future of ELT, making it imperative for us to adapt our teaching methodologies, all while ensuring ethical and responsible AI use.

The Growth of Constructive and Assistive AI

As introduced in chapter 1, constructive AI are AI agents that take input from the user and correct or modify it. While this most certainly includes tools like the image retouch features on most modern smartphones, here we will focus on language-centric constructive AI in keeping with the focus of the book. Indeed, constructive AI have been part of our workflows and technological affordances for quite some time. However, they often function in a much subtler manner than modern generative AI which has been responsible for the recent bout of AI anxiety in education and beyond (see D'Agostino, 2023). While the grandiose visions of AI often capture our imaginations – self-driving cars, humanoid robots, and virtual assistants – the delicate yet profound impact of supportive AI tools in everyday tasks is reshaping our interaction with technology. From the simple beginnings of AI-powered spelling and grammar checkers to sophisticated writing aids like Grammarly, and even the vigilant eyes of AI-driven plagiarism detectors, these tools are becoming indispensable for writers, students, and professionals alike. As we probe deeper into this topic, we will explore both the promising potential and the inherent limitations of these supportive AI tools.

Constructive AI & Productivity Software: Spelling and Grammar Checkers

The proliferation of the personal computer in the 1970s and 1980s brought with it an expanded access and use of productivity software – software for word processing, spreadsheet creation and analysis, presentation design, etc. And, in this vein, the introduction of grammar and spelling checkers in widely used productivity software stands out as a notable and storied advancement. Previously limited to basic spell checks, these tools have undergone significant evolution with the incorporation of AI technologies. Now, they not only address typographical errors but also provide sophisticated grammar suggestions, style enhancements, and tone insights. Their seamless inclusion in everyday software platforms, such as word processors and email clients, underscores the pervasive influence of AI-driven language tools. Transitioning to a more detailed examination, the subsequent discussion will highlight the instrumental role of these AI-powered checkers in language teaching and learning, explore viewpoints from students and educators, and critically evaluate the capabilities and constraints of these tools in educational contexts.

Spelling and grammar checkers have a history almost as long as that of the personal computer itself, with the first spellcheck program being developed in the 1960s and offering a straightforward, programmatic approach to correcting spelling errors by comparing the words in a text to a dictionary of known words to arrive at a conclusion about accuracy of spelling. These early versions could only provide a list of possibly misspelled words and would not be able to provide recommendations for corrections until much later as advances in NLP enhanced their abilities (Dale & Viethen, 2021; Haswell, 2005). Further advances in NLP technologies would see spell checkers gain further capabilities such as contextual awareness, which improved their ability to parse homophones, make recommendations about non-English text, and work across different varieties of English (e.g., British English, American English, etc.). Grammar checkers have a similar history to spell checkers, with the first one being developed in the early 1970s (see Heidorn et al., 1982). However, grammar checkers were more difficult to develop than spell checkers, as they needed to understand the meaning of sentences to identify grammar errors. Early grammar checkers were very simple, and they could only identify a limited number of grammar errors. However, as NLP technology improved, grammar checkers became more sophisticated and were able to identify a wider range of grammar errors (Dale & Viethen, 2021; Dobrin, 1990). Modern grammar checkers can identify a wide range of grammar errors, including subject-verb agreement, pronoun, verb tense, conjunction, punctuation, and sentence structure errors. The evolution of grammar checkers also mirrors that of spell checkers in their evolution from merely identifying errors to also providing suggestions for correcting grammar errors, again tied to the steady evolution of the underlying NLP technologies.

More recently, however, grammar and spelling checkers in most productivity software have received additional capabilities through the incorporate of AI as an underlying technology – this means that most modern grammar and spelling checkers have evolved also to make use of machine learning and big data analytics to offer even more robust and contextually aware recommendations to its users. Microsoft Editor, for example, has been AI-powered since about 2013, with a major upgrade in 2020 to make it competitive with Grammarly – a leading solution in the area of constructive AI since shortly after the company's founding in 2009 (Lytvyn, 2022; Microsoft, n.d.).

And here we turn our attention to stand-alone constructive AI tools like Grammarly and Quillbot, first emerging on the market in the late 2000s, but reaching maturity through the 2010s. As with more powerful grammar and spelling checkers, the emergence of more capable constructive AI applications was heavily reliant on advances that applied machine learning approaches to NLP applications fueled by the use of so-called big data to provide plenty of training data for both supervised and unsupervised machine learning to refine the underlying AI models that power these tools. As the training data set expands and is refined, we have seen the capabilities of these tools improve over time. Indeed, being an early adopter of Grammarly, I can personally attest to the fact that c. 2015, Grammarly felt far less useful than the Grammarly of today, which makes more meaningful and accurate recommendations. And this is born out in the research on constructive AI tools as well. As the model is refined over time, its capabilities tend to improve (e.g., Raheja & Kumar, 2024).

Perhaps because of our acceptance of grammar and spelling checkers as legitimate parts of the writing process, there was relatively little pushback against tools like Grammarly, Ginger, or Hemingway APP when they first launched, reflected to a certain degree in the popular press as well when compared to the hand-wringing that we saw upon the release of generative AI in the fall of 2022 (c.f., Pennington, 2019).

AI-based editors like Grammarly, Ginger, and Hemingway APP are often considered automated writing evaluation (AWE) tools – tools designed to provide students with more immediate feedback or actual scoring and assessment. Not all AWE tools are AI-powered, although all rely to varying degrees on the underlying technologies that make AI possible, such as NLP and ML. Here, we will focus primarily on AWE tools that have been used for pedagogical purposes, as opposed to evaluative and assessment purposes, which represents a much more fraught arena that will be discussed in greater detail in chapters 5 (assessment) and 6 (ethics) of this book. CALL and second language writing (SLW) researchers have explored a variety of applications of AWE systems to support students during L2 writing tasks. For example, Guo et al. (2021) looked at the actual impact of using AWE tools on students' error-correction strategies and accuracy in academic writing tasks, finding a marked improvement in using AWE tools, Grammarly in this case, to support L2 writers (see also Alhalangy & AbdAlgane, 2023; Barrot, 2023. Beyond this, other researchers have examined students' attitudes towards these tools (e.g., An et al., 2023; Han & Sari, 2022) and their impact on metacognitive skills development in L2 writing tasks (e.g., Azizah & Soraya, 2023; Koltovskaia, 2020). In both cases finding net positive impacts on students' learning, confidence, and L2 writing competency. However, many of these studies point to students being unsure of *how* to incorporate these tools into their writing processes in ways that support their long-term learning and success (see O'Neill & Russell, 2019). This points to the need for teachers to be trained in how to incorporate AWE tools into their pedagogical practices in meaningful ways that connect with real student need. And, in this area, we have seen some movement to better understand how teachers' own tech competency interfaces with pedagogical practices and can be used to create more inclusive classroom spaces for multilingual writers (e.g., Ghufron & Rosyida, 2018; Koltovskaia, 2023)

What remains consistent across not only this small cross-section of the rather considerable CALL and SLW research into AWE systems, like Grammarly, is that there was far less existential dread with these AI-powered systems than there has been with generative AI. Indeed, even the more cautious papers take a much more critical and open-minded approach to these kinds of tools. This is, perhaps, in part because of their familiarity – being near kin to "dumb" grammar and spelling checkers – and in part because they have been seen as less of a threat to the inherently human aspects of writing – creativity, emotion, and originality.

Beyond this grammar and style support, recent advances in AI have emerged to support users in variety of tasks. Platforms like *Elsa Speak* and *Correct Speak*, rather problematically use NLP and speech-recognition technology to help "normalize" accents (Becker & Edalatishams, 2019, Tan et al., 2022). An approach to constructive AI that has, quite rightly, been decried as dehumanizing (see Payne et al., 2023). However, this mirrors a long history of computer scientists and developers taking a rather simplistic see a problem, fix a problem approach – only seriously considering the interdisciplinary expertise needed to also ethically address social problems that their platforms either create or purpose to correct (see Christian, 2021; Mitchell, 2019). Perhaps less problematically, AI tools like *TALKPAL AI* purport to help guide learners and facilitate lifelong learning and instructional support for learners as they work through learning/acquiring a new language (Talkpal, 2023). Beyond this, one could point to constructive AI that aids in things like classroom management, student motivation, or plagiarism detection. However, I will save addressing these topics for later in this book as they are fraught applications of AI that, like accent reduction, perpetuates a problematic approach to students in the form of fueling (and feeding off of) a proverbial arms race between teachers and learners that simply erodes trust and threatens the human connection that making teaching and learning possible in the first place.

The Advent of Powerful Generative AI Models

More recently, advances in artificial intelligence have led to the emergence of powerful generative AI models that can handle everything from text generation (e.g., Claude 2.1), image generation (e.g., Stable Diffusion), audio (e.g., AudioCraft), and video (e.g., Synthasia). This new era in AI began with the development of generative adversarial networks (GANs) by Ian Goodfellow and his colleagues in 2014 (Goodfellow et al., 2014). GANs were a groundbreaking innovation, consisting of two neural networks – the generator and the discriminator – competing against each other. This setup enabled the generation of remarkably realistic images, catalyzing a new wave of creative and practical applications for AI. GANs, however, where only one cog in the vast machinery necessary to make modern, generative AI possible. Variational autoencoders (VAEs) were another pivotal development in generative models. Introduced by Kingma and Welling in 2013 (Kingma & Welling, 2013), VAEs are powerful in their ability to both generate new data and learn the distribution of a given dataset, making them valuable for tasks that require a deep understanding of complex data patterns. While GANs would come to be seen as the more powerful of the two technologies because of the clarity and detail in their outputs, VAEs are easier to train and less prone to model collapse, giving eventual rise to the VAE-GAN hybrid architecture in an attempt to gain the benefits of both. VAE-GANs have been used to great effect in platforms like OpenAI's Jukebox for music generation or highly specialized deployment to detect feature anomalies in patient MRIs (see Dhariwal et al., 2020; Li et al., 2021b).

The advancement of NLP brought about another significant milestone with the introduction of transformer models by Vaswani et al. in 2017 (Vaswani et al., 2017). These models, particularly notable for their ability to handle sequential data without needing to process it in order, revolutionized how machines understand and generate human language. The launch of OpenAI's Generative Pretrained Transformer series, especially GPT-3, demonstrated an unprecedented level of proficiency in generating human-like text (Brown et al., 2020), paving the way for a multitude of applications ranging from writing assistance to conversational AI. Indeed, it is the emergence of sentence transformers that have driven much of the work in generative AI. However, this has been enabled through the emergence of many of the technologies discussed throughout this book so far – from neural networks to deep learning paired with the emergence of big data and the compute resources to actually process it.

Today, we are witnessing the rise of multimodal generative models. These advanced AI systems are capable of understanding and synthesizing information across various formats – be it text, images, or sound – ushering in a new wave of AI applications that are more integrated and versatile than ever before. However, as we embrace these technological strides, we also face new challenges and responsibilities. The ethical considerations surrounding generative AI, including potential biases and the implications of its misuse, are increasingly coming to the forefront of AI research and application (Jobin et al., 2019).

However, given their relatively recent emergence there is relatively little history of generative AI in CALL or iCALL at the time of this writing. This is, in no small part, because we are currently living through this history and are navigating it is myriad pedagogical, professional, ethical, and ecological considerations. Certainly, we have seen the machinery of our shared discipline spinning to life to address precisely these questions with a number of books, workshops, and journal special issues being commissioned by publishers, professional organizations, and governments. It is against this backdrop that we could easily place the present monograph.

Conclusion

As we close this chapter, it is evident that the journey of AI in education has been both profound and transformative. Beginning with early experiments like ELIZA and PARRY, AI has steadily evolved, intertwining its capabilities with the educational landscape. The progression from expert systems in the 1970s to the sophisticated intelligent tutoring systems (ITS) of the 1980s and beyond illustrates a relentless pursuit of more personalized, responsive, and nuanced educational tools.

The emergence of AI in assessment and classroom management reflects a shift towards more efficient, data-driven, and student-centered approaches. Technologies like predictive analytics, while promising, bring with them a suite of ethical and practical challenges that educators and policymakers must navigate with care. The advent of tools like AI-assisted grammar and spelling checkers, and virtual assistants, marks a significant shift in how educational content is delivered and consumed. And, our current landscape, dominated by powerful generative AI models, is reshaping the contours of what's possible in education. With the ability to generate text, images, audio, and video, these models offer unprecedented opportunities for creative and engaging teaching methods. Yet, this new era also ushers in complexities surrounding ethical use, bias, and the potential impacts on the teacher-student dynamic.

As we transition to the next chapter, which will focus more specifically on AI in language teaching and learning and Computer-Assisted Language Learning (CALL), it is crucial to reflect on the historical journey of AI in education. This reflection not only provides context but also equips us with insights to navigate the unfolding future of AI in education. The key lies in balancing the innovative potential of AI with mindful consideration of its implications, ensuring that its integration into educational contexts is both ethical and effective. In embracing AI, educators are not just adopting new tools; they are participating in a rapidly evolving narrative that redefines the boundaries of teaching and learning. As we probe deeper into AI's role in language education, let us carry forward the lessons learned from its rich history, mindful of both its transformative potential and the responsibility it entails in shaping the future of education.

3

AI in Language Teaching and Learning

Introduction

Having examined the (surprisingly) long history of AI in education (AIED), we now turn our attention to how AI has been brought to bear, specifically in language teaching and learning. Admittedly, because of my own disciplinary positioning in ELT, you may notice that ELT-focused examples are given special focus throughout this, and subsequent, chapters. As we say in computer sciences, that is a feature and not a bug. However, special efforts have been made to consider AI in language teaching and learning more broadly to include examples from world languages instruction as well. To facilitate this discussion, this chapter will use two levels of distinction to render our conversation more knowable and accessible. The first is the already familiar distinction between teaching – what we as language educators do in the classroom to drive a change in our students – and learning – what our students are (we hope) doing as they engage with our teaching. For our second distinction, we will turn to computer sciences to borrow an organizational metaphor in keeping with the interdisciplinary nature of AIED conversations – a nature which likely must be maintained in applied linguistics and its allied disciplines in addressing the impacts and perils of AI in language teaching and learning.

In the field of computer science, the parent discipline of AI, there is a distinction between the work done to create the logic and processes that drive a system (backend development) and how information is presented to and manipulated by the user (frontend development). It is important to note that this is a porous metaphor even in computer science as in the case of Application Programming Interfaces, or APIs, which act as intermediaries between different services (e.g., your phone's weather app and a weather data service), allowing them to communicate and share information despite having different purposes and underlying infrastructure. We can see similar tasks in teaching and learning. Tasks like the administrative work of teaching, writing lesson plans, and engaging in curriculum design might be seen as backend tasks. Meanwhile, classroom teaching, designing curricular materials and learning assessments, and developing instructional activities can be seen as student-facing, frontend tasks. And, just as in software development, there is a significant porous border between the two filled with technologies like LMSs or paraeducators and tutors (see Paiz et al. forthcoming). While there may be some who take exception to the deployment of metaphors and concepts from the world of tech (see Bender, 2024), I would maintain that doing so provides us with powerful tools to engage in interdisciplinary dialogue. Beyond that, it empowers language teachers to engage with their peers in other disciplines and to better advocate for their proverbial seat at the table when engaging with AI systems designers and Ed Tech company representatives through the power of a shared lexicon. Problematic though this may be, anyone who has inhabited the proverbial power-under position knows that one must occasionally be able to speak the language of those in the power-over position to force them to listen and consider other perspectives (see Freire, 2000; hooks, 1994).

Therefore, this chapter will be organized around this metaphor, discussing the application of AI, particularly generative and constructive AI, to the teaching and learning of languages through the lens of frontend and backend work. As with chapter 2, this chapter aims to outline what it is that we, as a discipline, know about the current and emerging role of artificial intelligence in language education. To that end, this chapter will begin by looking at the proverbial backend of teaching second and foreign languages – the planning, design, and administrative work that language instructors and administrators must engage in be able to deliver meaningful instruction to students. While our students may encounter the fruit of backend processes, they are rarely directly engaged in these activities with us in any protracted manner. Then, the conversation will shift to look at frontend instructional activities and the impacts of AI in the classroom, focusing on what it is we are doing with our learners and in the materials and tools that we deploy to help facilitate instruction. Once this discussion is well in hand, we will have successfully set the stage for our collaborative wrestling with AI's sudden rise in importance in our daily and professional lives and to grapple with what, precisely *collaborative AI* means for us and the profession going forward.

AI on the Backend

In language teaching and learning, this most often connects to the subfield of iCALL, which focuses on how intelligent systems can support language teaching and learning. We often understand intelligent systems as those that may be built on one or more of the following technologies: AI, big data analytics, predictive analytics, natural language processing, and machine learning. These technologies serve to add the "intelligence" to traditional computer and CALL platforms. I will, of course, remind the reader that intelligent/intelligence here is a bit of a misnomer as AI systems aren't intelligent in the same sense as human beings, nor do computer scientists and AI designers really know the finer details of the shape or scope of the "intelligence" held by modern AI (see Li et al., 2021a; Mitchell, 2019 Zhang, 2020). Additionally, I would remind the more critically engaged reader to note that I will address some of the ethical concerns of AI in teaching and learning in chapter 6.

So, returning to the current discussion, some of the most common backend tasks that teachers engage in include curriculum development, lesson planning, materials creation, and analyzing student data to drive in-the-moment (online) decision-making. AI-powered curriculum development, as with much of the conversation on AI, is relatively new. Previous conversations have largely focused on how to evaluate and incorporate intelligent and AI systems into language teaching and learning (see Blake, 2007; Felix, 2005; Wang & Chiaráin, 2019; Ware, 2017). This is likely because, as we say in chapter 2, many AI systems before the advent of generative AI took the form of student-facing ITSs or teacher-facing predictive analytics tools, which could serve to inform aspects of curriculum design, but may have been more limited in their ability to be a more active collaborative partner supporting teacher's curriculum design processes.

With the advent of generative AI systems and the greater proliferation of predictive analytics tools built into LMSs like *Blackboard* or so-called "monitoring and analytics" tools like *PowerSchool*, AI is poised to become a more collaborative partner, offering more accessible recommendations to educators, empowering them to make data-driven decisions to support their learners (see Baskara, 2023; Kartal, 2023; Paiz, 2024a). Baskara (2023) offers a critical thought experiment on applying generative AI to curriculum development in EFL contexts. And, they quite rightly point to AI as a supplement to the teacher's expertise and knowledge of their learners and their context. They point to AI's ability to extend the teacher's existing abilities, empowering them to make impactful changes to their classroom curriculum while better managing the considerable demands on teachers' times, potentially helping teachers to forge a more humane work/life balance. Kartal (2023) collects diverse voices – both in terms of professional background and global contexts – to craft a thoughtful dialogue on how AI can certainly support teachers as they revise curriculum to stay relevant to students' needs, but that caution, and a critical eye, is most certainly warranted given the possible for underlying biases in the AI systems. This means that educators' expertise and skill for creative problem-solving remain vital to building language classrooms that challenge social inequalities and build more equitable spaces that empower all learners. In my own work in Bahrain with the Ministry of Education and the US Embassy, I have pointed to how generative AI tools like ChatGPT in Data Analysis mode or Rose.ai can enable teachers to make data-driven decisions about their educational practice by acting as a sort of data analytics expert – given that many of us view ourselves as expert language teachers and may feel less certain of our statistical or data science skills. Using AI in this capacity to support data-driven curricular revision can enable the educator to better advocate for themselves and their learners with other stakeholders who may question certain decisions.

Others have focused on the need of educators for targeted professional development for language educators to use AI collaboratively, as opposed to unilaterally, for sustainable curriculum development. Pokrivcakova (2019) proposes a wide array of areas in which teachers will need continued professional development and support to use AI tools in their professional practice – ranging from technical training to hands-on experience with AI systems. Meanwhile, Dai et al. (2022) outline a useful framework for thinking of how we support language teachers in using AI to support their professional practice by aligning AI systems to disciplinary values and institutional missions and building in space for student voices so that all stakeholders – students, teachers, the institution – can work with AI in a support capacity to build curricula that meet the real needs of our learners.

Another backend process where we are beginning to see explorations of AI supporting educators' expertise and practice is lesson planning. It is a more-or-less established fact that good teaching is often built on the foundation of good planning (Jones et al., 2011; Sawyer & Myers, 2018). Despite this critical role, early-service teachers struggle with developing robust lessons plans that can drive student engagement and connect classroom realities, learning objectives, and educational theory into a coherent classroom encounter that facilitates learning and student success (Jones et al., 2011; Stronge, 2018). Some of the early work on lesson planning points to AI's potential to help novice teachers navigate this challenge by acting as a sort of copilot, encouraging teachers to consider their goals for a lesson and how their domain expertise can be used to justify engaging pedagogical decisions (Huang & Li, 2023; Ji et al., 2023). Important elements of doing so effectively, however, include ensuring that the right AI tool is being used for the right task (Koraishi, 2023; Paiz et al., 2025) and ensuring that teachers are trained on how to use AI tools in ways that scaffold as opposed to replacing their expertise so that they continue to cultivate their skills as a professional educator (Amin, 2023; Lee & Zhai, forthcoming).

Examining teachers' perspectives has highlighted the fact that AI tools are seen as a way to increase efficiency and creativity, important gains when balanced against how "time-poor" many educators are in the face of growing class sizes and heavier teaching loads that pull time away from good planning design (van den Berg & Plessis, 2023; Riyadini & Triastuti, 2023). Additionally, language teachers report appreciating the perspective that AI tools can provide in attempting to create differentiated lesson plans for students of divergent proficiency levels or for neurodiverse learners (Paiz, 2024a). However, even in this regard, new challenges arise because of the very real potential for bias in the AI outputs and lack of trustworthy explainability in the recommendations that AI systems make to educators (Huang & Li, 2023; Riyadini & Triastuti, 2023).

Taken together, this all points to the very real need for a robust, disciplinarily situated framework for using AI in lesson planning for language teaching. At present, most of these frameworks are either highly theoretical or appear in institution-specific handbooks (e.g., Paiz, 2024b). Beyond this, we again see the need for continued professional development and training of both pre- and in-service teachers to leverage the benefits of AI tools to support their lesson planning while minimizing the potential risks introduced by bias in the training data of AI systems that could contribute to linguistic marginalization or cultural misrepresentation (Bjork, 2023; Sajid, 2023).

Another area where we have traditionally seen AI used to a great extent in language teaching and learning is in assessments and the evaluation of student capabilities. AI tools have been used to automate various aspects of assessment at least partially, such as the scoring of essays and open-ended questions (e.g., Goodwin-Jones, 2022; Huawei & Aryadoust, 2023; Richardson & Clesham, 2021). This helps teachers save valuable time and provides students with more immediate feedback (e.g., Ai, 2017; Edelblut, 2020; Lu et al., 2023). AI can even analyze pronunciation accuracy and fluency in real-time, allowing students to identify areas for improvement without direct teacher intervention (Liu & Quan, 2022; Zou et al., 2021). Additionally, AI-powered adaptive testing systems can tailor the difficulty of questions to the learner's demonstrated skills, ensuring an optimal level of challenge (Richardson & Clesham, 2021; Richardson, 2022).

More recently, we have begun to see work examining the impacts of generative AI on language teaching and learning, although many of these studies may be preliminary or exploratory in nature, given the time it takes for large-scale studies to be implemented. And, given the recent advent of LLM-based generative AI, there has yet to be time for considerable, robust longitudinal work to take place. Moqbel and Al-Kadi (2023), for instance, focus on how the rise of chatbot-based AI – which can be easily, if not effectively, used by most users raises the need for new assessment practices that better account for, if not incorporate this technology. Menaido (2023), on the other hand, points to the potential for tools like Google Gemini and Anthropic's Claude2.1 to empower language educators to create more meaningful and valid assessments that better connect with learners. Both sets of authors, however, rightfully point out many of the potential concerns about using generative AI systems that we have discussed in the previous chapter, looking at AI applied to teaching and learning more generally.

Still, it is important to remember that AI should augment, not replace, the role of skilled educators in assessment. Teachers remain crucial for providing nuanced feedback and addressing the broader context of a student's learning process. Furthermore, efforts must be made to minimize bias in the datasets used to train AI assessment tools to ensure fairness for all learners, as we have already see that some AI tools used (viz. AI detectors) are notoriously and dangerously biased again multilingual students – the exact populations that many of us (ELT professionals especially) are working with or are working to cultivate (Liang et al., 2023; Yan et al., 2024). As AI technology advances, we can expect even more sophisticated and impactful tools supporting language assessment in the future, which may democratize the process of creating valid and reliable assessments that truly support our learners, thereby driving lifelong learning and student success. Additionally, as AI, and especially generative AI, tools become more accessible, there is the possibility that certain efficiencies may permit educators – many of whom (myself presently included) teach very intensive schedules – to refocus on classroom instruction and connecting with students while coming to maintain a healthier work/life balance. That being said, we must remain vigilant to guard against the possible ethical concerns about data privacy and workplace exploitation.

AI on the Frontend

Continuing with our backend/frontend metaphor (see also Paiz et al. forthcoming), we now turn our attention to the proverbial frontend – those activities we do as teachers that our learners directly experience. This includes actions such as translating lesson plans into meaningful classroom instruction, deploying pedagogical materials to scaffold instruction and drive motivation/engagement, orchestrating student-teacher/student-student interactions, and utilizing a diverse array of formative and summative assessments to gauge student learning. Arguably, this is where the real impact of teaching is felt – where learning happens, and students can be nurtured from merely curious to lifelong learners (Darling-Hammond et al., 2020). It is also, sadly, where irreparable harm to learning processes can be done that drive students to, at best, disengage from the classroom and, at worst, drive them from the field of study altogether (Kremling et al., 2017). It is also, it seems, one of the areas where research into artificial intelligence, more generally, and generative AI, more specifically, has room for growth, especially when it comes to the purposeful deployment of AI tools to not only support student learning but also to drive students' acquisition of critical AI literacy.

To better situate the remainder of this book's intellectual labor against the backdrops of ELT and CALL, this section will begin by examining the current state of disciplinary knowledge about the application of AI to classroom learning and activities. From there, we will focus on the emerging use of AI tools to author educational materials that connect with students and help provide differentiated instruction. This section will then discuss how AI tools have been used to mediate both student-teacher and student-student interactions before concluding with a brief return to the front of the assessment – that is, when the assessment is in the room with the students, as opposed to the back work of analyzing the data generated during the assessment process.

The Machine Is in the Room: AI and Classroom Instruction

Much of the early work on AI discussed in the previous chapter has parallels in the language classroom, where we see AI-powered tools deployed during lessons to support student learning by providing for divergent learning pathways or by tailoring the kinds of problems that students see while practicing for an assessment as part of a larger CALL resource (e.g., Cui et al., 2018; Edge et al., 2011; Woolf et al., 2013). Cui et al. (2018), for example, provide a compelling example of how

AI-powered tools are being utilized in language classrooms to enhance student learning, highlighting the use of AI to support divergent learning pathways and tailor practice problems for assessments. Their approach demonstrates the practical application of AI in creating more personalized and adaptive learning experiences, underscoring how educators can better meet the needs of individual students by leveraging AI technologies. Such an approach can be vital to making language learning more engaging and effective. These themes of personalization, representation, and access in CALL and more general educational contexts recur in the research literature time and again, further underscoring the saliency of this possible contribution of AI systems to language teaching and learning (see also Chen et al., 2021). And, with the emergence of powerful and easily accessible LLM-based generative AI, we see educational scholars pointing to the possibility of further empowering teachers and learners to take greater agency in connecting with learners through personalized instructional content and learning pathways (Baskara, 2023).

Disciplinary understandings of AI systems to personalize the learning paths of our students or tailoring novel content to capture their interest and drive learner motivation is just the beginning, however. Edge et al. (2011), working with AI-driven, location-based services, described a possible use case that provides students with more contextually relevant language content based on their physical location in the real world to create more engaging and relevant language learning opportunities for learners and underscore the embodied nature of language and language learning. This work has since been extended also to consider the role of mobile technologies to enable educators to connect with students when and where they are at and through a means that is increasingly "natural" for learners whose daily lives are often mediated through mobile technologies (see Bernacki et al., 2020; Burston, 2014). As AI technologies become more deeply integrated into the mobile computing and communication resources that almost all of us carry with us in our daily lives, language educators and scholars will need to begin to grapple with that intersection between MALL, iCALL, and AI in Education better to understand their impacts on language learning and acquisition, and the better prepare future language teachers to leverage this platform to maximal effect (Counterpoint, 2023; Reuters, 2024).

Speaking of AI in education more broadly, Woolf et al. (2013) point to AI's potential to help students acquire the skills necessary to be critically informed and capable twenty-first-century citizens, as well as inculcating them with the habits of mind necessary to be lifelong learners.

These threads have also been picked up by the applied linguistics and (i)CALL communities. Dizon (2020), for example, examined the use of intelligent personal assistants to help students master pronunciation and speaking tasks in language-learning classrooms. This study found that while there was no significant impact on listening comprehension, the experimental group that interacted with Alexa showed more significant gains in L2 speaking proficiency than the control group. This suggests that intelligent personal assistants and voice-capable generative AI, like GPT-4, can be useful tools to enhance speaking skills, which are crucial for effective communication in the twenty-first century. The study highlights the potential of AI technologies to provide personalized and interactive language learning experiences, aligning with the goals of fostering key competencies and supporting continuous language development Meanwhile, Zhu and Wang's (in press) review of AI in language learning contexts reaffirms their ability to reinforce vital twenty-first-century skills for learners through a variety of processes. Getting students working together with AI tools in a task-based learning environment can help target critical thinking, communication, and collaboration while having students work on their own to evaluate AI-generated outputs for accuracy and linguistic and/or rhetorical appropriateness can foster critical thinking, information literacy, and communication skills. The authors aptly point out that, at present, the discipline appears to have a wealth of theoretical knowledge about AI tools and their potential for language teaching and learning; what is needed, however, is more practical research that can connect with language teachers and drive instructional excellence in the classroom. So, yes, the robot is in the room with us, but at present its impacts, potentials, and pitfalls remain a mystery – as do the pedagogically relevant ways in which that machine can be integrated meaningfully into teaching and learning to support equitable, accessible, and inclusive teaching and learning practices.

This issue is even more salient when we look only at generative AI tools in iCALL specifically and language teaching and learning more broadly. Granted, that can be somewhat forgiven because of the relative newness of generative AI tools at the time of writing, a body of robust literature on its direct classroom applications remains nascent. However, academic bloggers like Ethan Mollick and Brent Warner have regularly recommended classroom activities and assignment redesigns that incorporate AI, especially generative AI, into them. It should be noted, however, that even these "AI Power Users" point to the need for both more sustained inquiry into the impacts of AI tools on classroom instruction and dynamics *and* the need for practical pedagogical recommendations and activities that teachers of varying technical proficiencies can use *with* their learners (Warner, personal communication).

Towards Collaborative AI

Language teaching and learning, generally, and ELT, more specifically, are at an inflection point, one from which the path forward lies in fostering collaboration between AI systems and all stakeholders in the educational process. Importantly, this collaborative approach is one that has been advocated for by AIED specialists and the broader computer sciences discipline for some time in the form of *collaborative AI*, also known as human-AI collaboration or human-in-the-loop AI, which refers to the approach of designing AI systems that work together with humans to achieve better outcomes than either could achieve alone (Koch & Oulasvirta, 2018; Pasquale, 2020). The idea is to leverage the strengths of both artificial intelligence and human intelligence, creating a synergistic relationship that enhances decision-making, problem-solving, and task performance. Collaborative AI envisions a future where teachers, learners, and researchers work hand-in-hand with AI technologies and systems developers to create more effective, engaging, and equitable language learning experiences. Rather than viewing AI as a replacement for human teachers, Collaborative AI sees it as a powerful tool that can augment and enhance the work of educators. By leveraging the strengths of AI, such as its ability to provide personalized feedback, adapt to individual learning needs, and offer immersive, interactive learning experiences, teachers can create more dynamic and effective language classrooms.

However, the success of this integration relies heavily on the active participation and cooperation of all stakeholders. Teachers must be empowered with the knowledge, skills, and resources necessary to incorporate AI into their practice effectively. This requires a commitment to ongoing professional development and support from educational institutions and policymakers. Learners, too, must be engaged as active collaborators in this process. By involving students in the design, implementation, and evaluation of AI-powered learning tools, we can ensure that these technologies are meeting their needs and preferences. This learner-centered approach also helps to develop critical AI literacy skills, preparing students to navigate an increasingly AI-driven world. Finally, researchers will come to play a crucial role in the Collaborative AI ecosystem. By conducting rigorous, interdisciplinary research on the impacts and effectiveness of AI in language education, researchers can provide the evidence base necessary to guide the development and deployment of these technologies. This research should be grounded in the real-world experiences of teachers and learners, and should aim to address the ethical, social, and pedagogical implications of AI integration.

This book will aim to facilitate your exploration of Collaborative AI in ELT and CALL; my initial focus will be on the ELT context, but where possible, I will make connections to the larger realm of language teaching and learning. Throughout, it will be crucial to recognize that successfully integrating AI in the classroom requires a multifaceted approach. The upcoming chapters will explore the various aspects of this approach, drawing upon my experiences as the English Language Specialist for Bahrain on AI in Education with the US Department of State and my work in recreating EAP classes with explicit AI integration at George Washington University.

At this point, it may be helpful to review the roadmap for the remainder of this book. Chapter 4 will focus on the pedagogical approaches for AI integration, emphasizing the importance of combining human expertise with AI support to create a student-centered learning experience. This chapter will demonstrate how AI can be seamlessly integrated into teaching practices to enhance student outcomes by exploring techniques such as the flipped classroom model and using AI tools like Quizlet for pre-class vocabulary learning. Moving on to chapter 5, we will examine the role of AI in assessment and feedback within the ELT context. By leveraging AI-driven tools like automated essay scoring systems and adaptive quizzes, educators can provide timely, personalized feedback to students while managing their own workloads more efficiently. This chapter will highlight how AI can support both summative and formative assessments, ultimately fostering student learning and language acquisition.

Chapter 6 will tackle the critical issues of ethics and inclusion in an AI-rich world. As we integrate AI into ELT, it is essential to address concerns such as data privacy, digital equity, and the need for culturally sensitive and unbiased AI tools. This chapter will also discuss AI-related issues in academic integrity, acknowledging the potential challenges posed by the uncritical deployment of AI assistance by learners. Building upon the ethical considerations discussed in chapter 6, chapter 7 will explore the classroom and institutional policy considerations necessary for the successful implementation of Collaborative AI. By establishing clear guidelines and addressing professional anxieties, educators and administrators can ensure a smooth transition towards AI integration in ELT practices.

Chapter 8 will emphasize the importance of teacher professional development in the context of AI integration. As the AI landscape continues to evolve rapidly, it is crucial for educators to stay up-to-date with the latest advancements and best practices. This chapter will outline strategies for building AI literacy and competence among educators, ensuring that they can effectively leverage AI tools in the classroom. Finally, chapter 9 will look ahead to the future of ELT in an AI-driven world. By discussing emerging trends and technologies, such as advanced natural language processing and immersive virtual reality environments, this chapter will highlight the potential impact of AI on the field. However, it will also emphasize the enduring importance of human expertise and the need for a collaborative approach between educators and AI.

Throughout this book, we will explore the concept of Collaborative AI, which recognizes that the most effective integration of AI in ELT involves a synergistic relationship between human educators and AI technologies. By leveraging the strengths of both artificial intelligence and human expertise, we can create a future where AI enhances and transforms the language learning experience, ultimately benefiting both educators and students alike. The insights and experiences shared in the upcoming chapters will provide a roadmap for navigating this exciting, if not disruptive, moment in teaching and learning. Throughout, I will endeavor to provide practical and actionable advice for language teachers, researchers, and administrators based on my fieldwork providing teacher development, data analytics workshops, and policy consulting in the US, Asia, and the Middle East. Throughout, readers are encouraged to consider what localization of these recommendations to their respective local, institutional, and classroom (e.g., target language) contexts would look like.

4

Pedagogical Approaches for AI Integration: Human Expertise + AI Support

Previous chapters have sought to position this book against a shifting interdisciplinary backdrop, one marked by decided disruption and concerted change. They have also worked to equip the reader with an operative understanding of artificial intelligence without straying too far into the technical "weeds." The remainder of this volume will take a more applied approach to provide actionable recommendations for classroom and professional practice in CALL contexts. Here, I will pull heavily from work that I have done with the US Embassy in Bahrain, The Bahraini Ministry of Education, Bahrain Teachers College, the TESOL Research Collaboration Network (Vietnam), and several instructional support organs at George Washington University. As this is the case, you are likely to notice that many of the examples discussed focus on ELT contexts. Where possible, I will turn to the literature or my disciplinary peers to share insights on broader CALL contexts beyond English-centric ones.

A central goal of this chapter, then, will be to advance a pedagogical framework for language teaching and learning in the age of AI, one that, while language agnostic, is flexible enough to allow a diverse array of language professionals to find ways to meaningfully use AI tools, and especially generative AI tools, to support their instructional labor, drive learning and acquisition, and better prepare learners to live, be, and act on and in an increasingly AI-supported and nearly always tech-mediated world. A secondary goal will be to provide practitioners with useful examples of how to apply the approach advocate for herein. While examples may be crafted on particular platforms (e.g., GPT4ALL, GW's High Performance Computing Cluster) or using certain models (e.g., Gemma 7b, Mistral Instruct, Llama 70b, etc.), these are intended to serve as models as you work to integrate AI into your own practice.

At the core of every discussion in this chapter, and indeed the remainder of this book, will be the idea that AI should always be viewed as a *supplement* to human expertise and ability, not a *replacement for* it. At no point should you assume that the approaches advocated herein are meant to replace the irreplaceable work of the skilled and highly trained educator. Nor are students' abilities to use AI-powered tools a replacement for the domain, linguistic, or procedural knowledge needed to function in a second language, to be critical citizens, or to be productive members of a society. Indeed, meaningful AI integration should always stress the importance of taking a collaborative and complimentary view of AI in professional practice and human communication.

Collaborative AI & Pedagogy

To help guide the discussion that will occur in this chapter, a consolidated pedagogical framework can be a helpful tool for thought. To that end, this section will summarize one possible pedagogical framework for collaborative AI in language teaching and learning (Table 4.1, below), and each component of this framework will be further explored in subsequent sections of this chapter. It is important to bear in mind that this represents just *one possible* approach to AI integration in CALL contexts and should not be seen as *the* approach (see also Paiz, 2020). Indeed, educators should feel empowered to take the parts of the framework that work for their practice or their context and to modify what does not to tailor a solution to their teaching philosophy, student population, and material conditions.

Before outlining the framework let us begin by defining *collaborative AI* as an approach to artificial intelligence that stresses the importance of always keeping a human in the loop. Said another way, it is a view of AI as a technology that should exist synergistically with human beings, supplementing and extending their natural abilities while still creating space for human expertise, creativity, and agency. Indeed, the notion of collaborative AI is not unique to this text but is instead part of a small but growing voice in computer sciences and the fields of AI and human-computer interaction more specifically (see Koch & Oulasvirta, 2018; Saffiotti et al., 2020; Wang et al., 2021). Taking a collaborative stance on AI integration, then, creates space for more squarely ground the discussion of AI integration in disciplinary discourses by connecting it to existing theoretical frameworks on how people learn and acquire languages.

In this case, Atkinson's (2002) sociocognitive approach from applied linguistics equips us with a powerful theoretical tool to frame AI

Table 4.1 A Tabular Summary of an AI-integrative Pedagogical Framework for CALL Contexts

Framework Element	Description	Classroom Example
Sociocognitivism with Collaborative Triad	Knowledge construction involves a dynamic interplay between teacher, students, and AI where all participants can learn from and influence each other.	Students draft writing samples, AI provides feedback/suggestions, and teachers offer alternative perspectives or focus on areas AI might be less equipped to address (i.e., complex figurative language).
Teacher as Orchestrator and (Co-)Learner	Teachers foster a collaborative environment, model critical use of AI, and participate as co-learners, emphasizing that they too are learning alongside their students within this ever-evolving space.	Teacher transparently investigates AI responses that are unexpected or confusing, modeling inquiry and demonstrating that AI is not an infallible source of knowledge.
AI as Active Tool & Site of Inquiry and Critique	AI is used purposefully as a catalyst for discussion, language experimentation, and co-construction of knowledge rather than simply a source of answers or corrections.	Class identifies patterns of errors or limitations in AI output and develops strategies to work around them or provide corrective feedback to improve the models themselves (if applicable).
Emphasis on Metacognition & Transparency	All participants (even the AI, in a sense) are encouraged to reflect on their learning process.	Students keep reflective logs on AI interactions, identifying where it pushed their thinking and areas where they felt their own expertise was essential.
Focus on Meaningful Tasks	AI is integrated into authentic language activities, not just as a standalone skill.	Students collaborate on a multilingual website project, using AI tools to draft translations and humans to refine for cultural accuracy.
Emphasis on Collaborative Interaction	Learning activities prioritize peer-to-peer exchange and negotiation of meaning while leveraging AI tools.	Groups use an AI chatbot to role-play real-world scenarios, focusing on pragmatics (how language is used in context), social norms, and cultural variations.
Sociocultural Sensitivity	The sociocognitive lens highlights the impact of cultural background on language use and emphasizes awareness of potential biases inherent in AI.	*Class explores how AI-generated images might vary across cultures and analyze the potential biases built into the models.
Addressing Ethical Implications	Teachers emphasize responsible AI use, academic integrity, and transparency.	Class collaboratively develops guidelines for appropriate AI use within different types of assignments.

integration into CALL contexts. It is, therefore, the entry point for the pedagogical framework advanced here. Taking a sociocognitive approach to AI integration allows us to account for the tripartite collaboration between teacher – student – tool that must be facilitated for meaningful AI integration. A sociocognitive approach then accounts for how Knowledge construction involves a dynamic interplay between teachers, students, and AI where all participants can learn from and influence each other. The teacher plays a critical, if somewhat shifted, role in this collaborative triad.

In a pedagogical framework for collaborative AI in language teaching and learning, the teacher becomes an orchestrator and co-learner. As an orchestrator, the instructor becomes responsible for designing and managing the learning environment and creating the material conditions for successful AI integration into instructional tasks in a manner that supports learning outcomes, is aligned with disciplinary best practices, and complements human instruction and learning. Acting as orchestrator requires the teacher to make purposeful decisions about AI tool use and instructional design – an extension of their own critical AI literacy. Teacher as co-learner extends our collaborative framework to be about more than just teacher/AI or student/AI collaboration also to include instructor/learner collaboration. When in the co-learner role, the teacher may make use of student-centered instructional design decisions to leverage students' emerging AI literacy and knowledge of technology tools to experiment alongside students with AI tools to understand their capabilities and limitations better. Moreover, by modeling the habits of mind of a lifelong learner, the teacher-as-co-learner role also allows the instructor to encourage students to take greater agency over their learning and language acquisition trajectories. Finally, acting in the guide role, the teacher can provide feedback, guidance, and mentorship as students acquire not only linguistic ability but also the critical AI literacy needed to be successful learners in an increasingly AI-mediated social world.

The next element in the proposed pedagogical framework is to view AI as an active tool and a site of inquiry. This means viewing AI tools through a purpose-driven lens that drives us as educators and our learners to engage with these tools in modes that go beyond our typical use of large internet tools like search engines. We are not just seeking answers. We are, instead, using language to engage in meaningful dialogue with a computer system as an interlocutor. And this interlocutor, like all others, is one about which we must make regular judgments about trust, veracity, and reliability. This means, often then, that we must also view AI as a target of inquiry – something we can explore with our learners in dialogic ways, creating additional space for learning and language learning and use.

Given the legitimate concerns about the potential for learning loss from critics of AI in education (see Ahmad et al., 2023; Hoorn et al., 2021), there is the need for any AI-integrative pedagogy to make space for learners to reflect on their experiences, knowledge, and abilities and for increased transparency from all parties in the instructional encounter. This then means that focusing on students' metacognition and creating space for it throughout the curriculum becomes even more important in the age of AI. Students must be given an opportunity to grapple with their own learning and to receive meaningful feedback about how to improve their learning processes. Additionally, in an AI-integrative environment, both teachers and students must be transparent about their AI use to help build a culture of trust and to enable both instructor and learner better to assess learning trajectories.

Perhaps already stated, if somewhat tacitly, is that the greater integration of AI tools, especially generative and constructive ones, requires a concerted effort to incorporate them into meaningful languaging tasks. This will not only underscore the relevance of acquiring AI literacy and linguistic skills for our learners, but it will also help students to better consider how AI tools and human expertise can work collaboratively to facilitate greater human-human communication and connection in real-world ways aligned to their own potential future needs. This can be further extended by the next part of the proposed learning framework by emphasizing collaborative interaction – both human/computer and human/human. Taking this approach allows us to leverage the power of peer-to-peer interaction, which can help drive investment, engagement, and language learning, but to supplement it with AI tools to better prepare learners for the professional and social spaces that they will inhabit, further underscoring the value of acquiring linguistic skills and communicative competence because the AI really *cannot* "do it all" for you.

As we will explore further in chapter 6, AI is not a values-neutral technology. Indeed, no technology is ever values neutral. Each and every one is already/always implicated in the complex ecosocial tapestry of power-over and power-under, of privilege and marginalization. We can see this reflected in generative AI systems through the biases inherent in the systems because of their training data and the manner in which they are fine-tuned by their developers who are imbuing these tools with the same biases that drive them. And, this can even creep into wholly sub-symbolic systems trained entirely through unsupervised machine learning with little fine-tuning because the data used for training itself is often biased (see Crawford, 2020; Mitchell, 2019; Pasquale, 2020). This means that we as educators must make a concerted effort to ensure that our use of AI to support teaching and learning is done in a way that is sensitive to the sociocultural realities of our learners. Indeed, as a discipline, we have already accepted the importance of cultural (socio)cultural competence in language learning and acquisition (see Kramsch, 1993; Ortega, 2008). So, extending this focus on sociocultural sensitivity to AI integration in CALL contexts becomes even more salient as both teachers and learners will need to be able to leverage their own cultural understandings and social knowledge to ensure that the outputs of the AI tools that they are using are aligned to their needs, values, and social realities.

This brings us to the final component of this collaborative AI pedagogical framework, but one that will grow in importance as AI touches upon more and more aspects of our daily lives and as AI tools are refined and become more capable over time – namely that of addressing ethical considerations early, often, and explicitly in the language learning process. it is crucial for teachers and learners to engage in ongoing discussions and reflections about the ethical implications of these technologies. This involves considering issues such as data privacy, algorithmic bias, and the potential for AI to perpetuate or amplify existing social inequalities. By addressing these ethical considerations early in the learning process, teachers can help students develop a critical awareness of AI's benefits and limitations, as well as the skills and knowledge needed to use these technologies responsibly and equitably. Ultimately, addressing ethical considerations in a collaborative AI pedagogical framework is not to arrive at definitive answers or solutions but rather to foster a culture of ongoing inquiry, dialogue, and reflection. By empowering students to ask critical questions, consider multiple perspectives, and make informed decisions about the use of AI in their own lives and communities, language teachers can help prepare them to be responsible and engaged citizens in an increasingly AI-mediated world.

Exploring a Pedagogy of Collaborative AI

With this overview in hand, the rest of this chapter will provide more detailed explanations and examples of each component in the framework. The goal of this work is to create space for the reader to consider what this framework means in their own institutional context and in light of their own teaching philosophy. It is not meant to be read as a directive statement of *the* way to integrate AI into CALL contexts. Also, in the following sections, I will make use of an array of free and paid generative AI tools, in part to create exposure to the qualitative differences in capabilities between free and paid versions of generative AI tools, with the paid versions typically having larger context windows, more current knowledge bases, and better reasoning and analytic skills. I will ensure that I call out whether a tool was free or paid at the time of writing this book to help instructors and teacher-educators decide which tools, if any, they want to experiment with in their own practice. Additionally, the examples in the following sections will come from a variety of target language classes, but the majority are likely to focus on ELT contexts because of my own professional positioning.

Sociocognitivism and the Collaborative Triad

The sociocognitive perspective on second language acquisition first entered disciplinary discourses in the early 2000s as a response to the so-called social turn in second language studies (Atkinson, 2002; Block, 2003). Most sociocognitive perspectives begin by viewing language as a key tool for affiliative action; that is, language allows human agents to work together and to align with one another to carry out joint action. By way of example, consider the last time you built a piece of flatpack furniture with a friend or family member. You likely used language – both spoken and embodied (read: gestures) – to draw their attention to certain elements in your physical space, such as the hex key you need to turn a screw, a particular piece of laminated particle board to slot into tab A, or the inscrutable instructions printed on flimsy recycled paper. During this task, you are aligning to a shared goal (building a piece of furniture) and you are building, or perhaps testing, the affiliative bonds between you and the other party. Key here, from the sociocognitive perspective, is that language is being used to mediate this interaction with an end result being some change in your ecosocial space.

Beyond offering a new perspective on language and its role in facilitating alignment and mediating joint action, sociocognitivism also provides a theoretical framework that accounts for humans' use of tools to navigate, manage, and effect change on their ecosocial world (Atkinson, 2014, 2019; Huth, 2020). A tool can be understood as any affordance (e.g., a smartphone, pen, and notebook, gesture) that supports our existence in our eco-social spaces. More than this, however, we may use certain tools to off-load a portion of our cognitive burdens to extend our abilities, as long as that tool is readily and regularly accessible. A good example of this is the smartphone most likely sitting on your desk or in your pocket as you read this book. This device, its apps, and always on internet connection are likely almost always within arm's reach, and you probably use it a lot throughout the day to navigate your world and do what you need to do. Trying to find a new coffee shop that is not one decked out in green and mermaids? You probably open an app like Google Maps or Yelp. Trying to remember that who wrote that one article you read last week? You probably open a web browser and hit up your favorite search engine. You are likely not memorizing routes to locations anymore or may even find it harder to commit certain facts about your day to memory because you have come to offload a portion of your cognitive processes to this now vital affordance and its panoply of useful application. In this example, the smartphone and the internet have become not just mere tools but extensions of your cognitive apparatus – central affordances to support you as you go about your day.

By applying a sociocognitive approach to our present issue of meaningful AI integration, it is possible to cast new light on the potential role of AI in language teaching and learning. From this perspective, then AI becomes a key cognitive affordance to help us navigate our physical and social worlds and to affect change on our ecosocial spaces. As educators, generative AI tools can provide us with alternative takes on tried-and-true assignments as we work to stay relevant to our learners. As researchers, AI tools like rose.ai Julius.ai, or ChatGPT in Data Analytics Mode can help us to streamline exploratory data analysis or to plan visualizations that render our work more knowable and accessible to others. For learners, this means that multimodal AI, like ChatGPT 4.0 Omni or DuoLingo's chatbots may serve as an interlocutor tailor-made to support their learning and language acquisition, helping to mitigate the influence of the affective filter for some students. As with Atkinson's sociocognitive approach, AI tools must be sufficiently and regularly available for them to be considered a part of one's sociocognitive apparatus, This means that both the tool's provider must ensure sufficient up-time and educational institutions must work to ensure sufficient material support to ensure the proper infrastructure is in place so that instructors, researchers, and students have access to AI tools when they need them.

In the classroom, the integration of AI can significantly enhance the teaching and learning experience by complementing traditional pedagogical methods. For instance, when students draft writing samples, AI tools can be employed to provide immediate feedback and suggestions. This feedback can range from grammatical corrections and stylistic improvements to recommendations for enhancing clarity and coherence. By using AI for these initial stages of writing, students can engage in a process of iterative refinement, honing their writing skills through guided practice.

To implement this approach, educators can follow a structured process. First, introduce the writing assignment to the students, clearly outlining the objectives and guidelines. Encourage students to focus on getting their ideas down in the initial draft, emphasizing content over perfection. Once the drafts are complete, students can input their work into an AI writing tool, such as Grammarly or Hemingway, to receive instant feedback. The AI will analyze the text and suggest improvements on grammar, style, and clarity.

Students should carefully review the AI's suggestions, deciding which changes to accept or reject based on their understanding and judgment. This iterative revision process helps students learn from their mistakes and see tangible improvements in their work over time. After revising their drafts with AI feedback, students submit their work for teacher review. Teachers can then provide deeper, more nuanced feedback, focusing on areas where AI might be less effective, such as complex figurative language, cultural context, and thematic depth. The teacher's feedback highlights the strengths of the students' work and offers constructive criticism on areas for improvement. Students then incorporate this feedback into their final drafts, making thoughtful revisions that consider both the AI and teacher input. This balanced approach ensures that students benefit from the strengths of both AI (speed and consistency) and human teachers (insight and empathy), leading to a more comprehensive and effective learning experience.

This approach supports good language teaching pedagogy in several ways. By engaging in multiple rounds of revision, students refine their writing skills and develop a sense of autonomy and confidence. AI tools provide immediate, objective feedback on technical aspects of writing, allowing teachers to focus on higher-order skills and personalized instruction. This division of labor enhances the overall learning experience, as students receive comprehensive support that addresses both routine errors and complex writing issues. Furthermore, by deciding which AI suggestions to accept or reject, students develop critical thinking skills and learn to evaluate feedback, make informed decisions, and take ownership of their writing process. Integrating AI into the classroom also prepares students for a future where AI-human collaboration is common, making them adept at using AI tools to enhance their work while understanding the unique value of human insight. By following this structured process and understanding the pedagogical benefits, educators can effectively integrate AI into language teaching, creating a dynamic and supportive learning environment that enhances student outcomes. This alignment with the sociocognitive perspective highlights the potential of AI to transform language learning into a more efficient, personalized, and effective process.

Teacher as Orchestrator and (Co-)Learner

A pedagogical framework that seeks to foster an environment of collaborative AI in the language learning classroom requires us to reimagine the teacher's role in the classroom. This act is one that, in language education specifically and education more broadly, we are already rather familiar with because of global pandemics (Hill et al., 2020; Rosehart et al., 2022) or shifts towards more student-centered pedagogical practices (Froyd & Simpson, 2008; Keiler, 2018). Indeed, the collaborative AI pedagogical framework extends these shifts in the teacher's role by layers on AI tools and affordances to existing roles that the educator inhabits. Critical language pedagogies, tracing their lineage back to the Paolo Freire, have already advocated for student-centered classroom spaces where the instructor is more of a facilitator and coach (see Crookes, 2022; Norton & Toohey, 2004; Paiz, 2020); this is held in contrast to more traditionalist instructional paradigms with the educator held in a position of authority over both students and course content. Acting as facilitator, coach, and guide often requires the teacher to work collaboratively with learners to build a classroom community of learners engaged in joint action. It is a highly negotiated space and one responsive to the needs and interests of the community members. Pedagogies that support the collaborative AI require the instructor to also act as an *orchestrator* of students, curricular materials, learning activities, and AI to create a rich instructional encounter that supports students' learning while also preparing them to become more effective and agentive learners in an AI rich world where ready answers (but not necessarily deep understanding) are just a few keystrokes away. In the orchestrator role, the teacher coordinates various elements of the learning environment to create cohesive, engaging, and impactful educational experiences. This role involves strategic planning, seamless integration of resources, and dynamic adaptation to both the learners' needs and the evolving educational landscape, especially in AI-rich settings.

Being an orchestrator begins with the careful selection and integration of AI tools that enhance the learning experience. This involves choosing technologies such as intelligent tutoring systems, adaptive learning platforms, and virtual assistants that can provide personalized support and feedback to students. The instructor-as-orchestrator ensures that these technologies are not merely add-ons but are thoughtfully aligned with the learning objectives and curricular goals. This alignment ensures that the instructional design is enhanced, not distracted, by the use of AI, creating a cohesive and effective learning environment. Beyond this, the orchestrator also takes a central role in designing learning activities that leverage AI to create engaging, personalized, and immersive experiences. These activities are crafted to go beyond surface-level learning, encouraging students to engage in critical thinking, problem-solving, and the practical application of knowledge. By focusing on these higher-order thinking skills, the orchestrator ensures that students are not simply finding or memorizing facts but are developing a deeper understanding of the content and developing their own critical AI literacy skills in the process.

Given the seeming endemic rise in screen time, facilitating collaboration and interaction among students is another crucial responsibility of the orchestrator so that the language classroom can continue to leverage the advantage of language-in-use through social interaction as an instructional tool. To that end, the teacher works to set up collaborative projects and discussions that utilize AI tools to enhance communication and teamwork. Additionally, the orchestrator uses real-time data on student performance and interactions to dynamically form and reform student groups. This approach ensures that groupings (of both students and AI-powered tools) are always optimal for promoting productive and meaningful collaborative learning experiences while providing students with diverse perspectives and exposure to a variety of language forms and users. This, naturally, means that the teacher-as-orchestrator continuously monitors student progress using AI analytics, which allows for the provision of real-time feedback, interventions, and support. By creating adaptive learning pathways, the orchestrator adjusts the difficulty and focus of activities based on individual learner's progress and needs. This responsive approach ensures that each student receives the appropriate level of challenge and support, facilitating continuous growth and improvement.

An end goal of acting as orchestrator is to support learner agency and autonomy. They teach students how to use AI tools to monitor their own learning, set goals, and reflect on their progress. By fostering these self-regulation skills, the orchestrator helps students become more independent and effective learners. Additionally, they build AI literacy by helping students understand how AI works and how to critically evaluate AI-generated content and recommendations, empowering them to use AI tools responsibly and effectively. To help students become critical human agents and language users, the orchestrator is vigilant about the ethical implications of AI use in education. They ensure that AI tools are used in a manner that is fair, transparent, and respectful of student privacy. Moreover, the orchestrator creates an inclusive learning environment by ensuring that AI tools and activities are accessible to all students, supporting diverse learning needs and backgrounds.

This commitment to ethical and inclusive practices ensures that all students benefit from the technological advancements in education, fostering an equitable and supportive learning community.

Additionally, pedagogies that support the deployment of AI in language teaching and learning require the instructor to become a fellow learner alongside their students, in part because of how new the technology is and in part because of how quickly the technology evolves. For example, while drafting this book, OpenAI's ChatGPT saw three major model revisions and considerable expansion in its capabilities. This means that the potential pedagogical applications and even best practices for engaging with AI tools will continue to evolve. To both minimize the cognitive burden of the educator, and to further democratize classroom practices, learning how to ethically and meaningful engage with AI tools as part of the learning process can be very help. This may mean opening oneself to a position of greater vulnerability by sharing one's own missteps with learners so that they can "learn from you mistakes" and make more effective or ethical use of AI tools to *support* and *not replace* their learning.

By way of example, consider an advanced English language class, the teacher integrates an AI-powered language model, like Anthropic's Claude3Opus, to assist with writing exercises. One afternoon, during a session focused on essay writing, a student uses the AI to generate a response to a prompt about climate change. The AI's response is unexpected and somewhat confusing, leading the student to raise their hand and question its accuracy. Instead of providing the correct answer outright, the teacher sees this as an invaluable teaching moment. The teacher invites the class to join in a transparent investigation of the AI's response. The class examines the AI's response, breaking it down sentence by sentence. They compare it to the original prompt and consider the context. The teacher encourages them to identify any possible misunderstandings or errors in the AI's output by verifying its content against the collective knowledge of the class and reputable external sources, deepening their investigation. As they carry out the research and vetting, the teacher takes the opportunity to discuss the strengths and limitations of AI, highlighting the double-edged sword that LLM-based AI tools represent because of their quick, ready access to potentially flawed information. The teacher then asks the students to reflect on the process by considering what they learn from this investigation and how they can apply this critical approach to other AI-generated content that they encounter. Doing so helps to reinforce the critical AI literacy skills of the learners and reinforce the critical thinking and human-first creativity that we value in language teaching and learning context.

Through this collaborative effort, the class not only resolves the confusion but also learns a vital lesson about the nature of AI. They see firsthand that AI tools, while powerful, require human oversight and critical engagement. They learn to question and investigate AI responses, enhancing their understanding and critical thinking skills. The outcome of this exercise is multifaceted. Students come away with a deeper appreciation for the importance of critical thinking. They gain a better understanding of AI's workings and limitations, building their AI literacy. The collaborative investigation fosters a sense of community and shared learning, while encouraging students to become more independent and confident in using AI tools responsibly. The teacher, acting as both orchestrator and co-learner, has turned a moment of confusion into a powerful learning experience. They have shown the students that learning is a dynamic and interactive process, preparing them for a future where AI is an integral part of their educational and professional lives.

AI as an Active Tool & Site of Inquiry and Critique

Another component of a pedagogy of collaborative AI is utilizing AI as an active tool rather than merely a passive source of information. This can be extended by viewing AI resources as a site of inquiry and critique. Using AI as an *active tool* means engaging with AI systems dialogically and as an extension of, and not replacement of, one's own cognitive apparatus. This may require, both for ourselves and our students, unlearning certain digital literacy skills that have been acquired through sustained engagement with more traditional tools like Google search or research databases. Taking an active approach to using AI systems means that we deploy our own (emerging) expertise and perspectives alongside those provided as output from generative AI tools and then critically synthesize these disparate information streams together to arrive at either new knowledge or courses of action. Doing so can also encourage us to view AI and its outputs as *a site of inquiry and critique*. By engaging with AI as a site of inquiry, we use AI tools as a starting point for further investigation, driven by our natural human curiosity about a given topic or problem. To take this idea further, we question how the AI system arrived at its answer by considering what data may have been used and what biases and blind spots might be present. By taking this more critical, active approach to AI use, we are able to inhabit a more active, agentive position.

Putting this into practice can take a myriad of forms. Here, I will briefly outline three possible examples that readers are invited to consider in the context of their own professional practice, modifying as needed. Take a Japanese as a foreign language classroom. A traditional approach to using AI-power language tools would merely have students conversing with an AI chatbot in the target language. In a pedagogy based on collaborative AI, we instead design the activity to encourage students to engage in active interaction with the AI tools and to take agency over the interaction. The activity can begin by having students work together to research possible conversation topics and to explore possible language usages that may be helpful to them as they engage in conversational practice. From here, either alone or in small groups, learners can engage in the conversation with an AI chatbot in the target language, taking note of the content of the responses and the default language use of the AI tool (e.g., defaulting to more formal *-masu* verb endings). We may further encourage students to attend to places where the conversation with the AI tool deviated from their expectations – either straying off topic, being too formulaic/not sufficiently human-like, or containing linguistic errors. This active engagement, coupled with self-reflection after the activity is over can foster deeper learning on the part of the students and help them more effectively acquire the critical AI literacy skills needed to be successful learners in an AI rich world. This critical thinking can encourage students to view AI not just as a tool to be used, but also as a springboard for further investigation of language and culture.

A traditional approach to using AI-powered language tools in an Arabic as a second language classroom might have students using AI to generate arguments and rebuttals for a debate without further analysis or reflection. However, in a pedagogy based on collaborative AI, we design the activity to encourage students to engage in active interaction with AI tools and to take agency over the interaction. The activity begins with students working together to research debate topics relevant to the Arabic-speaking world. They identify key vocabulary and phrases that may be useful and explore cultural and contextual nuances that could influence the debate. This collaborative preparation phase not only builds a strong foundation for the debate but also enhances students' understanding of the cultural and linguistic context. In pairs or small groups, learners then use AI tools to generate arguments and counterarguments in Arabic. They take note of the AI's language use, argument structure, and any cultural references or idiomatic expressions. This active interaction with the AI tool helps students observe and understand how the AI constructs responses and uses language. During the debate, students actively engage with the AI-generated content, identifying areas where the AI's responses may lack depth, cultural relevance, or logical consistency. They critique the AI's arguments, discussing possible biases and inaccuracies. This critical analysis phase encourages students to think deeply about the quality and reliability of the AI's contributions. After the debate, students reflect on the strengths and weaknesses of the AI's contributions compared to their own and their peers'. This self-reflection phase helps them synthesize AI outputs with their own knowledge and develop a more nuanced understanding of the debate topic. By engaging in this reflective practice, students enhance their critical thinking and debate skills. Taking this more active, inquiry-based approach to using AI collaborative, Students learn to view AI as both a tool and a partner in the learning process, enhancing their critical thinking and debate skills. This approach fosters a deeper engagement with the Arabic language and culture, promoting active learning and AI literacy.

Adopting an active, inquiry-based, and critical usage of AI helps to support a pedagogy of collaborative AI in the classroom, and it has significant implications for critical AI literacy acquisition and overall language learning and teaching. This approach seeks to transform how students interact with AI, making them active participants in their learning journey. By engaging with AI tools as active collaborators, students develop a nuanced understanding of how these systems work. They learn to question the sources of AI-generated content, recognizing potential biases and data limitations. This critical engagement fosters an inquisitive mindset, encouraging students to not just accept AI outputs at face value but to probe deeper into the mechanisms behind these outputs. This process helps students become more discerning consumers of AI technologies, equipping them with the skills needed to navigate and critique the ever-evolving digital landscape.

Integrating collaborative AI pedagogy in language learning enhances both the teaching process and the students' learning experience. By using AI to generate conversational practice or debate content, students engage in real-time language use, which is crucial for language acquisition. This interaction helps them notice and analyze linguistic patterns, idiomatic expressions, and cultural nuances embedded in the AI-generated content. Moreover, the collaborative preparation and critical analysis phases of the activities promote deeper understanding and retention of the language being learned. For teachers, this approach provides a dynamic tool to facilitate language learning. It allows for the creation of more interactive and engaging lessons that can be tailored to the specific needs and interests of the students. Teachers can guide students in exploring language use in context, leading to more meaningful and practical language learning experiences.

This pedagogical approach also supports the development of collaborative AI pedagogy and habits of mind for our learners, which is essential in a world increasingly influenced by AI technologies. By working together to engage with AI tools, students learn to combine their cognitive abilities with AI-generated insights, fostering a partnership between human intelligence and artificial intelligence. This collaboration enhances their problem-solving skills and prepares them for future scenarios where AI will be a regular part of professional and personal decision-making processes. Moreover, the reflective practices embedded in this approach encourage students to synthesize AI outputs with their own knowledge and perspectives. This synthesis not only strengthens their individual critical thinking skills but also promotes a collaborative learning environment where ideas and insights are shared and developed collectively. By adopting a pedagogy of collaborative AI, educators can create learning environments that are dynamic, interactive, and reflective, ultimately preparing students to thrive in a world where AI is an integral part of everyday life.

Emphasis on Metacognition & Transparency

In a collaborative framework for AI integration, *metacognition*, or "thinking about thinking," remains as critical component of effective learning as it does in traditional language classrooms and CALL contexts (see Hauck, 2005; Wenden, 1998). It involves self-regulation and self-awareness of one's cognitive processes, and in language learning, it helps students to plan, monitor, and evaluate their learning strategies. For language teachers, metacognition can aid in strategic planning by helping to inform lesson planning and classroom management to improve student learning outcomes. In the context of AI, metacognition focuses on creating space for and value around deeply reflective practice (by the educator) and tool use (by both students and instructors). By emphasizing the acquisition of metacognitive skills and providing room for our students (and ourselves) to practice these skills in an AI-enhanced CALL context, we continue to place value on learning and human expertise while framing AI as a collaborative partner in such efforts – as opposed to a replacement for them.

To cultivate metacognitive abilities in an AI-rich environment, students could be encouraged to maintain reflective logs. These logs would serve as a space for students to document their experiences with AI tools, noting how they influence their thinking and language learning or use. Early on, it may be helpful to provide targeted prompts to guide students' reflections, such as:

- How did the AI tool challenge your understanding of the material?
- In what ways did you rely on your own knowledge to complete the task?
- What insights did you gain from the AI's feedback?
- In way ways was the AI ineffective in helping you learn? Or, how did it stand as a roadblock to your learning?
- What new linguistic items did you learn through your interaction with the AI and how confident are you that you can use these terms correctly in the future?

As the course progresses, students may be given greater flexibility in how they focus their reflections and may begin to consider how their language learning and improved critical AI literacy move outside of the language classroom to other classes they are taking, to their professional lives, or to their personal lives as they begin to exist in a world increasingly defined by AI-generated outputs. If you make use of a reflective final assessment, like the ones described in chapter 5, these reflections can be crafted as a powerful preparatory tool for learners.

Educators can, and perhaps early on in their own AI integration journeys should, join their students in writing regular reflections on their use of AI in and out of the classroom. Doing so can help language educators to better plan how to introduce different AI-powered tools to their learners and how to use them to support effective learning by scaffolding more traditional activities or creating new opportunities for authentic language engagement and interaction. For the instructor, such reflections may instead focus on instructional and classroom management issues, such as how engaging with AI has either expanded or limited their lesson planning efforts or delimited new paths to more inclusive and accessible activities and instructional design.

An added benefit to using reflection as a tool to help inculcate metacognitive strategies is that it can also be used as a platform to increase transparency. Transparency is key to building trust in AI tools and to maintaining trust and good faith in the classroom between all members of the instructional context (e.g., students/peers/teachers/parents). Indeed, while working with the US Department of State in Bahrain, a common request from students and teachers across K-12 and higher educational contexts was greater transparency. Teachers want students to be transparent about their AI use, and students and parents want teachers to be transparent about their AI policies and expectations. So,

Figure 4.1 Sample AI Use Footnote

everything about the company and produce a more reliable trading algorithm that may

---

[1] **No Gen-AI was used in this Reflective Journal, Just Grammarly to correct grammar and fix punctuation.**

in our pedagogy of collaborative AI *transparency* involves being clear and explicit about our use of AI, the potential impacts its use, or non-use, has had on our teaching (or learning), our rationale for using AI tools, how we have used AI tools in our work as instructors and learners, and our expectations about acceptable (and unacceptable) AI use.

This transparency can be supported in several ways. Take the ESL writing class as one example. There, transparency on the students' side can be supported by requiring AI-use statements on all assignments. Depending on the length of the assignment, these statements may be relatively short, appearing as a footnote (see Figure 4.1, below). In these short statements, students may merely outline what AI tools they have used (if any).

For longer assignments, the AI use statement can take on a more protracted and reflective form. One implementation of this is the AI Use Table included as an appendix (see Figure 4.2, below). In this example, students do not just list what tools they used, but also what stages of writing they used them in, how they used them, and – returning to metacognition from earlier – a reflection of the impact that using these tools had on their writing and learning.

Beyond requiring transparency for our learners, we should also provide them with transparency. Both transparency in our expectations of them and our rationale for holding them to that standard, whatever it may be, and transparency in our own use of AI tools. Beginning with the latter, being transparent with our learners about our own AI use can serve two purposes. First, it can help establish transparency as a key facet of trust in our classrooms. By being transparent with our learners about our own AI use, we set the stage for them to also be transparent with us. We disempower some of the negative mindsets about AI that they may have acquired in other settings, where AI has been cast as a crutch for those that are less-than-capable, or as a tool for only academic dishonesty. To do so, we may just include a syllabus statement outlining our own use of AI tools in preparing for the class (Figure 4.3, below).

Additionally, instructors should be transparent with their students about their expectations of learners' use of AI tools in their classroom and the consequences should they fail to meet those expectations. The

Figure 4.2 Sample AI Use Table

Appendix A: AI Assistance Statement

"In the spirit of professionalism and academic integrity, I hereby assert that I used the following AI agents to assist in drafting, revising, and editing this paper. The core ideas of this paper and the synthesis of evidence to support key ideas and an analysis of how that support functions are original to me. However, I did deploy AI agents during the following stages for specific purposes, as outlined in the table below."

Stage of Writing	AI Agent Used	Purpose/Method Used	Impact on Writing
Idea Generation	None	None	None
Research	Bing Copilot	Used to help generate an outline and discover topics to discuss.	Minimal, was only beneficial to framing my ideas.
Drafting	ChatGPT - 4	Used to generate some sample paragraphs where I sometimes became confused for how to progress.	I only paraphrased parts of the paragraphs that I decided to keep and used it only as inspiration for my own writing.
Revision	None	None	None
Editing	Grammarly-Premium	Used to check for grammar/syntax errors and provide minor sentence structure adjustments.	Effects were minimal and all the writing was all my own.

Figure 4.3 Sample of Instructor AI Transparency Statement in a Course Syllabus

AI Policy

Studends will be introduced to and are welcome to use an array of generative and constructive AI tools. However, students will be required to (A) fully disclose and reflect on their use of AI and its impacts on their learning and work, and (B) strictly adhere to any assignment-specific limitations placed on AI use. Failure to adhere to either part of this policy will lead to immediate reduction in the grade of the work in question by two letter grades. Repeated abuses of this policy will lead to referral to the Office of the Dean of Students for possible disciplinary action up to and including dismissal from the university due to academic integrity violations.

Instructor AI Transparency Statement

In this course, AI tools will be used to provide personalized feedback, support learning, and manage administrative tasks. All data collected will be handled with care to ensure privacy and fairness. Please engage critically with these tools and reach out with any questions or concerns.

syllabus statement in Figure 4.3 is a good starting point. But, it can be more effective to tailor AI policies to individual assignments or types of assignments. The goal here is outline in clear and accessible language for learners what kinds of AI tools can be used in a given assignment, if any, the acceptable ways of using those tools, and (most importantly) your rationale as a teacher for holding students to these expectations (c.f., Figures 4.4 and 4.5, below).

In a collaborative AI-integrated learning framework, metacognition – self-regulation and awareness of cognitive processes – remains

Figure 4.4 Sample AI Use Policy from a Weekly Reflective Assignment

AI-Use Policy:

The use of generative AI is expressly forbidden for this assignment series. The reasons for this is because reflective journals represent an intimate genre that AI simply cannot adequately replicate. Additionally, the focus in this assignment series is on the students metacognitive and reflective skills, as opposed to accuracy or analysis. Students are, however, permitted to use constructive AI for revision/editing. Students must include, as a footnote on the bottom of the first page, a statement asserting their use of AI and the stages of writing in which it was used.

Figure 4.5 Sample AI Use Policy from a Longer, Summative Assignment

AI Policy Specifics:

For this assignment, you are encouraged to use generative AI tools to brainstorm and explore topics, but you are not permitted to use them to draft your papers. Additionally, you may use constructive AI tools, such as Grammarly, to edit and refine your work. This policy is in place to ensure that your writing reflects your own understanding and effort, fostering genuine learning and skill development. Using AI tools appropriately helps you develop critical thinking and writing skills, which are essential for your academic and professional success. Further, you are required to include a reflective AI use table as an appendix to this assignment. Failure to do so will be considered an academic integrity issue and will lead to a grade of 0 until it is corrected.

Note:

Failure to adhere to the rules regarding the use of AI tools in the assignment, or any other stated requirements, may result in a reduction in grade or other penalties as outlined in GWU's Academic Integrity Code.

Sample AI-use Table - Required as an appendix

crucial for effective learning. For language teachers, it aids in strategic lesson planning and classroom management. In AI-enhanced contexts, fostering metacognition involves reflective practices, such as maintaining logs to document AI interactions and their influence on thinking. This promotes deeper engagement, critical thinking, and transparency, which are vital for building trust and enhancing learning outcomes. Educators should model and encourage these practices, ensuring AI is viewed as a collaborative partner rather than a replacement.

Focus on Meaningful Tasks

As language educators, many of us have been professionalized into the discipline at a time when communicative pedagogies and sociocognitive theoretical approaches are ascendant (see Atkinson, 2002; Savignon, 1987). We theorize, inquire, and teach in a field well into its post-social turn (Block, 2003), and many of our students have come to expect that our classes will be driven by rich interaction and engagement with not only the rules of language, but the language in use. Because of this, any meaningful integration of AI into language education generally, and into CALL more specifically, must maintain and extend the field's rich and sustained engagement with meaningful languaging tasks (see Ellis, 2017; Levy & Stockwell, 2013). As with previous elements in this pedagogical framework, we arrive again at a moment where our professional practice does not radically change just because of the advent and proliferation of artificial intelligence and AI-powered tools. Indeed, as before, to facilitate a collaborative approach to AI integration, a strong focus on meaningful languaging tasks must be maintained. Said more simply, just because AI is part many people's daily lives, increasingly coming packaged "on device" – as seen with Apple iOS 18, Microsoft's Surface CoPilot+ laptop series – doesn't mean that we shift our focus in the language classroom to solely focus on AI literacy or using AI tools for languaging and communicative tasks.

Instead, we must continue to design and deploy *meaningful tasks that are AI-aware to better support our learners throughout their learning process and* instill in them the critical habits of mind necessary to be effective learners in an age where AI tools are more than willing to just "spit out" a *seemingly* correct answer. This means that we must continue to intentionally design and implement educational activities that recognize and integrate the capabilities and limitations of AI tools. These tasks go beyond simply using AI as a tool for convenience and instead leverage AI to enhance the learning process in a thoughtful and pedagogically sound manner.

This begins with integrating AI in pedagogically sound ways that align with learning objectives.. For example, AI can be used to generate writing prompts or provide feedback that guides students in improving their writing skills. These tasks are designed to engage students actively, encouraging them to interact with AI outputs critically rather than passively accepting them. And it is this encouraging of critical engagement that is a key component of AI-aware tasks. Students should be prompted to critically analyze the responses generated by AI, questioning the sources, potential biases, and accuracy of the information provided. Reflective practice is essential, with activities including opportunities for students to reflect on how AI tools influence their learning and the quality of the outputs they receive. Indeed, this reflective practice may draw attention to times that AI should be eschewed entirely and may require us to redesign our learning and communicative tasks to limit students' abilities to utilize AI tools in their completion, as we see in in-person, oral examinations.

Crafting meaningful assignments also means working to promote inquiry and synthesis as our learners engage with our instructional spaces, whether that be computer-mediated, traditional in-person, or a blend thereof. AI-aware tasks should prompt students to use AI-generated information as a starting point for further investigation and exploration of topics. Students learn to combine AI outputs with their own knowledge and research, developing deeper insights and understanding. Doing so naturally brings us to the realm of ethical considerations (see also chapter 6). Meaningful tasks must incorporate discussions on the ethical use of AI, addressing issues such as privacy, bias, and the responsible and transparent deployment of AI technologies in ways that support lifelong learning as opposed to subverting. Here, using powerful stories that students can relate to can be very helpful. For example, while writing this book, I was also pursuing a second master's degree in applied computer sciences. One semester, I "over-relied" on AI to help me understand the sticky topics in one of my classes. Now, using AI to "help me learn" was, to me at the time, heaven-sent. I was able to do more, more effectively and efficiently. However, it severely limited my internalization of core competencies needed to call myself a CS student. This was made abundantly clear to me when I sat for the final exam and froze entirely. Narratives like this can serve as a strong cautionary tale for students and can show them the value in getting it wrong and in being reflective enough learners to learn not only from what we excel at but also from our AI missteps.

To better visualize this component of a collaborative AI pedagogy, consider an activity where groups of students work together with AI agents to complete a sustained communicative task, such as communicating with a pen-pal or developing a website. Here, we will take a closer look at a multilingual website project where students collaborate to create content in multiple languages. They use AI tools to draft translations of the website content. However, the task does not end with the AI-generated output. Students then work together to refine these translations for cultural accuracy, ensuring that the nuances and context of each language are preserved and correctly conveyed.

This project involves several key steps:

1. **Initial Translation:** Students use AI tools to generate initial translations of the website content.
2. **Critical Review:** Students critically analyze the AI-generated translations, identifying any inaccuracies or cultural insensitivities.
3. **Refinement:** Students collaboratively refine the translations, applying their linguistic and cultural knowledge to enhance the accuracy and appropriateness of the content.
4. **Reflection:** Students reflect on the process, discussing the strengths and limitations of the AI tools and the importance of human oversight in language translation.

Throughout this task, students engage with their peers and AI tools to develop a website for their chosen purpose in an iterative and dialogic manner. This may mean having to grapple with competing visions or

Figure 4.6 Sample Student Interaction Requesting a Cultural Recast in Claude3 Opus

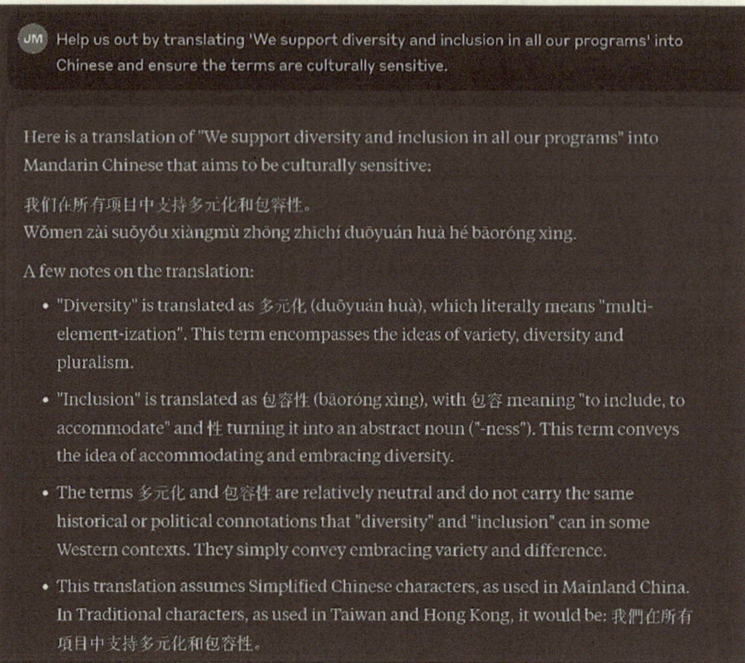

disagreements over intention or appropriateness of both student- and AI-generated content, both of which are valuable learning and languaging skills. For example, students may turn to AI and ask for help casting certain culturally loaded language into more accessible terms (see Figure 4.6, below). From there, students can be provided with off-line, non-AI supported space to discuss and debate the value (or lack thereof) of the AI-generated outputs to their completion of the task-based learning activity before returning to the AI tool with new prompts to seek clarification, gain perspective, draw new inspiration (see Figure 4.7, below).

This activity exemplifies the principles of designing meaningful tasks that are AI-aware. By engaging in this project, students actively interact with AI tools, critically evaluate AI outputs, and synthesize AI-generated information with their own expertise. They are encouraged to question the sources and biases of the AI-generated translations and apply their knowledge to improve the outcomes. This process not only enhances their language skills but also develops their critical AI literacy. Furthermore, this activity promotes ethical considerations by

Figure 4.7 Sample Student Interaction Requesting a Revision to Better Target a Sub-cultural Group on Google Gemini

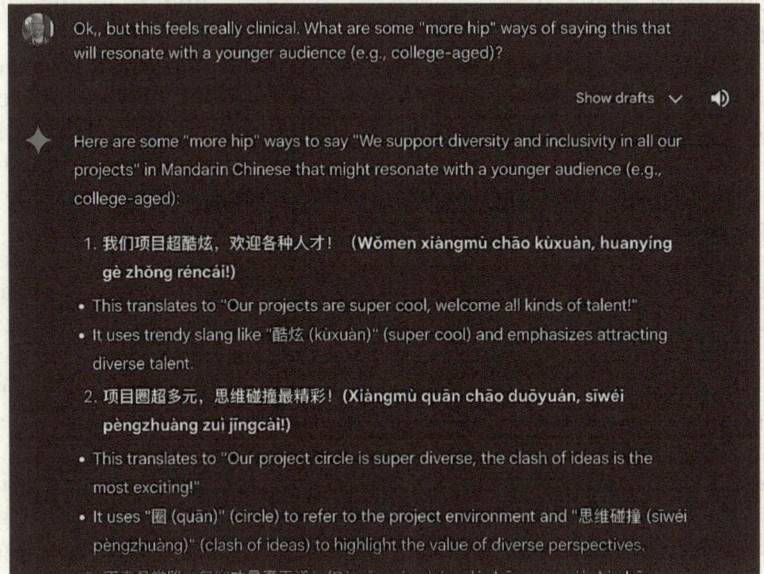

highlighting the importance of cultural sensitivity in translations and the role of human judgment in ensuring accuracy and appropriateness. By incorporating reflective practice, students gain a deeper understanding of the impact of AI on their learning and the quality of the outputs they produce.

Emphasis on Collaborative Interaction

Since about the 1980s, we have accepted the importance of the role of interaction in language teaching and learning (see Atkinson, 2002; Block, 2003). In the pedagogical framework proposed here, interaction remains an important element. This extends beyond focusing on the nature or quality of the student-student, student-teacher, or student-world interactions. It goes further to consider how we build collaborative interaction throughout instructional spaces in ways that link mind, body, tools, and world to support second language learning and acquisition. In this context, these four areas map to the cognitive, embodied, technological, and ecosocial spaces and affordances that we all make use of to navigate our daily lives. *Collaborative interaction* refers to the process whereby learners and instructors actively engage with each other and AI tools to jointly construct meaning, solve problems, and achieve common learning goals. This involves dynamic exchanges where participants share knowledge, negotiate understanding, and build upon each other's contributions.

Incorporating collaborative interaction into AI integration efforts can positively impact language learning. For example, it can encourage learners to use language in meaningful ways, promoting the development of communicative competence. By engaging in dynamic exchanges, students practice speaking, listening, reading, and writing in authentic contexts, which helps them become more proficient in using the language effectively and appropriately. Furthermore, learners develop critical thinking skills through the joint construction of meaning and problem-solving activities. They must analyze information, evaluate different perspectives, and synthesize ideas. This cognitive engagement deepens their understanding of language structures and functions, making their learning more robust and transferable. These aims are facilitated by leveraging peer-to-peer exchanges, allowing students to learn from one another. This social interaction creates a supportive learning environment where learners can share knowledge, offer feedback, and scaffold each other's learning. It also helps students build confidence in using the target language. AI enters the equation as a tool to allow learners to gain access to a vast array of resources and feedback mechanisms. AI can provide instant corrections, suggest alternative expressions, and simulate real-world language use scenarios. This integration helps learners refine their language skills and develop a more nuanced understanding of language use. By encouraging students to engage collaboratively with each other and with any AI tools we may be using, we can scaffold students' acquisition of strategic competence as they negotiate meaning, clarify misunderstandings, and reach mutual comprehension. This process is critical for language acquisition as it helps students become more adept at using language to convey and interpret meaning in diverse contexts.

By relying on collaborative interaction, this pedagogical framework seeks to enable language educators to continue to foster a sense of community and belonging among learners. By working together towards common goals, students build relationships and create a positive learning atmosphere. This sense of community enhances motivation and engagement, which are key factors in successful language learning. Additionally, learners may develop important lifelong learning skills such as teamwork, communication, and adaptability by engaging in collaborative interaction. These skills are essential not only for language learning but also for personal and professional growth in an increasingly interconnected and technology-driven world. It should be noted that all of these pedagogical goals are already aligned with accepted disciplinary best practices common in communicative language teaching-based paradigms that have been dominant through much of the social and post-social moments in modern language teaching and learning (see Block, 2003; Pennycook, 2021).

One example of a practical application of this element of the proposed pedagogical framework is the AI-Enhanced Role-Playing activity. In this activity, students use AI chatbots to role-play real-world scenarios in the target language, such as ordering food in a restaurant, checking into a hotel, or attending a job interview. This approach focuses on pragmatics – how language is used in context, social norms, and cultural variations.

The activity unfolds in several steps. First, students are divided into small groups and assigned specific roles and scenarios relevant to everyday situations in the target culture. They are provided with background information to understand the cultural and social norms involved. Next, students use AI chatbots to simulate the assigned scenarios, taking turns interacting with the chatbot in both customer/client and service provider roles. They pay attention to the chatbot's responses, focusing on language use, appropriateness, and cultural nuances. After the initial interaction, groups discuss the chatbot's responses, analyzing its language use and identifying any pragmatic errors or cultural insensitivities. They reflect on how the chatbot's responses align or differ from real-life interactions within the target culture. Based on their discussion, students collaboratively refine their language use and practice the role-play again, this time focusing on improving their responses to be more contextually and culturally appropriate. Groups rehearse the scenario, ensuring they incorporate proper social norms and cultural variations. Finally, groups re-enact the scenario, either with the AI chatbot again or with classmates playing the roles, and perform their refined role-plays in front of the class. The class provides feedback on language use, pragmatic appropriateness, and cultural sensitivity. A debriefing session follows, where students reflect on what they learned about language pragmatics, social norms, and cultural variations, and discuss the role of AI tools in their learning process.

This activity can aid in promoting communicative competence by engaging students in authentic language use and fostering critical thinking as they analyze and refine AI-generated responses. By focusing on pragmatics, social norms, and cultural variations, students gain a deeper understanding of how language is used contextually, enhancing their ability to navigate real-world interactions in the target language. This practical example illustrates how collaborative interaction, enhanced by AI tools, can be integrated into language learning to support communicative competence, critical thinking, cultural awareness, and teamwork.

Sociocultural Sensitivity

The role of one's social setting and (inter)cultural forces have come to be seen as playing an increasingly important role in language education in both traditional classroom settings and web-enabled CALL contexts (see Dooly & Vinagre, 2022; Kim, 2020; Levy & Stockwell, 2013). One could tie this, in part, to the so-called social turn in applied linguistics and language education (Block, 2003; Pennycook, 2021), but the importance of culture to language and communication is present even in more cognitivist interpretations of the field (Kramsch, 1993, 2014; van Lier, 2004). Given this reality, any attempts to integrate AI into language teaching and learning must continue to account for the roles of societal groups (e.g., student, youth, disabled, trans, working poor) and culture (both Big-C and little-c). From a collaborative AI framework, *sociocultural sensitivity* can be understood as working to highlight the impact of sociocultural background on language use/choice and on the AI tools that we choose to use, as they are themselves cultural products. Said more simply, it means creating space for ourselves and our learners to engage with the fact that technology is not values neutral (see Christian, 2021; Pasquale, 2020). Indeed, if we come to view them as cultural artifacts, it provides us with a new channel through which to understand the (sometimes) biased outputs that we receive from AI tools that may violate our needs or expectations.

Integrating sociocultural sensitivity when using generative AI in language classrooms requires thoughtful planning and execution to ensure that AI tools enhance cultural and social aspects of language learning. This is because AI platforms' societal and cultural biases can be deeply engrained and require a cultural insider of the target culture to suss out – further reinforcing the importance of a well-trained and supported professional language educator to help guide students as they acquire linguistic skills and the critical habits of mind necessary to engage with others and technology. Because it is a multivariate issue, there are many subparts that must be considered, some of which are discussed briefly below.

A first step is to select AI tools that offer diverse and inclusive content. Choosing platforms that have been rigorously tested for cultural biases is essential. Major platforms like Google's Gemini and Microsoft's

Copilot have made strides in reducing biases and improving inclusivity in their AI outputs (Bender et al., 2021). That being said, all AI systems are only as good as the training date used to build and fine-tune them. This means that even explicit attempts to create more inclusive and multicultural tools can fall flat if the fine-tuning data used reinforces stereotypes or cultural flattening. To begin to address this issue may require educators and students to generate prompts or dialogue scenarios as part of the AI prompting stream that include culturally relevant themes and contexts to refine the output of AI tools to be more culturally appropriate.

To actualize this in classroom, however, will require encouraging students to critically analyze AI-generated content for biases and cultural sensitivity is a valuable exercise. It helps develop critical thinking skills and understanding of cultural biases in technology. Students can work in groups to identify and discuss any biases, and suggest improvements for AI outputs (Christian, 2021; Pasquale, 2020). This work can be supported by Incorporating reflective exercises where students consider how their cultural backgrounds influence their language use and how AI tools might reflect or ignore these nuances. Reflective journals or discussion boards can facilitate deeper engagement with the cultural aspects of language learning.

One effective way to demonstrate the importance of sociocultural sensitivity when using AI tools in language education is through an engaging classroom activity that utilizes generative AI, such as DALL-E or Midjourney. This activity helps students understand how cultural contexts and biases can influence AI-generated outputs, highlighting the need for culturally sensitive use of technology in language learning. The objective of this activity is to illustrate the significance of sociocultural awareness when employing AI tools, allowing students to see firsthand how cultural contexts can shape AI outputs and emphasizing the importance of critically evaluating these tools.

To begin, the instructor should discuss the concept of sociocultural sensitivity and its relevance in language education, explaining that AI tools, such as image generators, are not culturally neutral and can reflect biases based on the data they were trained on (c.f., Figures 4.8 and 4.9, below). Students are then provided with a list of simple prompts, such as "draw a picture of a child making a snack," "create an image of a family having dinner," or "generate a picture of a classroom." Each student or group is assigned a specific prompt to use with the AI tool. They are encouraged to generate multiple images for each prompt to observe variations in the AI's interpretations. Once the images are generated, students analyze the outputs, considering how the AI depicts the scene,

Figure 4.8 Sample Images Created with DALL-E Using the Prompt "Draw a child making an after-school snack."

Figure 4.9 Sample Images Created with DALL-E Using the Prompt "Draw a Bahraini child making an after-school snack."

noting any cultural elements, biases, or stereotypes. The instructor facilitates a group discussion where students share their observations and insights, highlighting examples of cultural sensitivity or insensitivity in the AI-generated images. This prompts students to think critically about the potential biases in AI tools. To conclude the activity, the instructor leads a reflective discussion on the importance of sociocultural awareness in using AI tools. Emphasis is placed on the need for educators and students to critically evaluate AI outputs and consider cultural contexts. The discussion also covers how this understanding can be applied in language teaching and learning to create more inclusive and culturally responsive educational environments.

By engaging in this activity, students gain practical insights into how AI tools can reflect cultural biases and the importance of considering sociocultural factors when using these technologies in educational contexts. This hands-on experience helps them appreciate the complexities of integrating AI into language learning while fostering a more inclusive and culturally sensitive classroom environment.

Integrating sociocultural sensitivity into the use of AI tools in language education is not just an enhancement but a necessity. As AI becomes increasingly prevalent in educational contexts, it is imperative to acknowledge and address the cultural biases that these tools may carry. By critically engaging with AI-generated content, educators and students can develop a nuanced understanding of how cultural contexts shape technology and its outputs. This approach not only enriches the learning experience but also fosters critical thinking and cultural competence. Ultimately, by integrating sociocultural sensitivity into AI use in language classrooms, educators can create more inclusive and responsive learning environments. This prepares students not only to use AI tools more effectively and collaboratively but also to navigate a diverse and interconnected world with greater cultural awareness and sensitivity. As we move forward, it is essential to continue refining these practices and exploring new ways to ensure that technology in education serves all learners equitably and respectfully. The next section will discuss the need to consider the ethical implications of using AI in language education with our students, further underscoring the importance of thoughtful and responsible integration of technology in our teaching practices.

Addressing Ethical Considerations

Our exploration of a pedagogy of collaborative AI ends with what is perhaps the most pressing and significant issue in AI in education and society, that of AI ethics. This area has become so mission critical to AI development that an entire cottage industry and academic discipline have emerged in recent years with some very vocal proponents of stronger, more human-centered regulations to reign in AI developers who may be economically induced to act fast and break things, as opposed to acting purposefully and humanely (see Buolamwini, 2023; Mitchell, 2019; Pasquale, 2020). And, there are very real reasons to get the ethics question right because we have already seen so damningly what happens when we get it wrong – from Google's "gorilla-gate" to racially derived, algorithmically based pre-trial detention recommendations to horrific auto accidents (Mitchell, 2019; Pasquale, 2020). So, here, any pedagogical attempts to integrate AI into language teaching and practice must squarely and resolutely address its ethical implications. *Addressing ethical implications* entails a multifaceted approach that combines critical awareness, proactive measures, and ongoing evaluation. It involves:

1. Developing a deep understanding of potential AI biases and limitations
2. Implementing transparent policies for AI use in educational settings

3. Prioritizing student privacy and data protection
4. Ensuring equitable access and benefits across diverse student populations
5. Maintaining human oversight in key pedagogical decisions
6. Regularly assessing the impact of AI integration on learning outcomes and student well-being

This comprehensive approach aims to harness the benefits of AI in language education while mitigating risks and upholding ethical standards.

First and foremost, educators and institutions must develop a deep understanding of potential AI biases and limitations. This involves recognizing that AI systems, including language models, can perpetuate or even amplify existing societal biases present in their training data. For instance, an AI language tool might generate content that reflects gender stereotypes or cultural biases. By understanding these potential pitfalls, educators can better prepare to identify and mitigate such issues in the classroom. Consider, for example, an AI-powered writing assistant used in an English as a second language (ESL) course. If the AI model was primarily trained on texts from Western, English-speaking countries, it might struggle to accurately represent or understand cultural nuances from other regions. When asked to generate a story about a family dinner, the AI might default to describing a typical American or British meal, complete with culturally specific foods and customs. This could inadvertently reinforce Western-centric views and potentially alienate students from diverse cultural backgrounds. Moreover, the AI might use gendered language in ways that reinforce stereotypes, such as consistently depicting mothers as the ones preparing meals or fathers as the primary breadwinners. An educator aware of these biases could use this as a teachable moment, encouraging students to critically analyze the AI-generated content, discuss the biases they observe, and collaboratively rewrite the story to be more culturally inclusive and gender-neutral. This approach not only addresses the immediate issue of bias but also helps students develop critical thinking skills and cultural sensitivity that will serve them well in their language learning journey and beyond. By fostering this level of awareness and critical engagement, educators can transform potential ethical pitfalls into valuable learning opportunities, thereby enriching the language learning experience while simultaneously tackling important issues of bias and representation in AI systems.

As discussed previously, transparency is also crucial when implementing AI in educational settings ethically. Institutions should develop and communicate clear policies regarding AI use, outlining when and how AI tools will be employed in language instruction. This transparency extends to students as well, who should be informed about the role of AI in their learning experiences. For example, if AI is used to generate practice materials or provide feedback on writing assignments, students should be aware of this and understand the potential benefits and limitations of such tools. Furthermore, this transparency can actually enhance the language learning process in several ways. First, it allows students to engage more critically with the feedback they receive, understanding that while AI can provide valuable insights, it is not infallible. This encourages students to develop a more nuanced understanding of language, where they learn to balance AI feedback with other sources of input, including their own intuition and human instruction. Second, transparency about AI use can foster a sense of agency in students. When they understand how the AI works, they can learn to use it more effectively as a tool for their learning, rather than viewing it as an opaque authority. For instance, students might experiment with different pronunciations to see how the AI responds, deepening their understanding of phonetics in the process. Lastly, being open about AI use provides opportunities for meta-linguistic discussions about language technology, AI, and their role in modern communication. These discussions can enrich students' language learning experience, introducing them to relevant vocabulary and concepts that are increasingly important in our technologically driven world. By demystifying AI and encouraging critical engagement with it, educators can prepare students not just to speak a new language, but to navigate the complex, AI-infused linguistic landscape of the future.

Protecting student privacy and data is of paramount importance in the age of AI. As language learning increasingly incorporates digital tools and platforms, vast amounts of student data are being generated and potentially analyzed by AI systems. Educational institutions must implement robust data protection measures and ensure compliance with relevant privacy regulations. This includes being transparent about data collection practices, securing student information, and limiting data retention periods. Consider an Italian as a Second Language classroom in a European university that utilizes an AI-powered language learning platform. This platform might collect data on students' performance, including their writing samples, speaking exercises, and even their learning patterns and progress rates. Under the GDPR, the cornerstone of data privacy law in the European Union, the university has specific obligations to protect this data.

First, the university must obtain explicit consent from students to collect and process their data, clearly explaining what data is being collected, how it will be used, and for how long it will be retained. For instance, if the AI system analyzes students' Italian writing samples to provide personalized feedback, students must be informed of this and given the option to opt out without it affecting their education. Moreover, the university must ensure that the AI platform provider complies with GDPR requirements, including data minimization (collecting only necessary data), purpose limitation (using data only for specified purposes), and storage limitation (retaining data only as long as necessary). For example, while it might be tempting to keep all student data indefinitely for long-term analysis, GDPR principles would require the university to justify why this is necessary and to delete data that is no longer needed for educational purposes.

Ensuring equitable access and benefits across diverse student populations is another critical ethical consideration. While AI has the potential to personalize learning experiences and provide additional support, it is essential to ensure that these benefits are accessible to all students, regardless of their socioeconomic background or technological resources. This may involve providing necessary hardware or internet access to disadvantaged students or developing AI tools that can function effectively across a range of devices and bandwidth capacities.

Take a Korean as a Second Language class at a community college in the United States as an example. The instructor wants to incorporate an AI-powered language learning app that uses speech recognition to help students practice their pronunciation and conversational skills. However, the student population is diverse, including working adults, recent immigrants, and traditional college students from various socioeconomic backgrounds. Some students have the latest smartphones and high-speed internet at home, while others rely on older devices or have limited internet access. To address this disparity, the college could implement several strategies:

1. Device lending program: The college could establish a program that lends tablets or laptops to students who do not have suitable devices at home. These devices would come pre-loaded with the necessary AI language learning software.
2. On-campus AI labs: The college could set up dedicated computer labs with the AI language learning software installed, ensuring that all students have access to the technology during specific hours, regardless of their personal resources.

3. Offline functionality: The college could work with the AI tool developers to create an offline version of the app that students can use without constant internet connectivity. This version might have limited features but would still allow for essential pronunciation practice.
4. Partnering with local libraries: The college could partner with local libraries to provide access to the AI language learning tools, extending the reach beyond the campus and into the community.
5. Flexible AI system requirements: The college could prioritize AI tools that are designed to work effectively on a wide range of devices, including older smartphones and computers with lower processing power.
6. Data-light options: For students with limited internet plans, the college could work with the AI tool developers to create data-light versions that use minimal bandwidth while still providing key functionalities.

By implementing these measures, the college ensures that all students in the Korean language class can benefit from the AI-enhanced learning experience, regardless of their personal technological resources. This approach not only addresses the ethical imperative of equitable access but also enriches the learning environment by maintaining a diverse student body. It allows students from all backgrounds to engage with cutting-edge language learning technology, potentially increasing their motivation and success in mastering Korean. Moreover, this inclusive approach aligns with the broader goals of language education, which often include fostering cross-cultural understanding and communication. By ensuring that students from all walks of life can participate fully in the AI-enhanced Korean class, the college is better preparing them for a globalized world where technological literacy and language skills are increasingly intertwined.

Maintaining human oversight in key pedagogical decisions is essential to ensure that AI remains a tool in service of education rather than a replacement for human judgment. While AI can provide valuable insights and assist with tasks like grading or content creation, final decisions about curriculum, assessment, and student progress should remain in the hands of qualified educators. This human-centered approach helps to maintain the interpersonal and empathetic aspects of language education that are crucial for student engagement and motivation. By way of example, take the nuanced task of evaluating a student's progress in language acquisition. An AI system might efficiently analyze quantitative data such as test scores, vocabulary acquisition rates, or grammar accuracy in written assignments. However, language learning is a complex, multifaceted process that goes beyond these measurable metrics. A human educator can perceive and factor in qualitative aspects such as a student's growing confidence in speaking, their ability to navigate cultural nuances, or their creativity in using the language. They can also consider contextual factors like a student's personal challenges or learning style that may impact their progress. For example, an AI might flag a student's declining performance in written assignments, but a human teacher could recognize that this coincides with the student's increased willingness to take risks in oral communication, indicating a shift in learning focus rather than a deficit. This holistic, empathetic assessment is crucial in language education, where the goal is not just linguistic proficiency but also intercultural competence and communicative confidence. By maintaining human oversight, we ensure that the richness and complexity of language learning are fully acknowledged and supported, even as we leverage the analytical power of AI to enhance the educational process.

Finally, regularly assessing the impact of AI integration on learning outcomes and student well-being is necessary to ensure that the use of AI in language education is truly beneficial. This involves conducting ongoing research and gathering feedback from students and educators. Assessments should consider not only academic performance but also factors such as student engagement, motivation, and overall satisfaction with the learning experience.

As you can see, ethical concerns are multivariate, complex, and occasionally well hidden from surface-level observations. Because of this, considerable space has already been dedicated to ethical considerations here, and will be explored much more fully in chapter 6. Because of this, no extended discussion of classroom activities will be presented here. That being said, adopting this multifaceted approach advocated for here can allow language educators and institutions can work towards harnessing the benefits of AI while mitigating potential risks and upholding ethical standards. This balanced strategy allows for innovation in language teaching and learning while ensuring that the fundamental human elements of education are preserved and enhanced rather than diminished by technological advancements.

Conclusion

The pedagogical framework for collaborative AI in language teaching and learning presented in this chapter offers a comprehensive approach to integrating AI technologies into educational practices. By emphasizing sociocognitive principles, redefining the role of teachers, treating AI as an active tool for inquiry, focusing on metacognition and transparency, designing meaningful tasks, promoting collaborative interaction, maintaining sociocultural sensitivity, and addressing ethical considerations, this framework provides a robust foundation for educators navigating the complex landscape of AI in education. As we move forward in an increasingly AI-integrated world, it is crucial that we prepare our students not just to use these technologies, but to engage with them critically and ethically. This framework aims to strike a balance between harnessing the potential of AI to enhance language learning and preserving the irreplaceable role of human expertise and interaction in education.

However, it is important to recognize that this framework is not static. As AI technologies continue to evolve at a rapid pace, our approaches to integrating them into education must also adapt. Educators and institutions must remain flexible and open to refining these practices based on new developments and insights. While this chapter has laid out a comprehensive approach to AI integration in language education, the true test of its effectiveness lies in its implementation and outcomes. In the next chapter, we will explore the crucial aspects of assessment and feedback in AI-enhanced language learning environments. By examining how we can effectively evaluate student progress and the impact of AI integration, we can continue to refine our practices and ensure that our use of AI truly serves the goals of language education.

5

Assessment and Feedback in the AI-Assisted Classroom

Introduction

Artificial intelligence has played a role in testing and assessment for quite some time in language teaching and learning (see Brown, 2016; Malec, 2020). Perhaps one of the more common use cases has been in the form of automated essay scorer (AES) platforms (see Dikli & Bleyle, 2014; Fu et al., 2024; Li, 2023). Interestingly, many of these reports are light on technical details of the algorithms and models driving their platforms, and fewer still make their code available for inspection by the academic community, opting instead to merely report the findings of their research. However, scholarly attention to AES platforms has been sustained and varied regarding target language and use cases. In other cases, AI (and its underlying technologies) have been applied to the assessment of spoken languages to provide student feedback and scoring, in a similar vein to AES platforms (see Chandel et al., 2007; Lu & Bluemel, 2023; Zechner & Keelan, 2019).

The present chapter, however, does not seek to retread this ground. Instead, as with the previous chapter, it will seek to address new questions about AI and assessment and feedback that have arisen since the advent of generative AI. The question of what we, as language educators, do in light of generative AI is perhaps the most urgent. Related to it is the question of if, and if so how, we as language educators can leverage generative AI in assessment and feedback to drive better student learning outcomes and to do so in a more timely fashion, as providing meaningful feedback remains challenging for early-service educators (e.g., Zan & Yiğitoğlu, 2018) and is, perhaps, one of the largest proverbial "time sinks" for our labor (Henderson et al., 2019). Beyond the work of the language educator, however, there is also the question of what the emergence of generative AI means for those of us engaged in research and scholarship focused on language testing and assessment. This chapter will, instead, focus on addressing these more pressing questions, ones about which we as a discipline are actively grappling with at the time this book was drafted and about which research was just beginning to emerge (e.g., Hao et al., 2024; Moorhouse et al., 2023; Pack & Maloney, 2023; Smolansky et al., 2023). Continuing in the applied vein of much of the work in this book, I will seek to provide the reader with actionable strategies that they can modify and adapt to their own practice and contexts. Given the scope of testing, assessment, and feedback, this discussion will likely only begin to scratch the surface in the present chapter – one could, and perhaps should, dedicate an entire book to just this question. Before beginning this exploration, however, a better understanding of the challenges posed by generative AI in the testing and assessment space is needed. Additionally, some understanding of issues around using generative AI for learner feedback will also provide necessary framing for the applied discussion that will take up the bulk of the present chapter.

Generative AI Challenges to Testing, Assessment, and Feedback

Perhaps the single largest concern about the emergence of generative AI, and students' ready access to it, is that it will lead to significant increases in cheating as grade-motivated learners seek to gain an advantage (see Chen et al., 2024; Denkin, 2024; Lee et al., 2024). Indeed, the emergence of AI applications like CaktusAI, SmartSolv AI, and Solvely.ai all point to this as a legitimate concern. Indeed, SmartSolv AI had, at the time of writing this chapter, a series of advertisements on TikTok targeting college students as a tool to answer questions for them on their mid-term or final exams – all while guaranteeing higher scores and near-zero detectability. While troubling, I would encourage us to remember that platforms to subvert assessments are nothing new, as students highly motivated to cheat will find a way – even if it means paying someone else to take the exam for them or leveraging the exam banks rumored to exist at some fraternities and sororities. So, as educators who need to assess learning and development, challenges remain for us. What is new, however, is the speed and accessibility of a potentially potent tool for academic dishonesty.

Perhaps even more pressing for language education, where we purport to focus on connection and communication, is the question of authenticity in student work, which has become increasingly complex with the advent of generative AI (Ifelebuegu, 2023; Matheis & John,

2024). As these tools become more sophisticated, they blur the line between AI-assisted and independently produced language output. This ambiguity poses a significant challenge for educators attempting to gauge a student's true linguistic competence. For instance, a student might use AI to generate a flawless essay in their target language, complete with idiomatic expressions and cultural references that far exceed their actual proficiency level. How then do we distinguish between the student's genuine language skills and the AI's capabilities? This scenario not only complicates assessment but also raises questions about the very nature of language learning in an AI-assisted world. The dilemma extends beyond mere assessment; it strikes at the heart of our understanding of language acquisition and production in an AI-augmented world. As educators, we must grapple with redefining what constitutes authentic language use and how to foster genuine communicative competence in an environment where AI can seamlessly mimic human-like language production.

Equity concerns loom large in the AI-assisted learning landscape. While some students may have unfettered access to cutting-edge AI tools, others may find themselves at a distinct disadvantage due to technological or financial constraints. This digital divide threatens to exacerbate existing inequalities in educational outcomes, potentially widening the achievement gap between privileged and underprivileged learners (Holstein & Doroudi, 2022; Li, 2023). Consider, for example, two students in an advanced Spanish course: Student A has access to a premium AI language model that can generate nuanced, context-appropriate responses, while Student B relies on free, less sophisticated tools. When tasked with writing a complex argumentative essay, Student A can leverage their AI assistant to refine their arguments, suggest idiomatic expressions, and even tailor the language to a specific dialect or register. Student B, in contrast, might struggle with more basic language production, relying on simpler structures and vocabulary. This scenario presents a significant challenge for assessment. How can an instructor fairly evaluate these essays when the underlying support systems are so disparate? Moreover, this inequality extends beyond a single assignment, potentially influencing long-term language acquisition and academic performance. As educators, we must grapple with how to level this playing field without compromising the integrity of our assessments. This might involve rethinking our assessment strategies, perhaps focusing more on in-class, supervised work or oral examinations where AI assistance is less feasible. Alternatively, we might need to consider providing equal access to AI tools within educational settings, ensuring that all students have the same technological advantages. However, this approach raises its own set of logistical and ethical questions about the role of AI in language education.

Another challenge is the potential for student overreliance on AI tools – a paradoxical challenge of sorts. While these technologies offer unprecedented support in language learning, they also risk stunting the development of critical cognitive processes essential for genuine language acquisition. The ease with which students can generate AI-assisted responses may lead to a false sense of competence, masking underlying deficiencies in their language skills. For instance, a student might rely heavily on an AI tool for all their writing assignments, consistently producing polished essays that exceed their actual language proficiency. When faced with a spontaneous speaking task or a timed in-class writing assignment without AI assistance, this student may struggle significantly, revealing gaps in their true language abilities. This discrepancy not only complicates assessment but also potentially hampers the student's long-term language development by reducing opportunities for productive struggle and independent skill-building (see Klingbeil et al., 2024; Zhai et al., 2024). Educators must navigate this delicate balance, fostering AI literacy while ensuring students develop robust, independent language abilities.

Taken together, these challenges can create the sense that the validity of traditional assessment methods is under siege in the age of AI. Long-standing practices like essays, multiple-choice tests, and even oral examinations may no longer serve as reliable indicators of a student's language proficiency. We find ourselves at a crossroads as AI systems become adept at mimicking human-like responses across various assessment formats. This can create an entirely new challenge for us as educators – a crisis of faith in not only our assessment tools, but in the stock that we can place in their results. Beyond this, we also have to compete with the rapid evolution of AI capabilities, which adds another layer of complexity to assessment strategies. What seems like an effective evaluation method today may be rendered obsolete by tomorrow's AI advancements. This constant state of flux demands a level of adaptability from educators that is both exhilarating and exhausting. We find ourselves in an arms race of sorts, continually refining our assessment techniques to stay ahead of AI's ever-expanding capabilities. This reality may lead us, as a professional, to a reevaluation of which language skills we prioritize and how we assess them. Traditional benchmarks of language proficiency may need to be recalibrated in a world where AI can effortlessly generate grammatically correct sentences or provide instant translations. This shift may lead us to place greater emphasis on skills like critical thinking, cultural competence, and creative language use – areas where human cognition still holds a decisive edge over AI. As language educators, we must redefine what constitutes essential language skills in this new era. This means, then, that the opportunity for us lies in developing new evaluation paradigms that effectively measure language skills and learning in this evolving technological landscape, which will be a primary focus of this chapter.

Rethinking Assessment Strategies

That new assessment strategies are needed is already apparent across grade levels, disciplines, and institution types. We have seen this well reflected in blog posts and articles from outlets like *Inside Higher Education, AutomatED*, and a slew of others. Indeed, as I sit on university committees, a common refrain from the professors I work with have been that they need new tools to see if their students are actually learning what they are trying to teach them – and this is true from accounting to computer science, from public health to Swedish as a foreign language classes. Overall, most responses from instructional faculty have fallen into two domains – product-focused and process-focused. *Product-focused* assessment approaches will feel familiar to many of us. They are those traditional assessments of learning (e.g., the final exam; the term paper) that emphasize students showcasing what they have learned either through recall or application. Product-focused assessments tend to emphasize what the learner can produce, holding it to be a good measure of the students' cognitive state as a result of the learning process. *Process-focused* assessments are centered on how students use their cognitive apparatus to engage in problem-solving and seek to evaluate how students learn and may take the form of observation, simulation, or reflection.

Now, one could certainly take a product-focused approach to rethinking assessment in the age of AI. And I have seen instructors take a myriad of approaches to do. One EAP professor that I know requires students to write extensive essay exams on paper in class. I know of a high school computer science professor that does pen-and-paper exams as well now, having students write pseudocode instead of actual, executable computer code. Even in asynchronous, online classes, more instructors have turned to synchronous examinations where students must be present with their cameras and microphones on, use a locked-down web browser, and consent (sometimes tacitly) to being recorded – sometimes both their cameras and their screens/computer inputs. These are, in their own way, legitimate responses. Yet, they are ones that seek to maintain some semblance of the status quo, of how things have always been. In many cases, they introduce new burdens for learners that could negatively impact performance. For example, students writing by hand in a second language may struggle with the orthography of the L2. Speaking as an L2 learner of Japanese and Chinese, I can type them quite competently thanks to things like *romaji* and *pinyin* input. My handwritten capabilities are laughable, to be generous. If we were to add on to this the requirement that students write *legibly*, we can further hobble their ability to produce substantive, extensive output because we unnaturally slow down their production. In this case, we may just as well be assessing their ability to produce language or an essay and their penmanship (read: potential construct misalignment).

This is not to say that incorporating real-time, in-class assessments cannot work. Just that exceptional care is going to be needed to ensure the continued validity of the assessment while minimizing the likelihood that we are shutting out learners because of generational effects (e.g., a preference for typing over writing by hand), neurodiversity, or disability. To that end, this chapter will advocate primarily for a processed-focused approach to assessment in language classrooms. To help enumerate the possible forms that this can take, we will look at three examples of assessments strategies that language educators can use as a reference for their own professional practice, modifying to fit their unique linguistic and institutional contexts. To make these approaches, the implementation, and their potential benefits more salient for readers, they will be presented as a series of case studies utilizing different instructional contexts to add flavor to the base description.

Rethinking Assessment Case 1: Modifying Standard Examination Protocols

In the scenario for our first case, we're going to follow Professor Dongye, a Chinese as a second language professor who teaches *Advanced Chinese Language and Culture*, a 400/500-level course at a small Sino-American university in China. The class meets three times weekly for 90-minute sessions, catering to a diverse group of 12 students – seven undergraduates and five graduates – from various academic disciplines. Their majors span a wide range, including International Business, East Asian Studies, Computer Science, Political Science, Linguistics, Art History, and Environmental Science, reflecting the interdisciplinary appeal of advanced Chinese language skills. All students possess advanced Chinese proficiency, roughly equivalent to HSK 5 or 6, allowing Professor Dongye to conduct the class mostly in Chinese. The course aims to further develop their language abilities, focusing on mastering complex grammar structures, expanding vocabulary, and honing the ability to discuss abstract topics fluently in Chinese. The curriculum is rigorous and multifaceted. Students grapple with advanced subordinate clauses and sophisticated sentence patterns. They also build an extensive vocabulary that encompasses academic and professional terminology, idiomatic expressions, proverbs, and even contemporary slang and internet language.

Class activities are designed to challenge students' language skills in authentic contexts. They analyze current events, explore philosophical concepts, and discuss complex cultural phenomena. The coursework includes reading advanced Chinese texts ranging from news articles to academic papers and literature. Students also enhance their listening skills through podcasts and documentaries, engage in debates, deliver presentations, and write analytical essays and research papers in Chinese. Professor Dongye's teaching approach emphasizes authentic language use and deep cultural understanding. Students are expected to interact fluently in both formal and informal registers, preparing them for real-world application of their Chinese language skills across various professional and academic contexts.

Professor Dongye, recognizing the evolving landscape of language education in the age of AI, decides to innovate her midterm exam format. She aims to create an assessment that not only maintains academic integrity in the face of AI capabilities but also more accurately reflects the real-world application of Chinese language skills. Traditionally, the midterm exam had been a closed-book, in-class written test focusing heavily on grammar, vocabulary, and reading comprehension. However, Professor Dongye realizes that this format may no longer effectively measure students' true language abilities in an era where AI can easily generate grammatically correct responses or provide quick translations.

Instead, she designs a new exam format that emphasizes critical thinking, real-world application, and the ability to articulate complex ideas in Chinese. The exam questions are carefully crafted to require deep understanding and analysis, rather than simple recall or translation. For instance, one question might ask students to analyze a contemporary Chinese social issue, drawing on their knowledge of current events, cultural nuances, and advanced vocabulary. Another might present a complex business scenario, requiring students to draft a professional email that demonstrates not just language proficiency, but also cultural sensitivity and business etiquette. By modifying the exam in this way, Professor Dongye aims to assess not just her students' Chinese language skills, but also their ability to apply these skills creatively and critically in contexts that closely resemble real-world scenarios.

This approach aligns more closely with the course's overall goal of preparing students for advanced Chinese language use in their diverse future careers and academic pursuits. The new format challenges students to integrate their knowledge, provide personal insights, and use nuanced language in ways that are difficult to replicate with AI alone, thereby maintaining the exam's validity as a measure of true language proficiency.

To this end, Professor Dongye deploys the following exam protocol:

1. Students are allowed to use all resources they typically use for homework, including textbooks, notes, and the internet. However, the use of generative AI tools and communication with other students is strictly prohibited.
2. The exam consists of a series of application-based questions that require students to demonstrate their Chinese language proficiency in various scenarios, such as analyzing a piece of Chinese literature, responding to a complex business email, or explaining a cultural phenomenon.
3. Approximately halfway through the exam period, Professor Dongye begins conducting brief one-on-one interviews with each student. These interviews last about 5–10 minutes per student.
4. During the interview, students are asked to explain their thought process for one of the questions they have already answered. They must articulate how they arrived at their answer, demonstrating their understanding and language skills beyond simply repeating their written response.

The interview portion of Professor Dongye's exam protocol serves as a crucial component in addressing the challenges posed by AI in language assessment. This modification to the traditional exam format offers multiple benefits that enhance the overall evaluation process. The primary rationale behind the interview is to verify the authenticity of students' work and assess their real-time language production skills. By engaging students in spontaneous conversation about their written responses, Professor Dongye can confirm that they genuinely understand and can articulate their ideas in Chinese, rather than simply reproducing information from sources or potentially AI-generated content. This real-time interaction also evaluates students' ability to use Chinese spontaneously, a critical skill in real-world situations that is difficult for AI to replicate.

Moreover, the interview allows for a deeper assessment of students' critical thinking abilities in Chinese. Professor Dongye can probe students' thought processes, encouraging them to analyze and reflect on their responses in the target language. This approach not only evaluates language proficiency but also assesses higher-order cognitive skills essential for advanced language use. The conversational nature of the interview also provides an opportunity to check students' cultural competence. Through directed questions and discussion, Professor Dongye can gauge students' understanding of cultural nuances and sensitivity, aspects that may not be fully evident in written responses alone. This is particularly important in a language course that emphasizes deep cultural understanding alongside linguistic proficiency. Furthermore, the interview serves as a platform for evaluating students' metacognitive skills. By asking students to explain their approach to answering questions, Professor Dongye encourages them to think about their own thinking and learning processes in Chinese. This meta-level reflection is a valuable skill for advanced language learners and is challenging to assess through traditional written exams.

To facilitate these objectives, Professor Dongye prepares a range of questions designed to elicit thoughtful responses and encourage critical reflection. These questions might include asking students to walk through their thought process for a specific answer, discuss the sources or prior knowledge they drew upon and how/why they decided to use them in their response, or consider how they might approach the question differently. She might also ask how their response reflects cultural nuances discussed in class, what challenges they faced in articulating their ideas, or how their response might differ for various audiences. By incorporating these types of questions, Professor Dongye creates a comprehensive assessment that is much more difficult to replicate with AI assistance. This approach not only maintains the integrity of the exam but also provides valuable insights into students' language proficiency, critical thinking skills, and ability to engage in complex discussions in Chinese. Ultimately, this modified exam protocol aligns more closely with the course's goal of preparing students for advanced Chinese language use in diverse real-world contexts.

The approach to language assessment discussed in this offers valuable insights for language educators and teacher trainers grappling with the challenges posed by AI in education. Her modified exam protocol demonstrates the potential for creating more authentic, comprehensive evaluations of students' language abilities while maintaining academic integrity in an AI-augmented world.

The outcomes of this approach are largely positive. The interview component enhances the authenticity of the assessment, ensuring that students can genuinely articulate their ideas in Chinese rather than relying on memorized or AI-generated responses. It also provides a superior evaluation of spontaneous language use, critical thinking skills, and cultural competence – all crucial elements of advanced language proficiency that are difficult to assess in traditional written exams. Moreover, the format encourages students to develop metacognitive skills by reflecting on their own learning processes, a valuable ability for lifelong language learners. More specifically, this assessment method aligns closely with the principles of constructivist learning theory and communicative language teaching. By requiring students to explain their thought processes and defend their responses in real-time, Professor Dongye's approach fosters active construction of knowledge and meaning-making in the target language. The open-resource nature of the exam, combined with the prohibition on AI use, encourages students to develop critical information literacy skills – discerning which sources are reliable and relevant, and how to synthesize information effectively. This mirrors real-world language use scenarios where individuals must navigate vast amounts of information to communicate effectively. Furthermore, the interview component provides a unique opportunity for individualized feedback and assessment. Professor Dongye can tailor her questions to each student's responses, probing areas of uncertainty or encouraging deeper exploration of well-articulated ideas. This personalized interaction not only enhances the assessment's validity but also serves as a powerful learning moment, potentially boosting students' confidence in their Chinese language abilities and highlighting areas for future growth.

However, this approach is not without challenges. It requires a significant time investment from the instructor, potentially creating logistical issues in larger classes. Ensuring consistency across all interviews may prove difficult, and some students might find the format more stressful than traditional exams. Additionally, monitoring the use of permitted resources while prohibiting AI assistance during the open-book portion of the exam could present practical challenges. Indeed, these challenges highlight broader issues in assessment design and implementation in the age of AI. The time-intensive nature of individual interviews raises questions about scalability and equity in education. In larger classes or institutions with fewer resources, implementing such personalized assessments may be impractical, potentially leading to disparities in educational quality. The challenge of maintaining consistency across interviews also points to the subjective nature of language assessment, particularly when evaluating higher-order skills like critical thinking and cultural competence. This subjectivity, while valuable for capturing nuanced language abilities, may conflict with institutional demands for standardized, easily quantifiable assessment results. Furthermore, the difficulty in monitoring AI use during open-book portions of exams reflects a growing tension in education: how to leverage the benefits of AI as a learning tool while preserving the integrity of assessments. This challenge may necessitate a fundamental rethinking of what we consider "cheating" in academic contexts, and how we can design assessments that remain valid even with AI assistance.

Despite these hurdles, the case offers several important lessons for language educators. First and foremost, it underscores the need for adaptability in assessment practices. As AI technologies continue to evolve, educators must be willing to innovate and rethink traditional evaluation methods. This may involve focusing more on skills that AI cannot easily replicate, such as spontaneous language production, critical analysis, and cultural sensitivity. The case also highlights the importance of integrating real-world scenarios into assessments. By crafting questions that mirror authentic language use situations, educators can better prepare students for the complex linguistic challenges I will face in their future careers or academic pursuits. This approach aligns well with communicative and task-based language teaching methodologies, emphasizing practical application over rote memorization.

For those looking to implement similar strategies, it is crucial to consider the balance between technology use and assessment integrity. While embracing certain technological tools can enhance the learning experience, clear boundaries on AI use during evaluations are necessary. Educators should also prioritize individual interaction with students, as these conversations often provide invaluable insights into language abilities that written exams alone may miss. Additionally, adapting this approach to different contexts, scalability is an important consideration. While Professor Dongye's method works well for her small class, educators with larger groups may need to modify the concept. This could involve incorporating peer interviews, group discussions, or utilizing teaching assistants to help conduct individual assessments.

Ultimately, this case study serves as a call to action for language educators to reconsider their assessment practices in light of AI advancements. By focusing on evaluating skills that go beyond mere language production – such as critical thinking, cultural competence, and spontaneous communication – educators can create more meaningful and relevant assessments. This not only helps maintain academic integrity but also better prepares students for the complex, real-world language use they will encounter beyond the classroom.

Rethinking Assessment Case 2: Simulation-based Assessment

In our second case study, we turn our attention to Professor Carmen Vega, who teaches an advanced Business Spanish course at a mid-sized public university in the American Midwest. The course, *Spanish for International Business*, is a 300-level offering that meets twice a week for 75-minute sessions. Professor Vega's class consists of 20 undergraduate students, primarily juniors and seniors, representing a diverse mix of academic backgrounds. The majority are pursuing degrees in International Business or Spanish, but the class also attracts students from Economics, Marketing, and Global Studies programs. This interdisciplinary blend reflects the growing recognition of the importance of Spanish language skills in the global business landscape.

The students in Professor Vega's class have all completed at least two years of college-level Spanish or demonstrate equivalent proficiency, roughly corresponding to a B2 level on the Common European Framework of Reference for Languages (CEFR). This high-intermediate level allows Professor Vega to conduct the class entirely in Spanish, immersing students in the language as they explore complex business concepts and scenarios. The course aims to develop students' Spanish language skills within the specific context of international business. Objectives include mastering business-specific vocabulary and idioms, understanding cultural nuances in Spanish-speaking business environments, and honing communication skills for various professional scenarios such as negotiations, presentations, and formal correspondence. Additionally, the course integrates current events and case studies from the Spanish-speaking business world, encouraging students to apply their language skills to real-world situations. To facilitate these goals, Professor Vega utilizes a teaching approach emphasizes practical application and cultural competence. Students engage in a variety of activities including analyzing Spanish-language business reports, participating in mock negotiations, drafting professional emails, and delivering presentations on market trends in Spanish-speaking countries. The course also incorporates guest speakers from Spanish-speaking businesses and virtual exchanges with business students in Spain and Latin America, providing authentic interaction opportunities.

As the semester progresses, Professor Vega finds herself contemplating how to most effectively assess her students' progress in a way that truly captures their ability to apply their Spanish skills in realistic business contexts. Additionally, Professor Vega is acutely aware of the rapid advancements in AI language tools. She realizes that conventional exam formats are increasingly vulnerable to AI assistance, potentially compromising the authenticity of student work. For instance, AI can easily generate grammatically correct business emails or provide quick translations, making it difficult to gauge a student's true language abilities through these traditional means. The assessment challenge is further compounded by the specific needs of a Business Spanish course. Professor Vega knows that her students will need to navigate complex, nuanced business situations in their future careers, where language proficiency extends beyond mere translation or grammar knowledge. They need to demonstrate cultural competence, negotiate effectively, and adapt their language use to various professional contexts – skills that are difficult to assess through standard exams.

Additionally, Professor Vega recognizes the importance of preparing her students for the technological realities of the modern business world. While she wants to discourage over-reliance on AI tools for language production, she also understands that these technologies are becoming an integral part of the business landscape. The challenge, therefore, is to design an assessment that not only evaluates language skills but also assesses students' ability to use language resources (including technology) strategically and ethically in business contexts.

To address these challenges, Professor Vega decides to implement a comprehensive business simulation as the primary assessment tool for her course. This innovative approach aims to create an immersive, real-world environment where students can demonstrate their Spanish language skills in context, while also showcasing their business acumen and cultural competence. The simulation is designed as a semester-long project, culminating in a week-long intensive "business week" that serves as the final assessment. Professor Vega creates a detailed scenario involving a fictional Spanish multinational corporation, "GlobalHisp S.A.," facing a complex business challenge. The company, with operations across Spain and Latin America, is considering expansion into a new market while simultaneously dealing with a public relations crisis. She then dividers her students into small teams, each representing a different department within GlobalHisp S.A. (e.g., Marketing, Finance, Human Resources, Public Relations). Throughout the semester, teams work on various tasks related to their roles, building up to the final simulation week. These tasks include researching target markets, analyzing financial reports in Spanish, developing marketing strategies, and preparing press releases.

The simulation incorporates multiple elements to assess different aspects of students' language and business skills:

1. Written Communication: Students draft emails, reports, and proposals in Spanish, addressing various stakeholders within the company and external parties

2. Oral Presentations: Each team delivers several presentations throughout the semester, culminating in a final board meeting presentation during the simulation week
3. Negotiation Exercises: Students engage in role-played negotiations with other teams, simulating inter-departmental discussions and external business negotiations
4. Crisis Management: A surprise element is introduced during the simulation week, requiring students to respond quickly and appropriately in Spanish to an unexpected business challenge
5. Cultural Competence: The simulation includes interactions with "clients" and "partners" from different Spanish-speaking countries, requiring students to adapt their language and behavior to various cultural contexts
6. Ethical Decision-Making: Students face ethical dilemmas that require them to discuss and make decisions using appropriate Spanish business language and considering cultural implications

Throughout the simulation, Professor Vega allows limited use of online resources, including AI-powered translation tools, but with strict guidelines. Students must document and justify any use of these tools, explaining how they verified and adapted the AI-generated content to fit the context appropriately. By implementing this comprehensive simulation, Professor Vega aims to create an assessment environment that closely mirrors the complex, dynamic nature of international business conducted in Spanish. This approach not only evaluates students' language skills but also their ability to apply these skills creatively and critically in realistic business scenarios, addressing the limitations of traditional assessments in the age of AI.

Professor Vega's assessment strategy for the simulation is as comprehensive and multifaceted as the simulation itself. Throughout the project, she focuses on evaluating several key areas: language proficiency, communication skills, cultural competence, business acumen, teamwork and leadership, adaptive problem-solving, and ethical decision-making. This holistic approach allows her to assess not only students' Spanish language skills but also their ability to apply these skills effectively in a business context. To capture the complexity of student performance, Professor Vega employs a variety of assessment tools. She develops detailed rubrics for each major component of the simulation, including presentations, reports, and negotiations. These rubrics outline specific criteria for language use, content accuracy, and overall performance. Throughout the simulation, she takes observational notes on individual and team performances, paying close attention to language use, cultural sensitivity, and the implementation of business strategies.

Professor Vega also incorporates peer and self-evaluations, conducted in Spanish, to gain insights into team dynamics and individual contributions. Students compile portfolios of their work throughout the simulation, including written documents, presentation slides, and reflection pieces, which Professor Vega evaluates holistically. The final presentation to the mock board of directors is assessed not only by Professor Vega but also by guest evaluators from the Spanish-speaking business community, providing a real-world perspective on students' performances.

When it comes to grading, Professor Vega considers several factors to ensure a fair and comprehensive evaluation. She uses a progressive weighting system, where later tasks in the simulation carry more weight than earlier ones, allowing students to improve as they become more comfortable with the format. Grades are balanced between individual contributions and team outcomes. While language proficiency is crucial, Professor Vega also significantly weights the application of business concepts and cultural knowledge. She takes into account the effort and improvement demonstrated by students throughout the simulation, rewarding significant progress in both language skills and business acumen. Points are also allocated for creativity and initiative in addressing challenges within the simulation.

The debriefing session at the end of the simulation serves as a crucial opportunity for Professor Vega to provide actionable feedback. During this session, she highlights specific examples of effective language use, cultural competence, and business strategy observed during the simulation. She addresses common language errors or cultural misunderstandings, providing correct forms and explanations. Professor Vega discusses how students' decisions and strategies in the simulation might play out in real-world business scenarios, encouraging students to reflect on their learning experience and identify areas for growth. The debriefing of any simulation is a powerful moment of feedback and reflection. By incorporating one in this semester-long assessment, the instructor can ensure that the simulation serves not just as an evaluation tool, but as a powerful learning experience. It helps students connect their performance in the simulation to real-world business Spanish applications, reinforcing the practical value of the skills they have developed and providing clear direction for their continued growth in the field of international business Spanish.

The outcomes of Professor Vega's simulation-based assessment approach are largely positive, offering a rich and authentic evaluation of students' Spanish language skills in a business context. Students demonstrate increased engagement and motivation throughout the semester, as the real-world nature of the simulation makes the relevance of their language learning immediately apparent. The immersive experience leads to noticeable improvements in students' business Spanish proficiency, particularly in their ability to navigate complex professional scenarios and adapt their language use to different cultural contexts. Furthermore, the simulation proves effective in developing students' critical thinking and problem-solving skills in Spanish, as they are required to analyze business challenges, formulate strategies, and make decisions using their second language. The team-based nature of the project also enhances students' collaborative skills and their ability to communicate effectively in Spanish in a professional setting.

However, the approach is not without challenges. The intensive nature of the simulation, particularly during the "business week," can be stressful for some students, potentially impacting their performance. Additionally, ensuring equal participation and contribution within teams can be difficult, as some students may dominate while others struggle to keep up. Professor Vega also finds that assessing individual language progress within a group project setting requires careful attention and multiple assessment points. Another challenge lies in the scalability of this approach. While effective for a class of 20 students, implementing such an intensive simulation-based assessment for larger classes would require significant resources and coordination. Moreover, the complexity of the simulation means that considerable time must be devoted to explaining the project and its requirements, potentially reducing time available for other course content.

Reflecting on the implications of this case for broader language teaching practices, it is clear that simulation-based assessments offer a promising avenue for evaluating language skills in context. This approach aligns well with the growing emphasis on communicative competence and task-based language teaching in the field of second language acquisition. It also addresses the challenge of creating meaningful assessments in an age where AI can easily handle more traditional language tasks. The case underscores the importance of integrating content and language learning, particularly in courses designed for specific purposes like business Spanish. It suggests that language educators, especially those teaching advanced learners, should consider incorporating extended, complex tasks that mirror real-world language use scenarios in their assessment strategies. Furthermore, this approach highlights the potential for interdisciplinary collaboration in language education. By partnering with business faculty or professionals, language educators can create more authentic and relevant learning experiences for their students.

Several key lessons emerge from this case study. First, authentic, context-rich assessments can significantly enhance student engagement and learning outcomes in language courses. Additionally, while technology and AI pose challenges for traditional assessment methods, they also open up opportunities for more complex, realistic language use scenarios in assessment. Moreover, effective language assessment in the AI age may require a shift from evaluating discrete language skills to assessing holistic language use in complex situations. This shift aligns with the real-world demands students will face in their professional lives. We must also acknowledge that providing ongoing feedback and opportunities for reflection is crucial in complex assessment scenarios. The debriefing sessions in Professor Vega's simulation play a vital role in helping students understand their progress and areas for improvement. Finally, while simulation-based assessments offer many benefits, they require careful planning, clear communication of expectations, and ongoing support for students. Educators considering similar approaches should be prepared to invest significant time in design and implementation, but the rich learning outcomes can make this investment worthwhile.

Taking a simulation-based assessment approach offers a compelling model for language educators grappling with the challenges of teaching and evaluating language skills in the age of AI. By creating an immersive, semester-long business simulation, she has developed a comprehensive assessment tool that not only evaluates students' Spanish language proficiency but also their ability to apply these skills in complex, real-world business scenarios. This approach addresses many of the limitations of traditional language assessments, particularly in the face of advancing AI technology, by focusing on holistic language use, cultural competence, and critical thinking skills that are difficult for AI to replicate.

The success of this assessment strategy, despite its challenges, underscores the potential for similar approaches across various language teaching contexts. It highlights the importance of authentic, context-rich assessments in enhancing student engagement and learning outcomes. Moreover, it demonstrates how educators can leverage the realities of an AI-augmented world to create more meaningful and relevant learning experiences. As language education continues to evolve, approaches like Professor Vega's simulation-based assessment may become increasingly valuable in preparing students for the complex linguistic and cultural demands of their future professional lives. While implementing such comprehensive assessments requires significant investment in terms of time and resources, the rich learning outcomes and authentic evaluation of students' abilities make it a worthwhile consideration for language educators seeking to innovate their assessment practices.

Rethinking Assessment Case 3: Reflective Exit Exams/Defenses

Our third case study focuses on Professor Alex Chen, who teaches English for Academic Purposes (EAP) at a large public university in the United States. Professor Chen's courses, EAP 1015, 6010, and 6111, are foundational writing courses designed for international students and non-native English speakers pursuing undergraduate and graduate degrees across various disciplines. These classes meet two times a week for 75-minute sessions and typically has an enrollment of 14 students per section. The students in Professor Chen's class represent a diverse range of linguistic and cultural backgrounds, with varying levels of English proficiency, but mostly in the high-intermediate to advanced proficiency bands. While all students have met the university's minimum English language requirements, their actual competencies in academic writing can differ significantly. The course aims to develop students' academic writing skills, critical thinking abilities, and understanding of academic conventions in the American university context.

As the semester progresses, Professor Chen becomes increasingly concerned about the impact of generative AI on traditional writing assessments. He observes that some students are relying heavily on AI tools for their assignments, potentially masking their true writing abilities and hindering their long-term language development. Moreover, he realizes that conventional writing assignments may no longer effectively measure students' genuine understanding and application of course concepts in the age of AI. To address these challenges, Professor Chen decides to implement a reflective exit exam as the final assessment for his course. This oral exit exam is designed to evaluate students' comprehension of academic writing concepts, their ability to articulate their learning journey, and their capacity to apply course material in a spontaneous, conversational setting.

The assessment is structured as a one-on-one conversation between Professor Chen and each student, lasting approximately 15–20 minutes. During this time, students are expected to discuss various aspects of academic writing, reflect on their learning experiences, and demonstrate critical thinking skills. Throughout the exam, students are encouraged to provide specific evidence for any claims that they might make. This evidence may take the form of references to their work for the class, or even drawing attention to specific passages of a text. The exam is holistically assessed, focusing on the depth of students' responses, evidence of learning, and proof of critical engagement with course themes and content (see also, Table 5.1, below.

Table 5.1 Assessment Heuristic for Reflective Oral Exit Exam

Grade Band	Depth of Responses	Evidence of Learning	Critical Engagement
A	Responses are thorough, nuanced, and demonstrate a comprehensive understanding of concepts. Student provides detailed examples and explanations.	Clear and substantial evidence of significant learning and growth throughout the course. Student can articulate how their understanding has evolved.	Demonstrates high-level critical thinking, connecting course themes in innovative ways. Critically evaluates concepts and applies them to novel situations.
B	Responses are clear and show good understanding of concepts. Examples are relevant but may lack some detail.	Evidence of learning is present and student can discuss their progress, but may not fully elaborate on the process.	Shows good critical thinking skills, making connections between course themes. Some evaluation of concepts, but may not always reach the deepest levels of analysis.
C	Responses demonstrate basic understanding of concepts. Examples may be general or lack specificity.	Some evidence of learning is present, but student struggles to articulate how their understanding has changed over time.	Basic critical thinking is evident. Student can discuss course themes but may struggle to make deeper connections or evaluations.
D	Responses are superficial and may contain misunderstandings of key concepts. Examples are vague or irrelevant.	Little evidence of learning or growth throughout the course. Student struggles to discuss their progress.	Limited critical thinking. Student struggles to engage with course themes beyond surface level or to make connections between concepts.
F	Responses are unclear, incorrect, or absent. Student unable to provide relevant examples.	No clear evidence of learning or growth. Student unable to discuss their progress in the course.	No evidence of critical engagement with course themes. Unable to discuss concepts beyond basic recall.

To prepare students for this novel assessment approach, Professor Chen provides detailed guidelines, including:

1. An explanation of the assessment format and its objectives
2. Advice on reviewing course materials and reflecting on personal learning experiences
3. Suggestions for developing critical thinking and oral communication skills
4. Tips for engaging in respectful academic dialogue

Beyond these general guidelines, provided to students from day one on the course CMS, Professor Chen also incorporates regular reflective exercises into the class that first model for students the kinds of responses that he expects on the reflective exit exam and provides students space to "try on" this mode of reflection and critical response. These "reflective moments" take varied forms during the course of the semester. One for that they take is a bi-weekly writing assignment where students write a formal 400–600 word reflection of their learning, their struggles, and the plans for continued development in the coming weeks. More regularly, Professor Chen includes "mini-reflections" after key points in the lesson – varying between quiet, internal reflection upon a targeted question and more open-ended discussion of a reflective prompt in the final 10 minutes of class. Then, in the week before the reflective exit exam, Professor Chen dedicates an entire class period to helping students better understand the assessment format by holding an in-class discussion and activity period. During this period, the students have space to clarify the assessment protocol and practice responding to reflective questions. To help achieve the latter objective, Professor Chen uses an in-class activity wherein students first work in groups to develop 3–5 questions *they think* they will encounter on the exam before splitting from their groups to ask their questions to 2–3 other students. During this time, they are advised to pay attention to what they think makes a stronger response versus a weaker one while talking to their peers. This all culminates in a class discussion of best practices to do well on the oral exit exam.

The actual assessment consists of a series of open-ended, reflective questions. For example:

- Describe how your writing process has evolved over the course of the semester, focusing on what drove the change and the impacts you perceived that it had on your writing.

- Tell me about a challenge that you faced in completing the requirements of this course and discuss how you've overcome it if you did, or the impacts of the challenge on your ongoing intellectual labors?
- Talk to me about one concept from our class that you think will help you in other classes. How and why?

These questions are designed to elicit responses that demonstrate not only students' understanding of course content but also their ability to apply this knowledge to their own experiences and future academic endeavors. During the assessment, which takes place in Professor Chen's office, he merely asks the question before falling silent and allowing the student to answer to the best of their abilities. During this time, he takes notes on the students' responses and identifies potential follow-up questions to help the student dig deeper if needed. These notes then become tools to use in providing feedback to the student after the assessment is over.

Professor Chen finds that this assessment approach offers several benefits. Firstly, it significantly reduces the possibility of AI-generated responses, as students must engage in real-time, spontaneous conversation. Secondly, it allows for a more nuanced evaluation of students' understanding, as Professor Chen can ask follow-up questions or seek clarification when needed. Thirdly, it encourages students to reflect deeply on their learning process, promoting metacognition and self-awareness. Indeed, the majority of students leave the assessment saying one of two things, unprompted, "Wow, that was easier than I thought it would be" or "Huh. I have never had the chance to think about my classes like this and how they connect to the rest of my studies." This speaks to the potential power of this assessment method as a sort of capstone for a course that can, especially for advanced learners at the university-level get them thinking about how their learning transfers from one course to another.

However, this assessment method also presents challenges. Some students, particularly those less confident in their spoken English, find the format anxiety-inducing – up until the moment the moment that they finish the examination and Professor Chen signals its formal close. This is often marked by audible sighs of relief. Additionally, the one-on-one nature of the assessment is time-consuming for Professor Chen, requiring careful scheduling and potentially limiting the depth of assessment possible in larger classes. Indeed, as Professor Chen is a teaching professor, he teaches four sections of EAP each semester. This amounts to about 56 students on average, meaning that the exit exams take about 50–60 hours of labor just during the week of exit exams. This includes administering the exams to the students, writing up notes, crafting feedback, and assessing student performance.

To address these challenges, Professor Chen implements several strategies. He incorporates practice sessions throughout the semester, allowing students to become more comfortable with academic discussions in English. He also provides heuristics that clearly outline the assessment criteria, helping students understand what is expected of them. To manage time constraints, he schedules the assessments over the course of a week, using office hours, regularly scheduled course meeting times, and other available time slots. This creates considerable flexibility for the students, but also greatly increases the amount of time that Professor Chen must be on campus compared to a "regular" teaching week.

The outcomes of this assessment approach are largely positive. Students demonstrate a deeper engagement with course material and show improved ability to articulate complex ideas about writing. The reflective nature of the questions encourages students to take ownership of their learning process, leading to more meaningful and lasting understanding of academic writing concepts. Moreover, the format helps identify areas where students may be over-relying on AI tools, allowing for targeted intervention and support.

This case study offers several important lessons for language educators grappling with assessment in the age of AI. Firstly, it highlights the value of oral assessments in evaluating genuine understanding and language proficiency. Secondly, it underscores the importance of reflection and metacognition in the learning process. Lastly, it demonstrates how innovative assessment methods can not only evaluate student learning but also enhance it by promoting deeper engagement with course material. For educators considering implementing similar assessment strategies, several key considerations emerge:

1. Clear communication of expectations and assessment criteria is crucial for student success
2. Incorporating reflective practices throughout the course can prepare students for this type of assessment
3. Time management and scheduling are important factors, especially for larger classes
4. Flexibility in questioning allows for a more comprehensive assessment of student understanding
5. This approach may require additional support for students who struggle with oral communication

In conclusion, Professor Chen's reflective oral exit exam offers a promising model for assessment in language courses, particularly in the context of increasing AI capabilities. By focusing on students' ability to articulate their learning, apply concepts to personal experiences, and engage in academic dialogue, this approach provides a more holistic and authentic evaluation of student progress. While it presents certain logistical challenges, the benefits in terms of student engagement, metacognition, and genuine demonstration of learning make it a valuable tool in the modern language educator's assessment toolkit.

A Principled Guide to Feedback in the Age of AI

Up until this point, much of our discussion has focused on assessing student learning. This largely mirrors conversations we have witnessed play out in the literature and in trade publications over the past two to three years at the time of writing this chapter (see Abdous, 2023; Nadeem et al., 2024; Supiano, 2023). However, the actual assessment instrument, or a more extensive protocol, is just one part of the issue in teaching and learning. Particularly in language education, we are well aware of the important role that feedback plays in not only supporting our assessments of students' learning but also in fostering their continued development (Hattie & Timperley, 2007; Gibbs & Simpson, 2005; Lee, 2008; Lyster & Ranta, 1997). Because of this reality, it is necessary for an AI-integrative pedagogical or professional practice in language teaching and learning more generally and in CALL contexts more specifically to directly engage with the intersection of assessment, feedback, and artificial intelligence.

More specifically, feedback is a crucial element in the educational process because it can serve as an accessible bridge between teaching and learning. Effective feedback provides learners with clear information on their current performance, identifies areas for improvement, and offers concrete suggestions for how to enhance their skills. This targeted guidance helps learners to understand their strengths and weaknesses, fostering a sense of self-awareness that is essential for continuous improvement. One of the key reasons feedback is so vital is its ability to transform assessments from mere evaluative tools into learning opportunities. While assessments measure what learners know and can do at a particular point in time, feedback extends this by explaining why they have achieved certain results and how they can progress further. For instance, Ellis (2009) highlights that corrective feedback in language education helps learners notice the gaps in their knowledge, prompting them to adjust their language use and internalize correct forms. This iterative process of receiving feedback, making adjustments, and receiving further feedback creates a dynamic learning environment where improvement is continuous and self-directed.

Moreover, feedback supports the development of learner autonomy. As Nicol and Macfarlane-Dick (2006) argue, effective feedback practices encourage students to take responsibility for their own learning. By providing detailed, actionable insights, feedback empowers learners to set their own goals and monitor their progress, which is particularly important in language learning where self-regulation and practice are key to achieving fluency. Feedback also plays a crucial role in maintaining learner motivation. According to Hyland and Hyland (2006), feedback that is constructive and encouraging can boost learners' confidence and willingness to engage with challenging material. When students see that their efforts are recognized and that they are making tangible progress, they are more likely to remain motivated and committed to their studies.

In the context of AI-integrative pedagogical practices, the role of feedback becomes even more critical. AI tools can provide immediate, personalized feedback that is tailored to the individual learner's needs, but these rapid response capabilities must be balanced with both instructor expertise and direct instruction and training of the learner in how to utilize these capabilities effectively. The feedback capability of modern LLM-based AI systems may serve to enhance the traditional feedback loop by making it more responsive and specific, thereby accelerating the learning process. However, it also necessitates a thoughtful integration of AI systems with pedagogical strategies to ensure that the feedback provided by AI is meaningful and effectively supports learner development.

To contribute to the meaningful integration of AI into language teaching practices, the remainder of this chapter will focus on principles and strategies that language educators can use when it comes to building appropriate AI integration into their classrooms. Continuing in the vein of building an environment of collaborative AI, the remainder of this chapter will explore general approaches to leveraging AI for feedback in language learning, emphasizing how these technologies can complement, rather than replace, traditional instructor feedback. In doing so, this section will address potential challenges and ethical considerations that arise when integrating AI into feedback processes.

To ground our discussion in practical applications, the following sections will examine conceptual scenarios of AI-assisted feedback in various language classroom contexts. These examples, primarily drawn from experiences with current commercial and open-source LLM platforms, will illustrate how AI principles can be effectively applied across different language skills – writing, speaking, reading, and listening – and how they can support differentiated instruction and personalized learning. Moreover, this section will discuss strategies for training students to effectively interpret and apply AI-generated feedback, recognizing that the successful integration of these technologies requires not only instructor proficiency but also student engagement and understanding.

While exploring these topics, I would encourage you to also consider how AI-driven feedback can be integrated with the assessment strategies discussed earlier in this chapter, creating a cohesive approach to language teaching and learning in the age of AI. This chapter will also provide guidelines for evaluating and implementing AI feedback principles based on specific learning objectives and student needs, acknowledging that the application of AI in education requires careful consideration of pedagogical goals and contexts. Throughout this discussion, I will emphasize the importance of balancing AI-enhanced feedback with instructor expertise and judgment. While AI offers powerful capabilities for providing rapid, personalized feedback, it is crucial that language educators maintain their central role in guiding student learning and development. By adopting a collaborative approach that leverages the strengths of both AI-enhanced methods and human instruction, we can create more effective, engaging, and equitable language learning environments.

Principles for Effective Generative AI Use to Support Feedback in the Language Classroom

To begin the conversation, I would first draw our attention to a set of shared principles that can guide professional practice. The hope in doing so is that we can make reasoned, informed use of AI to supplement our expertise and to create a more equitable working environment – as it is a matter of fact that language educators are often working in peripheral/marginalized positions (e.g., adjunct/part time/contracted) that come with an outsized teaching/student load with an, at times, markedly lower salary than their faculty peers in more "traditional" roles (read: tenure/tenure-track). It is also a matter of disciplinary fact that feedback is one of the most labor-intensive parts of the instructional process – and one that, speaking from personal experience, we language educators take very seriously (e.g., Yu, 2021). We often provide more feedback in our classes than students might see in any of their other classes combined during an instructional unit. By way of personal anecdote, in a single semester as a student in one of my EAP classes, I will typically receive between 12–20 pages of written feedback from me in the form of memos, marginal comments, and in-line markup. As a student in applied computer sciences, unless I went to office hours, I received about 500 words of written feedback across the entire semester. So, the potential of AI to help support professional educators, while potentially creating space for better work-life balance, or at least more time on direct instruction, preparation, and continuing professional development, is certainly worth exploring (c.f., Deeva et al., 2021; Taskıran & Goksel, 2022).

The first principle is that of **complementarity**, or the view that artificial intelligence, in all things, should enhance and extend instructor feedback rather than replace this important intellectual labor outright. This principle recognizes the unique strengths and limitations of both AI systems and human agents and advocates for a synergistic approach that leverages the best of both (see also Pasquale, 2020). More specifically, complementarity means using AI to augment the feedback process in ways that support and amplify the instructor's expertise and individual insights. For instance, AI can be used to offer recommendations on how to present feedback to learners to better support neurodiverse learners, or to quickly come up with example text, freeing the instructor to focus on identifying underlying issues in the student's work and formulating an instructional plan to help better support that learner.

The importance of this principle in language education cannot be overstated. While AI tools have made remarkable strides in language processing and generation, they lack the depth of understanding, empathy, and contextual awareness that human instructors bring to the learning process. For example, we as a field have come to accept that language learning is not just about acquiring vocabulary and grammar; it involves developing cultural competence, nuanced communication skills, and the ability to express complex ideas effectively. These aspects often require the guidance of an experienced human instructor who can provide personalized feedback based on a holistic understanding of the student's progress, challenges, and goals. Moreover, the principle of complementarity acknowledges the irreplaceable role of human interaction in language learning. The rapport between instructor and student, the motivational aspect of personalized encouragement, and the ability to adapt teaching strategies in real-time based on student responses are all crucial elements that AI, in its current form, cannot fully replicate – although admittedly AI companies, like OpenAI are certainly trying if their tutoring demos are to be believed (OpenAI, 2024).

Complementarity, therefore, requires us as practitioners to find and strive for an appropriate balance between AI support and instructor labor. Maintaining said balance once it is found will likely represent an ongoing effort on the part of the instructor *and their learners* as they work together towards thoughtful implementation and adjusting to student need and course objectives. One potentially effective approach is to adopt a layered approach. In this model, AI systems provide an initial layer of feedback, addressing fundamental aspects of language use such as grammar, vocabulary, and basic structure. This AI-generated feedback can be made immediately available to students, allowing them to make preliminary revisions and improvements to their work. Subsequently, human instructors can focus their attention on higher-order concerns such as content development, argumentation, cultural nuances, and stylistic refinement. In a writing assignment, for example, an AI running locally on the instructor's device using a platform like GPT4All might first analyze a student's essay, highlighting grammatical errors, suggesting vocabulary improvements, and noting issues with sentence structure or coherence. The student could then revise their work based on this feedback before submitting it to the instructor. The instructor, freed from the need to address these basic issues, can then provide more in-depth feedback on the essay's arguments, use of evidence, and overall effectiveness in addressing the assignment prompt.

The principle of complementarity in AI-assisted feedback offers a potentially powerful approach for supporting neurodiverse learners in language classrooms. By combining teacher expertise with AI capabilities, we can create more accessible and actionable feedback, tailored to the unique needs of students with conditions such as autism spectrum disorder, ADHD, or dyslexia. Consider a scenario where a language teacher, Professor Chen, is providing feedback on an essay written by Alex, a student with ADHD. Professor Chen has extensive experience in language instruction but finds it challenging to consistently frame feedback in a way that Alex can easily process and act upon. After carefully reviewing Alex's essay, Professor Chen drafts detailed feedback addressing various aspects of the writing, including content development, argument structure, and language use. However, instead of sending this feedback directly to Alex, Professor Chen utilizes Generative AI to recast teacher feedback for neurodiverse learners. In this case,

Professor Chen could construct a prompt like the one below to prime the AI system to assist in this effort:

> I need to recast the following feedback for a student with ADHD in my advanced ESL writing class. The student's name is Alex. Please restructure my feedback to be more accessible and actionable, keeping in mind the following guidelines:
>
> 1. Break down lengthy comments into shorter, more digestible points
> 2. Incorporate visual elements like color-coding or simple diagrams where appropriate
> 3. Provide specific, actionable steps for each point of feedback
> 4. Use clear, concrete language, avoiding idioms or abstract concepts
> 5. Suggest multimedia elements (e.g., short video explanations) where they might be helpful
> 6. Maintain a positive and encouraging tone throughout
> 7. Prioritize the most important points if the feedback is extensive

The AI system analyzes Professor Chen's feedback and restructures it in a format more suitable for a student with ADHD. It breaks down lengthy comments into shorter, more digestible points. The AI also incorporates visual elements, such as color-coding or tiered lists with emojis, to help organize the feedback visually. Additionally, it suggests specific, actionable steps for each point of feedback, helping Alex understand not just what needs improvement, but how to go about making those improvements. This may, for instance, take a comment from Professor Chen on the need for better paragraph structure and recast it as: "Action Step: Organize your ideas. 1) Identify the main point of each paragraph. 2) Highlight it in yellow. 3) Ensure supporting details in blue." This step-by-step approach can be particularly helpful for students who struggle with executive functioning. Moreover, the AI tool can adjust the language of the feedback to be more concrete and literal, which can be beneficial for students on the autism spectrum who might struggle with abstract or idiomatic language. It might also suggest incorporating multimedia elements, such as short video explanations or audio clips, to cater to different learning styles and attention spans.

The complementary use of teacher expertise and AI in this manner offers several advantages. It allows for the nuanced, context-aware feedback that only a human teacher can provide, while leveraging AI to make this feedback more accessible and actionable for neurodiverse learners. It helps maintain consistency in feedback delivery, which can be particularly important for students who thrive on routine and clear expectations. Additionally, it saves time for the teacher, allowing them to focus more on the content of their feedback rather than the mechanics of how to present it for different learning needs. This approach also promotes a more inclusive classroom environment. By using AI to adapt feedback for neurodiverse learners, teachers can ensure that all students have equitable access to constructive criticism and guidance, regardless of their neurological differences. Over time, this can lead to improved learning outcomes and increased confidence for neurodiverse students in their language learning journey.

The second principle that can be used when applying generative AI to support feedback in language classes is ***transparency***. Here, transparency refers to the need for clear and open communication about how, when, and why AI is being used to support feedback processes. This is not merely about *disclosure*; it is instead about fostering an environment of trust, understanding, and active engagement with a technology that is increasingly shaping educational processes (see Johnson, 2024). Driving the need for transparency is, first and foremost, that our stakeholders – students, parents, administrators – may harbor legitimate concerns (and the occasional misconception) about AI's role in education. Moreover, we must consider our ethical due diligence when using AI-powered tools in our classes. This necessitates an ongoing and dialogic approach to transparency about AI as a tool to support providing timely and accessible feedback to our learners.

Implementing transparency in the classroom involves more than a one-time announcement. It requires ongoing dialogue and clear delineation of AI's role throughout the course. This might involve explaining to students how AI algorithms analyze their work, what aspects of feedback are AI-generated versus instructor-generated, and how the instructor uses AI to inform their overall assessment. For instance, an instructor might say, "The initial grammar and vocabulary feedback you receive is generated by an AI tool. I then review this feedback, make adjustments if necessary, and add my own comments on your argument structure and content." The benefits of doing so are manifold. Primarily, it builds trust between instructors and students. Specifically, when students understand the feedback process, they are more likely to engage with and trust the feedback they receive. Transparency can also be used to enhance students' digital literacy and critical thinking skills. By understanding how AI is used in their education, students are better prepared to navigate and evaluate AI-assisted processes in their future academic and professional lives. Moreover, transparency can be used to help improve students' understanding and engagement with feedback. When students know that certain aspects of feedback are AI-generated, they may approach it differently – perhaps with more objectivity or with an understanding of its limitations. This awareness can lead to more thoughtful engagement with feedback and potentially more effective learning outcomes.

However, maintaining transparency is not without its challenges. One primary difficulty is balancing detail with clarity in explanations. While it is important to be thorough, overwhelming students with technical details about AI algorithms may be counterproductive. Instructors must navigate the fine line between providing sufficient information and avoiding cognitive overload. For instance, explaining that an AI uses "natural language processing" might be appropriate, but requiring students to understand the parse trees or vector space models in the name of better grasping the intricacies of transformer models and neural networks could confuse rather than clarify. This challenge is particularly acute in language classrooms where students' proficiency levels vary. An explanation that is clear to an advanced learner might be incomprehensible to a beginner. Instructors must therefore adapt their explanations to suit their audience, potentially necessitating multiple versions of the same information tailored to different proficiency levels. Moreover, the language used to describe AI processes can itself be a barrier. Terms like "algorithm," "machine learning," or "neural network" might be unfamiliar or intimidating to some students, especially those from non-technical backgrounds. Instructors need to find ways to explain these concepts using accessible language without oversimplifying to the point of inaccuracy. Another significant challenge is the rapid evolution of AI technologies. The field of AI is advancing at an unprecedented pace, with new models, techniques, and applications emerging regularly. This means that instructors must continuously update their understanding and explanations of the AI tools they use. What was cutting-edge one semester might be outdated the next, requiring constant vigilance and professional development on the part of educators. This rapid change also makes it difficult to provide students with stable, consistent information about AI tools. An instructor might explain how an AI writing assistant works at the beginning of a semester, only to find that a major update has significantly changed its functionality mid-course. This can lead to confusion and potentially erode trust if not handled carefully.

Furthermore, the proprietary nature of many AI tools adds another layer of complexity to transparency efforts. Commercial AI products often do not disclose the full details of their algorithms or training data, citing intellectual property concerns. This can limit how much information instructors can provide to students about the inner workings of the AI tools they are using. This lack of much needed transparency and explainability from AI systems designers means that there is also the challenge of conveying the limitations and potential biases of AI systems. While it is important for students to understand these aspects, explaining them without undermining confidence in the AI-assisted feedback process requires careful messaging. Instructors need to strike a balance between fostering critical thinking about AI and maintaining its effectiveness as a learning tool.

Consider the case of Professor Garcia, who teaches an advanced Spanish composition course. At the beginning of the semester, she introduces the AI writing assistant that will be used in the course, explaining its capabilities and limitations. She demonstrates how she will use the AI to provide initial feedback on grammar and vocabulary, which she will then review and supplement with her own comments on content and style. Throughout the semester, she regularly reminds students of this process and encourages them to ask questions about the AI-generated feedback they receive, even going to far as to build reflective assignments and "feedback dialogues" into class sessions. To provide students a safe space to voice more critical thoughts, Professor Garcia also implements an anonymous mid-semester survey to gather students' thoughts on the AI-assisted feedback process. Based on the responses, she adjusts her approach, providing more detailed explanations of certain AI-generated comments that students found confusing. By maintaining this level of transparency, Professor Garcia not only builds trust with her students but also helps them develop a nuanced understanding of AI's role in language learning.

Beyond building trust in both AI-powered educational systems and in an AI-inclusive pedagogical practice, language educators should also seek to continue instilling critical habits of mind in their learners, even during the feedback stage of the learning and assessment processes. Here, helping students to evaluate feedback critically, whether human-, AI-, or hybrid-generated is a key step. To that end, a collaborative view of AI and feedback in language teaching and learning should be governed, in part, by a principle *of critical engagement and evaluation*. This principal advocates for encouraging students to thoughtfully analyze and assess all feedback, rather than accepting it unquestioningly. By promoting this approach, we not only enhance the effectiveness of AI-assisted feedback but also cultivate essential digital literacy and critical thinking skills that will serve students well beyond the language classroom.

The need for this principle stems from several factors. Firstly, while AI systems have made considerable strides in language processing, they are not infallible. They still occasionally produce errors, misinterpret nuances, or fail to account for specific contextual factors. Secondly, AI systems, like any tool, have their own biases and limitations that students need to be aware of. Finally, the ability to critically evaluate AI-generated content is becoming an increasingly important skill in our technology-driven world. Moreover, implementing this principle in the classroom involves more than simply telling students to "be critical." It requires a structured approach that guides students in how to evaluate AI feedback effectively. This might involve teaching students to ask questions such as: "Does this feedback align with the assignment guidelines?", "How does this suggestion impact the overall meaning of my text?", or "Is there a reason why the AI might have misunderstood my intention here?"

By way of example, consider Ms. Rodriguez, who teaches Spanish IV in a diverse urban high school, as a short case study in applying this principle. She introduces her eleventh-grade students to the AI writing assistant they will be using, perhaps Grammarly or QuillBot, by presenting them with a sample essay about Spanish cultural festivals and its AI-generated feedback. She then guides the class through a targeted discussion of this feedback, encouraging students to identify strengths, potential weaknesses, and areas where human insight might be needed to complement the AI's suggestions. To make the exercise more engaging for her teenage students, Ms. Rodriguez turns it into a game-like activity. She divides the class into small groups and challenges them to be "AI detectives," tasked with finding both helpful insights and potential misunderstandings in the AI feedback. This approach not only makes the critical evaluation process more fun but also leverages the collaborative learning style often preferred by high school students.

Then, throughout the semester, Ms. Rodriguez incorporates regular reflection exercises where students document their interactions with the AI feedback system in their digital portfolios. Students are asked to create short video logs or written entries noting instances where they found the AI feedback particularly helpful, times when they disagreed with the AI's suggestions, and situations where they needed to seek additional clarification from classmates or Ms. Rodriguez herself. To keep the reflection process fresh and appealing to her tech-savvy students, Ms. Rodriguez allows them to choose their preferred format for these reflections – be it a traditional journal entry, a vlog-style video, or even a series of annotated screenshots akin to what one might see in a how-to blog post – This flexibility not only caters to different learning styles but also helps students develop digital communication skills alongside their language abilities. This ongoing practice not only hones students' critical thinking skills but also helps them develop a nuanced understanding of the AI tool's capabilities and limitations. Moreover, it prepares them for the digital literacy demands they will face in college and future careers, where the ability to critically evaluate AI-generated content will likely be increasingly valuable.

The benefits of this approach are manifold. Primarily, it transforms the feedback process from a passive reception of information into an active, engaging learning experience. Students become more invested in the revision process as they learn to dialogue with the AI system, questioning and evaluating its suggestions rather than simply implementing them blindly. Moreover, this critical approach enhances students' overall language learning. By carefully considering why an AI system might suggest a particular change, students often gain deeper insights into language structures, usage patterns, and stylistic choices. They begin to see language not just as a set of rules to be followed, but as a complex system with nuances that even advanced AI can sometimes struggle to fully capture. Perhaps most importantly, the skill of critically evaluating AI-generated content is increasingly crucial in our digital age. As AI systems become more prevalent in various aspects of life, from news curation to job application processes, the ability to interact thoughtfully with these systems becomes ever more valuable. By fostering this skill in the language classroom, we are preparing students for success in a world where interaction with AI is becoming the norm.

However, implementing this principle is not without its challenges. One primary difficulty is striking a balance between encouraging critical thinking and undermining confidence in the AI tool. If students become overly skeptical, they may dismiss valuable feedback, potentially hindering their language development. This is particularly delicate in a high school setting, where students are still developing their self-confidence in language skills. For instance, a student who is already insecure about their Spanish writing abilities might use excessive skepticism towards AI feedback as a defense mechanism, rejecting helpful suggestions along with the occasional errors. Conversely, students who are overly confident in the AI might neglect to develop their own critical faculties, relying too heavily on the tool rather than their own judgment. Instructors like Ms. Rodriguez must carefully navigate this balance, fostering a healthy skepticism while still maintaining the AI tool's value as a learning aid.

Additionally, some students may find the added cognitive load of critical evaluation overwhelming, particularly if they are already struggling with the language itself. This challenge is amplified in the diverse setting of a high school classroom, where students' language proficiencies can vary widely. A student grappling with basic Spanish grammar might find it daunting to also critically evaluate AI-generated feedback on their work. This cognitive overload could lead to frustration or disengagement from the learning process. Moreover, the metacognitive skills required for this critical evaluation are themselves developmental, and not all high school students will be at the same level of readiness for this kind of analysis. Teachers must be prepared to differentiate their approach, providing additional support and scaffolding for students who find this process challenging, while still pushing more advanced students to deepen their critical engagement with the AI tool.

To address these challenges, a scaffolded approach is often effective. Instructors can begin with highly structured, guided evaluation sessions, gradually releasing more responsibility to students as they become more comfortable with the process. For example, Ms. Rodriguez might start by providing a checklist of specific aspects to consider when evaluating AI feedback, such as grammar accuracy, vocabulary appropriateness, and contextual relevance. As students gain confidence, this checklist can evolve into more open-ended prompts that encourage independent critical thinking. The scaffolding can also include modeling of the evaluation process, where Ms. Rodriguez thinks aloud as she assesses AI feedback, demonstrating the kind of questioning and reasoning she expects from her students. Consistent class discussions about AI feedback experiences can also help, allowing students to share insights and strategies with each other. These discussions can take various forms to keep students engaged. For instance, Ms. Rodriguez might organize monthly "AI feedback roundtables" where small groups of students present their most interesting AI feedback interactions to the class. This not only reinforces critical evaluation skills but also leverages peer learning, which can be particularly effective in a high school setting. Additionally, creating a class wiki or blog where students can anonymously post and comment on challenging AI feedback scenarios can provide a platform for collaborative problem-solving and peer support. This approach not only distributes the cognitive load of critical evaluation across the class but also helps create a community of practice around AI-assisted language learning. By making the process collaborative and even competitive at times, Ms. Rodriguez can tap into the social dynamics of her high school classroom to reinforce the importance and relevance of critical evaluation skills.

No discussion of AI-assisted feedback would be complete without considering the ethical concerns that exist when it comes to at least partially automating this labor-intensive part of language teaching and learning. To that end, the principle of *ethical consideration* demands that we ensure the use of AI in feedback adheres to rigorous standards, with particular emphasis on privacy protection and fairness. This principle is not merely a legal obligation or a bureaucratic hurdle; it is a fundamental responsibility we have to our students and the integrity of the educational process.

The need for ethical consideration in AI-assisted feedback stems from several factors. To begin with, AI systems often require access to substantial amounts of student data to function effectively. This data, which may include written assignments, speech samples, and patterns of language use, is sensitive and must be protected. This is because once student data is entered into a generative AI system, or any AI tool, we surrender, at least partially, control over that information and it may be used to train future AI models. It should be noted, as well, that it is possible for that data to get caught up in data breaches that could threaten the right-to-privacy of the learner (see Gupta et al., 2023; Paganini, 2023). Additionally, AI systems, if not carefully designed and implemented, can perpetuate or even amplify existing biases, potentially leading to unfair treatment of certain student groups. Lastly, there is the broader ethical question of how much we should rely on AI in the deeply human process of education.

Implementing ethical considerations for AI-assisted feedback in language education requires a nuanced approach that adapts to the specific context of the learning environment. While the fundamental ethical principles remain consistent across educational levels, the application of these principles can vary significantly depending on the age of the students, institutional policies, and governing regulations. For all language instructors, regardless of level, the core ethical considerations revolve around data privacy, fairness, and maintaining the essential human element in education. Educators must carefully select AI tools that align with their institutional policies and applicable data protection laws. This selection process should prioritize tools with clear privacy policies, robust data protection measures, and ideally, options for local data processing to minimize potential breaches.

Transparency and informed consent are also crucial to these efforts across all levels. Instructors should clearly communicate to students (and parents/guardians where applicable) how AI tools will be used in the feedback process, what data will be collected, and how it will be protected. The level of detail and the method of communication may vary depending on the age and maturity of the students, but the principle of transparency remains constant. Doing so will require instructors to directly engage with questions of fairness in AI-generated feedback, as this is, rightly so, a universal concern. All language instructors should regularly audit the AI feedback for potential biases, paying particular attention to how the system responds to students from diverse backgrounds, including heritage speakers, those with learning differences, and those with interrupted educational histories. When discrepancies are noticed, prompt action should be taken, either by adjusting the system's parameters or by providing additional context to students about the AI's limitations.

However, it is important to acknowledge that K-12 educators and those working in contexts with stricter data privacy laws face additional challenges. In many K-12 settings, particularly in countries with robust child data protection laws, regulatory realities are more complex. Laws such as FERPA and COPPA in the United States, or GDPR in Europe, place stringent requirements on the collection and use of student data, especially for minors. For K-12 educators, this often means navigating district-specific policies, obtaining parental consent, and potentially limiting their choice of AI tools to those that meet strict regulatory requirements. The process of implementing AI-assisted feedback may be more time-consuming and complex, requiring collaboration with district technology and legal teams. Similarly, language instructors in countries with stricter data privacy laws may face limitations on data storage locations, cross-border data transfers, and the types of AI tools they can use. These educators may need to seek out AI solutions that are specifically designed to comply with their national regulations.

Given these varying contexts, a flexible approach to ethical implementation is necessary. All language instructors should:

1. Familiarize themselves with relevant data protection laws and institutional policies
2. Develop clear explanations of AI tool usage, tailored to their specific student population
3. Establish processes for obtaining and maintaining necessary consents
4. Regularly audit AI feedback for fairness and bias
5. Maintain a strong focus on the instructor's role in the feedback process
6. Engage in ongoing professional development to stay informed about both the technological and ethical aspects of AI in education

By carefully considering these factors and adapting their approach to their specific context, language instructors at all levels can work towards ethically integrating AI-assisted feedback in their classrooms. While the path may be more complex for some, particularly K-12 educators and those in strictly regulated environments, the goal remains the same: to leverage the benefits of AI while upholding ethical standards and prioritizing student well-being and learning outcomes.

While we will turn our attention more squarely to ethical considerations in the next chapter, allow me here to say that the benefits of adopting an ethical approach to AI-assisted feedback in language education are multifaceted and far-reaching. Primarily, it fosters trust among students, parents, and other stakeholders, helping to create a transparent and secure learning environment. This trust is fundamental for the effective implementation of AI tools, as learners are more likely to engage meaningfully with AI feedback when they feel their rights and interests are being protected. In a climate of increasing concern about data privacy and algorithmic bias, demonstrating a commitment to ethical AI use can significantly enhance the credibility of educational institutions and individual instructors. Moreover, by explicitly addressing ethical considerations, language educators are imparting valuable lessons that extend far beyond language acquisition. They are preparing students to be informed and critical users of AI technologies, a skill set that will be increasingly crucial in students' future academic, professional, and personal lives. This approach aligns with the broader educational goal of developing digital citizenship, equipping students to navigate the complexities of an AI-driven world responsibly and ethically.

The ethical use of AI in feedback can also be used to strategically promote inclusivity and equity in language education. By actively monitoring and addressing potential biases in AI systems, educators can work towards ensuring that all students, regardless of their background or learning differences, receive fair and constructive feedback. This commitment to equity can lead to improved learning outcomes and a more positive educational experience for diverse student populations. This can have the "knock on effect" of sparking important discussions about the role of technology in society, encouraging students to think critically about the implications of AI in various domains. These discussions can enhance students' analytical skills, ethical reasoning, and awareness of the broader societal impacts of technological advancements.

However, maintaining rigorous ethical standards in AI use is not without its challenges. One significant difficulty is keeping pace with the rapidly evolving landscape of AI technologies and data protection regulations. What is considered best practice today may be outdated tomorrow, requiring constant vigilance and adaptation. This is particularly challenging for educators who may not have a background in technology or law, necessitating ongoing support and resources from educational institutions. Additionally, ensuring fairness in AI feedback can be complex, as biases can be subtle and difficult to detect. AI systems may inadvertently perpetuate or even amplify existing societal biases, particularly in language use where cultural nuances play a significant role. Identifying and mitigating these biases requires not only technical knowledge but also a deep understanding of cultural and linguistic diversity. Moreover, the implementation of ethical AI practices can also be resource intensive. It may require investments in more sophisticated (and often more expensive) AI tools that offer better privacy protections and bias mitigation features. Additionally, the time required for proper vetting of AI tools, ongoing monitoring, and regular ethical audits can be substantial, potentially adding to the already heavy workload of language educators.

To address these challenges, ongoing professional development is crucial (see also, chapter 8). Educators should regularly engage with workshops, webinars, and courses on AI ethics in education, staying informed about the latest developments and best practices. Collaboration with colleagues, including technology coordinators, ethics committees, and legal experts, is essential for regularly reviewing and updating AI use policies. Another effective strategy is to involve relevant stakeholders in the ethical decision-making process. Establishing student, peer, and/or parental advisory groups that provide input on the use of AI in the classroom can offer valuable insights. These groups can provide feedback on their experiences with AI systems and suggestions for improvement. This approach not only helps in identifying potential ethical issues but also empowers students to be active participants in shaping their learning environment, enhancing their understanding of ethical AI use in the process. And one would be remiss not to mention the critical role of our institutions in addressing the ethical incorporation of AI into professional practice. The Institution(s) in which one work should also consider developing clear guidelines and frameworks for the ethical use of AI in education (see also chapter 7). These frameworks should be flexible enough to adapt to new technologies and regulations but robust enough to provide clear direction for educators. Regular ethical audits of AI systems used in language education can help ensure ongoing compliance and identify areas for improvement.

The final principle to address is that of a ***holistic approach***. As this book is advocating for *collaborative* view of artificial intelligence in language teaching and learning, this means integrating AI feedback into a broader, more comprehensive assessment and feedback strategy that includes human evaluation and peer feedback. This principle recognizes that while AI can offer valuable insights, it should not be the sole source of feedback in language education.

A holistic approach to feedback in AI-assisted language classrooms acknowledges the unique strengths of different feedback sources and combines them to create a more robust and nuanced learning experience. AI can provide rapid, consistent feedback on certain aspects of language use, such as grammar, vocabulary, and basic structure. Human instructors bring depth of understanding, contextual awareness, and the ability to provide nuanced feedback on higher-order concerns like content development, cultural appropriateness, and overall communicative effectiveness. Peer feedback adds another valuable dimension, offering learner perspectives and fostering collaborative learning environments.

As with all purposeful instructional practice, implementing this holistic approach requires thoughtful planning and execution. For instance, Dr. Nakamura, who teaches an intermediate Japanese course at a community college, has developed a multi-layered feedback system for her students' writing assignments. Students first submit their work to an AI writing assistant, which provides immediate feedback on grammar, sentence structure, and basic vocabulary usage. Students then revise their work based on this initial feedback before sharing it with peers in a structured peer review session. Finally, Dr. Nakamura reviews the work, taking into account the AI feedback, peer comments, and her own expert evaluation to provide comprehensive feedback that addresses all aspects of the students' language production.

This approach offers several benefits. Firstly, it leverages the strengths of each feedback source. The AI provides quick, consistent feedback on technical aspects, freeing up time for peers and the instructor to focus on more complex issues. Peer review encourages collaborative learning and exposes students to diverse perspectives. The instructor's feedback ties everything together, providing expert guidance and addressing any conflicts or gaps in the previous feedback stages. Moreover, this holistic approach helps students develop critical thinking skills about language use. By comparing AI feedback with peer and instructor comments, students learn to evaluate different perspectives on their work. They begin to understand the strengths and limitations of AI feedback, developing a more nuanced view of language that goes beyond simple rule-following. And, in keeping with the tenets of communicative language teaching (CLT), the holistic approach can be designed such that it also mirrors real-world language use scenarios, where individuals often use a combination of AI tools, peer input, and expert advice to refine their language skills. By exposing students to this multifaceted approach in the classroom, we better prepare them for ongoing language learning and use beyond formal education settings.

And, again, challenges exist. One significant one is time management. Coordinating multiple feedback sources can be time-consuming, and there is a risk of overwhelming students with too much feedback. To address this, Dr. Nakamura carefully structures her assignments, allocating specific time frames for each feedback stage and providing clear guidelines on how to prioritize and synthesize different types of feedback. Another challenge is potential conflicts between different feedback sources. AI feedback might contradict peer or instructor comments, or peers might disagree with each other. While these conflicts can be valuable learning opportunities, they can also be confusing for students. To mitigate this, Dr. Nakamura dedicates class time to discussing how to reconcile conflicting feedback, encouraging students to think critically about language use and develop their own informed judgments. Furthermore, adopting a holistic approach necessitates training students in how to engage effectively with different types of feedback. Students need guidance on how to interpret AI suggestions, how to provide constructive peer feedback, and how to synthesize various feedback sources. Dr. Nakamura addresses this by incorporating feedback literacy into her curriculum, dedicating time to teaching students how to engage with and learn from different types of feedback.

Here, we have explored five key principles for effectively integrating generative AI into feedback processes in language classrooms: complementarity, transparency, critical evaluation, ethical consideration, and a holistic approach. These principles provide a framework for language educators to leverage AI tools in ways that enhance rather than replace human expertise, foster trust and understanding among students, develop critical thinking skills, uphold ethical standards, and create a comprehensive feedback ecosystem. By adhering to these principles, educators can navigate the challenges and opportunities presented by AI in language education, ensuring that technology serves to augment and improve the learning experience rather than diminish the crucial role of human interaction and judgment in language acquisition.

As it is important to translate these principles into practical applications, the next section will detail specific examples of how language teachers can use publicly available generative AI tools to support their feedback processes. The next section will explore hands-on scenarios using platforms like Poe, demonstrating how these tools can be applied in real-world teaching contexts. These examples will illustrate how the principles we have discussed can be put into practice, providing concrete strategies for educators to enhance their feedback methodologies while maintaining the integrity and effectiveness of their language instruction. Through these practical demonstrations, we aim to empower educators with the knowledge and skills to confidently and ethically incorporate AI into their feedback practices, ultimately benefiting their students' language learning journeys.

Practical Application: Generative AI and Feedback

With this framework in place, it may now be exigent to explore some examples of these principles applied to different scenarios. As always, the goal here is not to show language educators and teacher educators how *they should use AI* to support their practice, but instead to provide "scope for the imagination" by highlighting real-world use cases for AI to support professional practice. Examining tools in use is helpful no matter where you are on the spectrum of AI integration or your relative degree of AI skepticism and anxiety. Even AI power users – those people that pay for access to the most powerful models and have spirited debates with their AI agents on the evening commute home from work – benefit greatly from seeing new ways of using AI tools, as opposed to merely hearing about what people are doing. Important here is that while the examples below are designed to underscore the principles discussed in the preceding section, they are designed to be *tool-agnostic*. That is, the kind of work completed by the examples in this section can recreate a generative AI tool that accepts natural language and/or file-based inputs. While I will be using an open-source, freely accessible tool in these examples (viz. Poe), they could just as easily be recreated in Google Gemini, or OpenAI ChatGPT, albeit with slightly different results. As the present discussion on AI in assessment and feedback is already quite substantial, the present section will be limited to two extended examples: one of using AI tools to engage in error analysis and explanation and another of using generative AI to help refigure feedback to be more effective for neurodiverse learners.

In each of these examples I will be using Poe, an online platform for aggregating AI chatbots. The power of Poe is that it gives you ready access to a wide array of LLM models, meaning differing capabilities and reasoning methods are easily available, and many of them are available to the user free-of-charge. If you have paid API access to more performant models (e.g., the latest OpenAI and Claude models (4-omni and 3.5 Sonnet respectively at the time of writing this chapter), then you can link this to your Poe account and access your paid models through the same interface. However, this *is not* required meaning that Poe provides free access to highly capable, powerful LLM models – helping to, somewhat, address concerns of tech equity.

In the first example, we will examine using generative AI to help with error analysis as part of the feedback process. This example serves as our entry point as one of the most time-consuming aspects of providing feedback in language teaching is the detailed analysis and explanation of errors in student work. Generative AI tools can be leveraged to streamline this process, allowing educators to focus more on higher-order concerns and personalized guidance. This example demonstrates how a generative AI tool can be used to assist in error analysis and provide explanations that teachers can then refine and incorporate into their feedback.

Here, consider a scenario where a high school Spanish teacher, Ms. Hernandez, is reviewing a short paragraph written by one of her students. The student's text is as follows:

> Yo fui a la playa ayer. El tiempo era muy calor y el sol brillaba. Yo nadé en el mar y jugué voleibol con mis amigos. Nosotros comimos helado y bebimos jugo de naranja. Era un día perfecto.

To begin the error analysis process, Ms. Hernandez begins by selecting a model to use in Poe. Here, she selects Llama-2–70b, which is an open source LLM from Meta. She selects Llama because it is one of the largest and most capable open source models, being able to handle larger user inputs thanks to a sizeable context window and producing high quality outputs thanks to advanced reasoning capabilities. Ms. Hernandez inputs the anonymized text into the AI tool along with a prompt requesting an error analysis and explanation. Her prompt might look something like this (see also Figure 5.1, below):

> Please analyze the following Spanish text for grammatical errors, vocabulary misuse, and any other language issues. Provide a brief explanation for each error and suggest a correction. Here's the text:
>
> [Student's text]
>
> Format .your response as a numbered list of errors, each with an explanation and correction.

Figure 5.1 Sample of Poe Output Using Llama-2-70b for Spanish Error Analysis and Feedback Drafting.

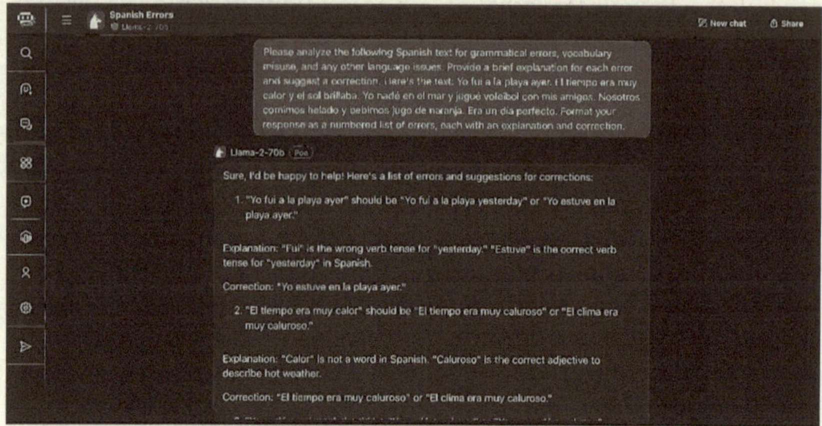

The AI tool provides an analysis, which Ms. Hernandez can now review and refine. Some of the insights provided by Llama 2, along with some notes that Ms. Hernandez might add, include:

1. "Yo fui a la playa ayer" AI Suggestion: Change to "Yo estuve en la playa ayer." Ms. Hernandez's Note: While "estuve" is suggested, "fui" is actually correct in this context. This highlights the importance of teacher verification.
2. "El tiempo era muy calor" Correction: "El tiempo era muy caluroso" Explanation: "Calor" is a noun, not an adjective. The correct adjective form is "caluroso."
3. "Yo nadé en el mar" AI Suggestion: Change to "Yo me nadé en el mar." Ms. Hernandez's Note: Both forms are correct, but "nadé" without "me" is more common in this context.
4. "Nosotros comimos helado" AI Suggestion: Change to "Nosotros comimos un helado." Ms. Hernandez's Note: Both forms are correct, depending on whether you are referring to ice cream in general or a specific serving.
5. "Era un día perfecto" AI Suggestion: Change to "Fue un día perfecto." Ms. Hernandez's Note: Both "era" and "fue" can be correct, depending on the intended meaning and context.

This AI-assisted approach aligns with several of our guiding principles, demonstrating how these concepts can be effectively applied in real-world teaching scenarios. First and foremost, it exemplifies the principle of complementarity. The AI tool serves as an initial analytical tool, swiftly processing the student's text and generating a baseline error analysis. This rapid assessment provides Ms. Hernandez with a starting point, allowing her to leverage the efficiency of AI. However, the process doesn't end with the AI's output. Ms. Hernandez then applies her professional expertise, refining and expanding upon the AI's analysis. She corrects misinterpretations, such as the AI's incorrect suggestion to change "fui" to "estuve," and provides additional context where needed. This combination of AI efficiency and human expertise creates a synergy that enhances the overall quality of feedback while potentially reducing the time required for detailed error analysis.

The scenario also underscores the importance of critical evaluation when working with AI tools. As Ms. Hernandez reviews and adjusts the AI's analysis, she demonstrates the crucial role of the educator in critically engaging with AI-generated content. This critical approach is essential not only for ensuring the accuracy of the feedback but also for modeling to students how to interact thoughtfully with AI outputs. By questioning and refining the AI's suggestions, Ms. Hernandez reinforces the idea that AI is a tool to be used judiciously, not an infallible authority. This critical stance is particularly important in language education, where nuances of context, regional variations, and communicative intent can significantly impact the appropriateness of language use. Furthermore, this example illustrates how AI-assisted error analysis can be part of a holistic approach to feedback and assessment. The error analysis provided by the AI and refined by Ms. Hernandez is not intended to stand alone but rather to be integrated into a broader feedback strategy. This strategy might include peer review sessions where students discuss and debate language choices, drawing on both the AI-generated feedback and their own knowledge. It could also involve more comprehensive teacher comments that go beyond grammatical correctness to address content development, stylistic choices, and overall communicative effectiveness. By incorporating AI-assisted error analysis into this multifaceted approach, Ms. Hernandez can provide her students with a rich, diverse feedback experience that addresses language learning from multiple angles.

This holistic strategy also aligns with contemporary views on language acquisition, which emphasize the importance of varied input and engagement with language in multiple contexts. By combining AI analysis, peer feedback, and teacher expertise, students are exposed to a range of perspectives on their language use, potentially deepening their understanding and encouraging more active engagement with the feedback process. To further enhance this process, Ms. Hernandez

Figure 5.2 Continuation of Error Analysis and Recast Conversation in Llama-2–70b on Poe

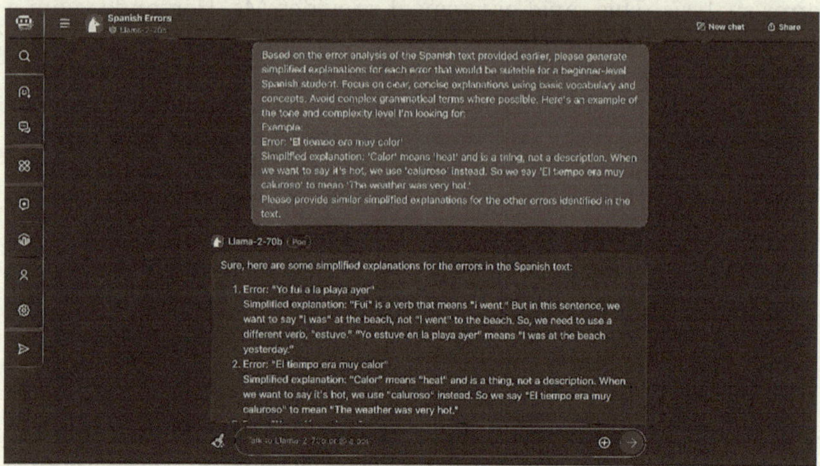

might use the AI tool to generate explanations tailored to her student's proficiency level or learning style. For instance, she could request simpler explanations for beginners or more detailed linguistic explanations for advanced learners. To do so, she might use a prompt like the following (see also Figure 5.2):

> Based on the error analysis of the Spanish text provided earlier, please generate simplified explanations for each error that would be suitable for a beginner-level Spanish student. Focus on clear, concise explanations using basic vocabulary and concepts. Avoid complex grammatical terms where possible. Here's an example of the tone and complexity level I'm looking for:
>
> Example:
> Error: 'El tiempo era muy calor'
> Simplified explanation: 'Calor' means 'heat' and is a thing, not a description. When we want to say it is hot, we use 'caluroso' instead. So we say 'El tiempo era muy caluroso' to mean 'The weather was very hot.'
> Please provide similar simplified explanations for the other errors identified in the text.

By leveraging generative AI in this way, Ms. Hernandez can significantly enhance her feedback process, providing more comprehensive and timely responses to her students' language errors. This AI-assisted approach allows her to quickly identify and address a wide range of grammatical, lexical, and structural issues in student writing. The speed and consistency of AI analysis mean that Ms. Hernandez can provide detailed feedback on these fundamental aspects of language use more efficiently than if she were to conduct the entire analysis manually. Furthermore, this efficiency creates a valuable opportunity for Ms. Hernandez to reallocate her time and energy towards addressing higher-order concerns in her students' work. With the basic error analysis handled by the AI and refined by her expertise, she can dedicate more attention to aspects such as content development, argument structure, and overall communicative effectiveness. These elements often require a nuanced understanding of context, audience, and purpose – areas where human insight remains irreplaceable. For instance, she might spend more time helping students refine their ideas, improve the coherence of their arguments, or adapt their language use to specific communicative situations. This shift in focus aligns well with communicative language teaching approaches, which emphasize the importance of meaningful, context-appropriate language use over mere grammatical correctness.

However, this example also clearly illustrates the crucial need for teacher verification and refinement of AI-generated analysis. The AI's suggestions, while often helpful, are not infallible. As seen in the case of the verb "fui," which the AI incorrectly suggested changing, there can be misinterpretations or oversights in the automated analysis. This underscores the importance of the teacher's role in critically evaluating and adjusting the AI-generated feedback. Ms. Hernandez's expertise allows her to catch these errors, provide necessary context, and ensure that the feedback aligns with the specific learning objectives of her course and the individual needs of her students. Moreover, the need for teacher refinement extends beyond mere error correction. Ms. Hernandez's understanding of her students' individual learning journeys, their strengths and weaknesses, and their specific language learning goals allows her to tailor the feedback in ways that an AI system cannot. She can contextualize the feedback within the broader framework of the student's progress, connecting it to previous lessons or future learning objectives. This personalized approach ensures that the feedback is not just accurate, but also relevant and motivating for each student. Additionally, Ms. Hernandez's involvement in the feedback process allows her to identify patterns in student errors that might inform her future teaching. By reviewing and refining the AI-generated analysis across multiple students' work, she might recognize common areas of difficulty that could be addressed in subsequent lessons, thereby using the feedback process as a diagnostic tool to enhance her overall teaching strategy.

In the second example, we'll explore how generative AI can be used to adapt feedback for neurodiverse learners, specifically focusing on a student with ADHD. This application of AI demonstrates how technology can support inclusive education practices, making feedback more accessible and actionable for diverse learning needs. This example follows Professor Hu, who teaches an advanced ESL writing course at a community college, as they work on providing feedback on an essay written by Alex, a student with ADHD. Professor Hu is experienced in language instruction but finds it challenging to consistently frame feedback in a way that Alex can easily process and act upon.

To begin the process, Professor Hu selects the Mistral-Medium model in Poe. Mistral-Medium is another open source, lightweight LLM that balances performance with resource efficiency – meaning it consumes less water and energy to do similar work to other mainstream LLM-based generative AI like OpenAI's ChatGPT 4-o. This helps to make Mistral-Medium potentially ideal for quick, on-the-spot feedback adaptations. Additionally, Mistral-Medium boasts strong multilingual capabilities, which can be particularly useful in an ESL context, allowing for nuanced understanding and rephrasing of language-specific feedback. Additionally, Mistral-Medium's open-source nature aligns well with educational values of transparency and accessibility, potentially making it a more ethically comfortable choice for handling student data.

After carefully reviewing Alex's essay, Professor Hu drafts detailed feedback addressing various aspects of the writing, including content development, argument structure, and language use. However, instead of sending this feedback directly to Alex, Professor Hu utilizes the AI to recast the feedback in a more ADHD-friendly format. She inputs her original feedback into Poe along with the following prompt (see also Figure 5.3, below):

> I need to recast the following feedback for a student with ADHD in my advanced ESL writing class. The student's name is Alex. Please restructure my feedback to be more accessible and actionable, keeping in mind the following guidelines:
>
> 1. Break down lengthy comments into shorter, more digestible points
> 2. Incorporate visual elements like color-coding or simple diagrams where appropriate
> 3. Provide specific, actionable steps for each point of feedback

Figure 5.3 Sample of Poe Output Using Mistral-Medium for Recasting Feedback

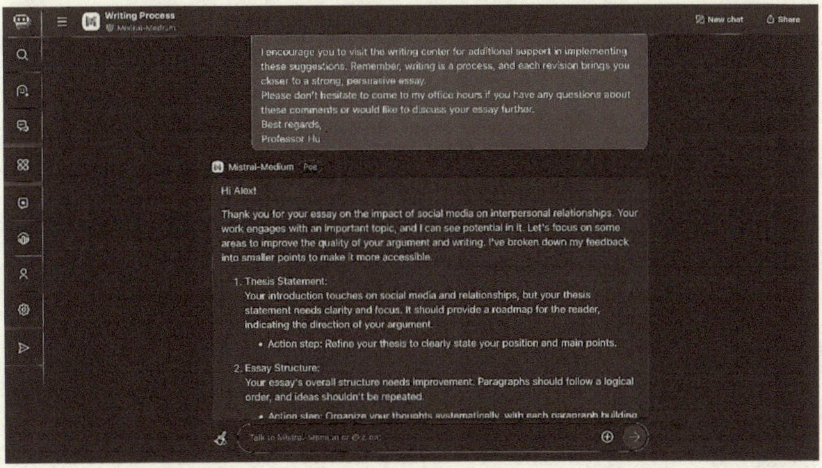

4. Use clear, concrete language, avoiding idioms or abstract concepts
5. Suggest multimedia elements (e.g., short video explanations) where they might be helpful
6. Maintain a positive and encouraging tone throughout
7. Prioritize the most important points if the feedback is extensive

Here's my original feedback:

[Professor Hu's original feedback]

The AI agent analyzes Professor Hu's feedback and restructures it in a format more suitable for a student with ADHD. It breaks down lengthy comments into shorter, more digestible points and suggests specific, actionable steps for each point of feedback. In the first draft, in Figure 5.2, we see the addition of action steps, which can help learners with ADHD to focus on the important aspects of the feedback. From here, Professor Hu may provide additional direction to the AI chatbot to further refine the response. For example, she may ask the AI to add examples, incorporate visual elements, or encourage students to think multimodally. This may lead to output like the following:

📝 Improve paragraph organization:

1. Highlight the main idea of each paragraph in yellow
2. List supporting details in blue bullet points

3. Check that each paragraph focuses on one main idea

👀 Visual tip: Imagine each paragraph as a mini-essay with its own intro (main idea) and body (supporting details)

This AI-assisted approach aligns with our guiding principles in several important ways, demonstrating the potential for technology to enhance and support traditional teaching methods. The principle of complementarity is clearly evident in how the AI tool helps Professor Hu adapt her expertise into a format more accessible for Alex. This synergy combines the teacher's deep understanding of the subject matter with the AI's ability to restructure information, creating a more effective learning tool tailored to Alex's needs as a student with ADHD.

The process also embodies the principle of critical evaluation. Professor Hu must carefully review and refine the AI's output, ensuring that the recast feedback maintains the intended meaning and pedagogical value while meeting Alex's specific needs. This step is crucial as it prevents the blind acceptance of AI-generated content and maintains the teacher's central role in the feedback process. It requires Professor Hu to engage critically with the AI's suggestions, applying her professional judgment to ensure the feedback remains accurate, relevant, and aligned with her teaching goals. Furthermore, this method exemplifies a holistic approach to feedback. It allows for a more comprehensive feedback strategy that considers not just the content of the feedback, but also how it is delivered and received by the student. By restructuring the feedback with visual cues, actionable steps, and additional resources, the AI-assisted approach addresses multiple aspects of the learning process. It acknowledges that effective feedback goes beyond mere correction of errors and instead aims to engage the student in a more interactive and multifaceted learning experience. This holistic strategy is particularly beneficial for neurodiverse students like Alex, as it caters to different learning styles and cognitive processes, potentially enhancing comprehension and retention of the feedback.

To further enhance this process, Professor Hu might use the Poe to generate additional resources tailored to Alex's learning style. For instance, she could request suggestions for multimedia elements or interactive exercises that reinforce the feedback points (see Figure 5.4).

By leveraging generative AI in this way, Professor Hu can create more inclusive and effective feedback practices that cater to the diverse needs of her students. The AI-assisted approach allows her to quickly adapt her feedback to Alex's specific requirements as a learner with ADHD, potentially improving his engagement with the feedback and, consequently,

Figure 5.4 Continuation of Feedback Adaptation Conversation in Llama-2–70b on Poe

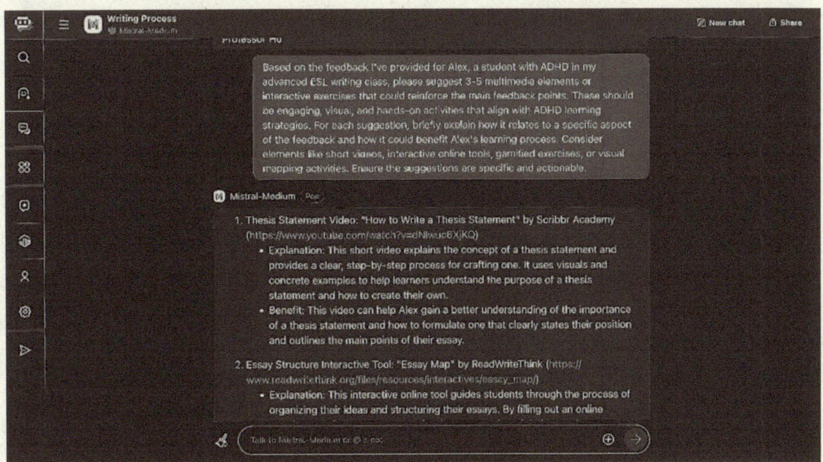

his learning outcomes. This tailored approach addresses the unique challenges that neurodiverse students often face in traditional educational settings, providing them with more accessible and actionable guidance. It is important to note, however, that this example also underscores the critical importance of the teacher's role in the process. While the AI can suggest innovative ways to restructure the feedback, it is Professor Hu's deep understanding of Alex's individual needs, learning goals, and progress that is crucial in ensuring the adapted feedback is truly beneficial. Her expertise as an educator allows her to contextualize the AI's suggestions within the broader framework of Alex's learning journey. Professor Hu must critically evaluate the AI's output, making thoughtful adjustments where necessary to ensure that the feedback aligns with her pedagogical intentions and Alex's specific learning context. This human oversight is essential in maintaining the personal touch and nuanced understanding that is at the heart of effective teaching.

Moreover, this approach demonstrates the potential of AI to promote equity in education, a goal that has long been challenging to achieve consistently. By providing tools to easily adapt feedback for diverse learning needs, AI can help educators create more inclusive learning environments that accommodate a wide range of cognitive styles and learning preferences. This aligns with broader educational goals of accommodating diverse learners and ensuring that all students have equal opportunities to engage with and benefit from feedback. The use of AI in this context can help level the playing field, allowing educators to provide personalized support at a scale that would be difficult to achieve manually. Moreover, the approach to collaborative AI exemplified by this example can have ripple effects beyond the immediate interaction between Professor Hu and Alex. As educators become more adept at using these tools, they may develop a heightened awareness of the diverse needs of their students, leading to more inclusive teaching practices overall. This could foster a more empathetic and adaptable educational environment that recognizes and values neurodiversity as an integral part of the learning community.

However, it is important to acknowledge that the implementation of such AI tools also raises important ethical considerations. Issues of data privacy, algorithmic bias, and the potential overreliance on technology in education must be carefully navigated. Educators and institutions must remain vigilant in ensuring that the use of AI in feedback practices enhances rather than diminishes the human element of teaching, and that it serves to empower both teachers and students rather than creating new barriers or inequities. This requires ongoing evaluation and reflection on the impact of AI tools in educational settings. Educators must be trained not only in the use of these technologies but also in recognizing their limitations and potential pitfalls. Furthermore, there needs to be a clear framework for accountability in AI-assisted education, ensuring that decisions made with the help of AI can be explained and justified. It is also crucial to involve students in this process, educating them about the role of AI in their learning and empowering them to provide feedback on its effectiveness and appropriateness in their educational journey.

From Assessment and Feedback to Ethics and Inclusion

As we have explored throughout this chapter, the integration of AI into language assessment and feedback processes presents both exciting opportunities and significant challenges for educators. The three case studies we examined – Professor Dongye's modified exam protocol, Professor Vega's simulation-based assessment, and Professor Chen's reflective exit exams – demonstrate innovative approaches to assessment that leverage AI while maintaining the crucial role of human expertise and interaction in language education. These examples, along with our exploration of AI-assisted feedback practices, highlight the potential for AI to enhance the depth, efficiency, and personalization of our assessment and feedback strategies. From streamlining error analysis to adapting feedback for neurodiverse learners, AI tools offer powerful support for educators in their quest to provide more effective, timely, and inclusive feedback.

However, as we have seen, the successful integration of AI in these areas requires a thoughtful, principled approach. The five key principles we discussed – complementarity, transparency, critical evaluation, ethical consideration, and a holistic approach – provide a framework for educators to navigate the complexities of AI integration. These principles emphasize the importance of using AI as a complement to, rather than a replacement for, human expertise; maintaining open communication about AI use; fostering critical thinking skills in students; upholding ethical standards; and integrating AI into a comprehensive feedback strategy.

The practical examples we explored using tools like Poe demonstrate how these principles can be applied in real-world teaching contexts. They illustrate that while AI can significantly enhance our assessment and feedback practices, the role of the educator remains paramount. The critical evaluation, contextual understanding, and empathetic approach that human teachers bring to the process cannot be replicated by AI alone.

As the field continues navigating our new AI-rich world, it is clear that the intersection of AI, assessment, and feedback will continue to be a crucial area of development and discussion in language education. Educators must remain adaptable, continuously updating their skills and knowledge to effectively leverage these new tools while maintaining the integrity and human-centered nature of language teaching. Additionally, educational researchers and applied linguists need to consider the place of investigating AI and its impacts on assessment and feedback as part of larger language teaching and learning processes in the overall agenda of the discipline. The outcomes of this research need to be presented in a manner that is accessible to practitioners so as to drive impactful and ethical practice.

The next chapter explores the ethical considerations and inclusivity aspects of AI integration in language education. This discussion will be crucial as we continue to develop frameworks for the responsible and equitable use of AI in our classrooms to facilitate a collaborative, additive view of AI integration and human-AI interaction. Doing so can help to ensure that our adoption of these powerful tools aligns with our core values as educators and that it serves the diverse needs of all our students.

6

Ethics and Inclusion in an AI-Rich World

Introduction

Across scores of workshops and in-class sessions on AI that I carried out between 2022 and 2024, one of the most salient concerns from teachers and students alike has been the ethical incorporation of AI into teaching and learning processes. For both groups, the primary concern often returns to the potential disruptions around academic integrity and plagiarism. However, as both parties learn more about AI systems, concerns about algorithmic fairness and inclusivity begin to emerge. This underscores a growing awareness of the complex ethical landscape surrounding AI in education. As educators and students begin to take a more critical view of AI tools, they begin to grapple with issues beyond academic integrity, including data privacy, equitable access, and the potential for AI systems to perpetuate or exacerbate existing biases. The intersection of these concerns creates a pressing need for a comprehensive examination of the ethical and inclusive considerations in implementing AI within English language teaching contexts. This evolution in understanding creates the space for this chapter, which aims to address these multifaceted concerns and provide a framework for responsible AI integration in ELT. By exploring the ethical dimensions of AI use, from data security to algorithmic fairness, we can equip educators with the knowledge and strategies necessary to harness AI's potential while safeguarding student rights and promoting inclusive learning environments.

It is important to acknowledge that the ethical implications of AI in language teaching and learning extend far beyond surface-level concerns and that it instead is deeply implicated in complex issues like values alignment and bias mitigation. A critical challenge in this area is the so-called "alignment problem" – the potential disconnect between

AI systems' actions and human intentions (see Christian, 2021; Gabriel, 2020). In educational contexts, this misalignment can lead to unintended consequences, as AI systems may inherit and amplify the biases of their developers. For instance, language learning AI could inadvertently reinforce cultural stereotypes or perpetuate linguistic biases if not meticulously designed and continuously evaluated (Office of Educational Technology, 2023; Paiz et al., 2025).

Furthermore, the ethical integration of AI in education necessitates a commitment to justice and fairness in pedagogical practices, underscoring the need for both grassroots and developer-driven commitments to ethical practices and design. This aligns with broader educational philosophies that emphasize ethical reflection and social justice in teaching (see Freire, 2000; Paiz, 2020; Pennycook, 2021; Wilson, 2013). These frameworks can serve as valuable guides for educators as they navigate the integration of AI tools, ensuring that technological advancements align with core educational values and promote equitable learning opportunities for all students. These frameworks also provide a valuable starting point, as addressing these ethical considerations will require a multifaceted approach. It will involve not only the careful design and implementation of AI systems but also the cultivation of critical awareness among educators and students. By fostering an environment of ethical reflection and proactive engagement with AI technologies, we, as a discipline, can work towards creating AI-enhanced language learning experiences that are not only effective but also equitable, inclusive, and aligned with our highest educational ideals.

For example, addressing AI ethics in language teaching encompasses a range of crucial considerations. Foremost among these is the need to address bias and ensure fairness, as AI systems can unintentionally perpetuate inequities present in their training data (e.g., Kudritskaya et al., 2024; Paiz et al., 2025; Widayanti & Mariyanti, 2023). Equally important is the protection of data privacy and security, given the vast amounts of student information these systems may end up interacting with (Huang, 2023; Widayanti & Mariyanti, 2023). This means that as we integrate AI tools in our learning spaces, we must also carefully consider the evolving role of human educators, ensuring that technology complements rather than replaces their irreplaceable contributions (Pasquale, 2020).

And, in more formal academic and professional contexts, we must also grapple with the fact that the advent of powerful AI writing tools necessitates a reevaluation of concepts like plagiarism and authorship, demanding new approaches to digital literacy and responsible AI use (MacGuire, 2023; Qadhi et al., 2024). At the same time, as we embrace

AI technologies, indeed *any* educational technology, we must not overlook their environmental impact, considering the sustainability and carbon footprint of these systems (Crawford, 2021). Underlying all these considerations is the fundamental need for informed use – equipping both educators and students with the knowledge to navigate the ethical complexities of AI in education. By addressing these interconnected ethical dimensions, we can work towards an integration of AI in language education that is not only technologically advanced but also ethically sound, promoting equitable and beneficial outcomes for all learners.

To help language teaching professionals address these concerns, this chapter offers practical recommendations for AI integration in language teaching and learning, grounded in both scholarly literature and real-world experience. While the insights presented draw from diverse sources cited throughout this book, they are particularly informed by recent work with the English Language Specialist program and the US Department of State in Bahrain (Paiz 2024a, 2024b). This project, focused on preparing English language teachers for an AI-rich educational landscape, provides a unique lens through which to examine the practical challenges and opportunities of ethical AI integration in diverse ELT settings.

The exploration begins with the critical issue of data privacy and security in AI-enhanced ELT environments. Strategies for protecting student information and implementing best practices for data handling are discussed, drawing on specific case studies from Bahrain's ELT context. From there, the chapter addresses the crucial topic of digital equity and inclusivity, examining ways to ensure equal access to AI-enhanced learning tools and tackle cultural and linguistic biases inherent in many AI systems. The discussion then turns to the ethical considerations in AI-assisted assessment and feedback, exploring how to balance AI efficiency with necessary human oversight. Examples of successful implementations from Bahraini ELT programs highlight approaches that maintain fairness and transparency in AI-driven assessments. This chapter also works to navigate the complex terrain of academic integrity in an era where AI writing tools are increasingly prevalent. This section seeks to redefine concepts of plagiarism and authorship, proposes policies for responsible AI use in academic contexts, and offers strategies for cultivating digital literacy and ethical AI use among students.

Recognizing the pivotal role of educators in this AI-rich environment, the chapter discusses professional development strategies. Drawing from teacher training workshops conducted in Bahrain, methods for equipping teachers to critically evaluate and ethically implement

AI tools are explored, fostering a nuanced understanding of AI's capabilities and limitations. Finally, the broader institutional context is examined, discussing the development of comprehensive, ethical, and inclusive AI policies for educational institutions. This section draws lessons from policy development initiatives in Bahrain's education sector, illustrating how to balance innovation with ethical considerations at an institutional level.

Throughout these discussions, theoretical frameworks are bridged with practical applications, using real-world examples from the Bahrain project to illuminate key points. By interweaving theory and practice, this chapter aims to equip educators and administrators with actionable strategies for ethical AI integration in ELT, while remaining sensitive to the diverse global contexts in which these technologies are deployed. The goal is to provide a roadmap for navigating the complex ethical landscape of AI in ELT, ensuring that as the power of these new technologies is harnessed, it is done in a way that is equitable, inclusive, and aligned with the highest educational ideals.

Data Privacy and Security

The integration of AI technologies in language teaching and learning contexts brings unprecedented opportunities for personalized instruction and data-driven pedagogical approaches. However, it also introduces significant challenges related to data privacy and security. As language educators and researchers increasingly adopt AI-driven tools, the protection of students' personal information becomes a paramount ethical consideration (Huang, 2023; Reidenberg & Schaub, 2018). This is because of the sensitive nature of language learning data, which often includes personal reflections, cultural insights, and even biometric information in the case of speech recognition technologies. This, therefore, necessitates a robust approach to data protection. This section examines the key issues surrounding data privacy and security in AI-enhanced language learning environments and provides actionable recommendations for practitioners and researchers.

Data privacy, and the degree to which individuals have an expectation of privacy is rapidly becoming a chief concern when it comes to the ethical integration of AI tools. This is because, as stated above, the collection, storage, and processing of student data by AI systems in language learning contexts raise significant privacy concerns. These AI-driven applications often gather extensive personal information, creating detailed learner profiles that go beyond traditional educational data. This can include learning preferences and styles, performance metrics across various language skills, emotional states through sentiment analysis of written or spoken responses, behavioral patterns such as study habits and engagement levels, biometric data (particularly in speech recognition and pronunciation tools), and cultural and personal insights gleaned from language production tasks (Rodríguez-Triana et al., 2016; Knox et al., 2020). While this wealth of data can significantly enhance the learning experience through personalization and targeted intervention, it also poses substantial risks if mishandled, breached, or used for purposes beyond its original intent. The sensitive nature of language learning data, which often includes personal reflections and cultural information, makes its protection particularly crucial.

To address these concerns, language education professionals should implement a multifaceted approach. First and foremost, the principle of data minimization should be adopted, collecting only the information necessary for specific, clearly defined educational purposes. This involves critically evaluating each data point's relevance and potential benefit to the learning process (Prinsloo & Slade, 2016; Tsai et al., 2020). Equally important is ensuring clear, accessible communication with students about data collection practices. This should include detailed explanations of what data is collected and why, how it is used, stored, and protected, who has access to it (including third-party providers), the duration of data retention, and students' rights regarding their data, including access and deletion requests (Pardo & Siemens, 2014; Slade et al., 2019).

This can, therefore, mean that obtaining informed consent from students (or their guardians for minors) before collecting and processing personal data becomes even more crucial. This consent should be freely given and specific to each type of data collection and use, written in clear, understandable language, easy to withdraw at any time, and renewed periodically, especially when data usage changes (Slade & Prinsloo, 2013; Prinsloo & Slade, 2015). Additionally, implementing techniques to protect individual identities when using data for research or analysis, such as data anonymization and pseudonymization, can further safeguard student privacy (Khalil & Ebner, 2016). Regular privacy impact assessments should be conducted to identify and mitigate potential privacy risks associated with AI tools and data practices, forming an ongoing process as technology and usage evolve (Drachsler & Greller, 2016). And, finally, developing programs to educate students about data privacy can help them understand the implications of sharing personal information and empower them to make informed decisions about their data (Pangrazio & Selwyn, 2019).

By implementing these strategies, language educators can harness the power of AI-driven tools while upholding ethical standards and respecting student privacy. This balanced approach not only protects students but also builds trust in the educational use of AI technologies, potentially leading to greater engagement and more effective learning outcomes. Here, an example of what this application looks like may be helpful. By way of example, consider your typical integrated skills ESL classroom, where you want to introduce an AI-powered writing app to help support student learning.

Before introducing the app to your students, you begin by reviewing its data collection practices outlined in the end user agreement, or EULA. Choose an app that only collects essential data for improving language learning outcomes. For instance, it might track vocabulary acquisition, grammar accuracy, and speaking fluency, but avoid unnecessary data like location or personal preferences unrelated to language learning. From there, you prepare a clear, jargon-free document explaining what data the app collects, how it is used, and who has access to it. Include information on data storage and deletion policies. You then present this reinterpretation document to your students in class, allowing time for questions and discussion. Then, you would then create a simple consent form for students (or their guardians) to sign. This form should outline the app's data practices and give students the option to opt out of data collection while still using the app's core features.

In class, when you introduce the tool to your learners, you should begin by demonstrating how to use the app's privacy settings. Show students how to view their data, change sharing preferences, and request data deletion if desired. To facilitate this, you can develop a mini lesson on digital privacy in language learning. Discuss the benefits of data collection for personalized learning, but also potential risks. Encourage critical thinking about what information students are comfortable sharing. As a student engages with the AI tool(s) you use in the class, you should regularly check in with students about their comfort level with the app's data practices. Be prepared to address concerns and adjust usage if necessary. By taking these steps, you create a transparent, ethical environment for using AI in your language classroom, empowering students to make informed decisions about their data while benefiting from AI-enhanced learning tools.

While we have the most control over what happens at the local level, in our own classrooms, we must not overlook the fact that these classrooms exist in rich institutional contexts, and for those of us working in remote environments, our work may cross national boundaries. Given this oft international workplace, we must acknowledge the need for a comprehensive understanding of and compliance with various data protection regulations. This is particularly crucial in the context of

AI-enhanced language education, where data collection and processing are often more extensive and complex than in traditional teaching methods. This, naturally, introduces considerable complexity into the work of ethically integrating AI tools into language teaching and learning contents. Fortunately, however, the GDPR in the European Union has emerged as a global benchmark for data privacy standards (Voigt & Von dem Bussche, 2017). Its emphasis on user consent, data minimization, and the right to be forgotten has influenced data protection policies worldwide. Meanwhile, in the United States, the California Consumer Privacy Act (CCPA) has set new standards for data protection, while Canada's Personal Information Protection and Electronic Documents Act (PIPEDA) provides another model for safeguarding personal information.

For language educators, navigating this complex regulatory landscape can be challenging but is essential for ethical practice. To ensure compliance and protect student data, educators should take several proactive steps. First, it is crucial to develop a working knowledge of relevant data protection laws, both in the educator's jurisdiction and those of their students. This is particularly important for online language courses that may have a global student base. Educators should familiarize themselves with key concepts such as data subject rights, consent requirements, and data breach notification procedures (Sclater, 2016). Next, clear data governance policies should be developed and implemented. These policies should outline how student data is collected, used, stored, and protected. They should also detail the procedures for responding to data subject requests, such as access or deletion requests. These policies should be living documents, regularly reviewed and updated to reflect changes in regulations or teaching practices (Williamson, 2017). To that end, regular audits of AI tools and platforms used in language teaching are essential. These audits should assess compliance with data protection standards and identify any potential vulnerabilities. This process might involve reviewing the privacy policies and data handling practices of third-party providers, ensuring that data processing agreements are in place, and verifying that data transfers (especially international transfers) are conducted in compliance with relevant regulations (Rubel & Jones, 2016).

To make these recommendations actionable, educators could create a "Data Protection Checklist" for each AI tool or platform they use. This checklist could include items such as whether the tool allows for data minimization, if student data can be easily exported or deleted upon request, and whether the tool's privacy policy aligns with the institution's data governance policies. For instance, a language instructor considering the adoption of an AI-powered pronunciation app might develop a checklist that includes the following items:

1. Does the app allow users to control which data is collected (e.g., voice recordings, usage patterns)?
2. Can students easily access and download their own data from the app?
3. Does the app provide a clear process for students to request deletion of their data?
4. Is the app's privacy policy written in clear, accessible language that students can understand?
5. Does the app comply with relevant data protection regulations (e.g., GDPR, CCPA) applicable to our student population?
6. Are there options to anonymize or pseudonymize student data for analysis purposes?
7. Does the app provider offer a detailed data processing agreement that aligns with our institution's policies?
8. Is there transparency about how the AI algorithms use student data to generate feedback?
9. Are there safeguards in place to prevent unauthorized access to student voice recordings?
10. Does the app allow for regular data audits by our institution?

By systematically working through such a checklist, educators can ensure they are thoroughly evaluating the data protection aspects of AI tools before implementing them in their language classrooms. This process not only helps in selecting appropriate tools but also in identifying potential areas of concern that may need to be addressed with students or the tool provider.

As thinking about data and data privacy may be new to many educators, creating a "Data Protection 101" training module for language educators can be immensely helpful. This module could cover basic principles of data protection, key regulations, and best practices for protecting student data in AI-enhanced language teaching contexts. Establishing a process for conducting privacy impact assessments before implementing new AI tools in the language classroom is another important step. This could involve a cross-functional team including educators, IT professionals, and data protection experts. To illustrate this concept, consider the experience of a university language department implementing such a training module. The department developed a comprehensive online course for its faculty, combining video lectures, interactive quizzes, and practical exercises. The module began with an overview of data protection principles, explaining concepts like data minimization and purpose limitation in the context of language learning. It then probed into key regulations, using case studies to demonstrate how GDPR or CCPA might apply to common scenarios in language classrooms.

The training also included a segment on conducting privacy impact assessments. Faculty members were guided through a hypothetical situation: introducing an AI-powered writing assistant in their courses. They learned to identify potential privacy risks, such as the tool's data retention policies or its use of student writing samples to improve its algorithms. The module emphasized the importance of collaborating with IT staff and legal experts during this process. To make the training more engaging, the department incorporated role-playing exercises. Educators practiced explaining data rights to students and responding to data access requests. They also participated in a simulated meeting with an edtech vendor, learning to ask critical questions about data handling practices. Upon completing the module, educators reported feeling more confident in their ability to navigate data protection issues. Many expressed surprise at the complexity of the topic but appreciated its relevance to their teaching practice. The training not only improved the department's overall compliance but also sparked ongoing discussions about ethical data use in language education.

Finally, developing clear communication materials for students explaining their data rights and how to exercise them is essential. This could include guides on how to request access to their data, how to withdraw consent for data processing, and how to raise concerns about data handling practices. To bring this recommendation to life, imagine a language program creating a user-friendly digital guide for students enrolled in AI-enhanced courses. This guide, accessible through the program's learning management system, would serve as a central resource for all data-related matters. It might begin with an engaging infographic illustrating the journey of a student's data through various AI tools used in the course, demystifying the often-opaque process of data collection and utilization.

The guide could then offer step-by-step instructions for students to exercise their data rights. For instance, it might walk students through the process of requesting a comprehensive report of their personal data, complete with screenshots of relevant interfaces and explanations of what each data point represents in the context of their language learning journey. Similarly, it could outline the procedure for withdrawing consent for specific types of data processing, explaining the potential impacts on the personalized learning experience. To address concerns about data handling, the guide might feature a mock-up of a data concern submission form, accompanied by examples of valid concerns and the program's commitment to addressing them promptly. This section could also include anonymized case studies of past data-related issues and their resolutions, demonstrating the program's transparency and responsiveness.

By providing such clear, accessible information, the language program would not only fulfill its ethical obligations but also empower students to engage more critically and confidently with AI-enhanced learning tools. This approach could foster a culture of data awareness among students, potentially leading to more informed discussions about the role of AI and data in language education.

In conclusion, while AI technologies offer transformative potential for language education, their adoption must be tempered with a strong commitment to data privacy and security. By implementing these recommendations, language educators and researchers can harness the benefits of AI-driven tools while upholding ethical standards and protecting student privacy. As the field continues to evolve, ongoing dialogue and research into best practices for data protection in AI-enhanced language learning environments will be essential to ensure responsible and ethical integration of these powerful technologies. While data privacy and security are certainly critical in an AI-enabled learning environment, it is far from the only concern. In the next section, I will turn our attention to issues of digital equity and inclusivity, extensions of ongoing conversations about more general tech equity that have centered on students' access to reliable, and powerful-enough computing and network resources.

Digital Equity and Inclusivity

The rapid proliferation of AI technologies in educational contexts has the potential to exacerbate existing disparities, creating new barriers for marginalized learners while simultaneously offering unprecedented opportunities for personalized and adaptive learning. This tension underscores the urgent need for a thoughtful and proactive approach to ensuring that AI-enhanced language learning environments are accessible, culturally sensitive, and equitable for all students. To address this issue, we need a robust set of tools-for-thought to grapple with them, render them more knowable, and to effect change – in this case: digital equity and inclusivity. The concept of *digital equity* in education extends beyond mere access to technology; it encompasses the ability to fully participate in and benefit from digital learning experiences. In the context of AI-enhanced language learning, this principle takes on new dimensions. Educators must consider not only the physical accessibility of AI tools but also their cognitive accessibility, cultural appropriateness, and potential for bias. Language educators and researchers bear the responsibility of critically examining the AI technologies they employ, ensuring these tools serve to bridge rather than widen educational gaps.

This section explores three interconnected facets of digital equity and inclusivity in AI-enhanced language education. First, it explores the incorporation of accessible AI technologies for learners with disabilities and learning differences, examining how adaptive interfaces, natural language processing, and other AI-driven innovations can be leveraged to create more inclusive learning environments. Next, it addresses the critical issue of cultural sensitivity and bias in AI tools, exploring strategies to mitigate algorithmic prejudice and ensure that language learning technologies respect and reflect the diversity of student populations. Finally, this section discusses comprehensive strategies for promoting equal access to AI-enhanced learning, considering factors such as socioeconomic disparities, technological literacy, and infrastructure limitations.

The exploration draws upon emerging research in the field of AI ethics in education, as well as established principles of universal design for learning and culturally responsive pedagogy. By weaving together theoretical frameworks with practical examples and actionable recommendations, this section aims to equip language educators with the knowledge and tools necessary to harness the power of AI in ways that promote equity and inclusion. As educators navigate this complex landscape, the goal is not only to avoid perpetuating existing inequalities but to actively leverage AI technologies as a means of creating more just and accessible language learning opportunities for all students.

Driving Equity and Inclusivity for Learners with Disabilities and Learning Differences

The incorporation of accessible AI technologies for learners with disabilities and learning differences represents a critical frontier in the pursuit of digital equity in language education. As AI-enhanced tools become increasingly prevalent in language classrooms, it is crucial to ensure that these technologies do not inadvertently exclude students with diverse learning needs. Instead, when thoughtfully implemented, AI has the potential to dramatically improve accessibility and learning outcomes for a wide range of learners.

Take the ability to create applications with adaptive interfaces as one such example. Adaptive interfaces powered by AI offer one promising avenue for enhancing accessibility and addressing diverse learning styles. These interfaces can dynamically adjust to individual user needs, offering customized font sizes, color contrasts, or simplified layouts for students with visual impairments or learning disabilities. For instance, Rajapakse et al. (2018) demonstrated the efficacy of an AI-driven adaptive interface in improving engagement and performance among dyslexic language learners. The system's ability to tailor its presentation based on real-time user interactions proved particularly beneficial for students with varying levels of reading proficiency.

Beyond visual adaptations, AI-powered NLP technologies are opening new doors for learners with auditory processing difficulties or speech impairments. Text-to-speech and speech-to-text functionalities, enhanced by machine learning algorithms, can provide real-time transcriptions or vocalizations, making language content more accessible across modalities. Jeon et al. (2023) found that integrating AI-driven speech recognition into language learning platforms contributed to some improvements comprehension and participation rates among students with hearing impairments and those for whom the target language was particularly challenging phonologically.

Moreover, for learners with attention deficit disorders or those who benefit from more structured learning environments, AI can offer personalized pacing and content sequencing. Adaptive learning systems, such as those described by Khawaja and Karimi (2024), use machine learning algorithms to analyze a student's performance patterns and adjust the difficulty and presentation of language tasks accordingly. This dynamic adaptation can help maintain engagement and reduce frustration for learners who might otherwise struggle with a one-size-fits-all approach.

However, the implementation of these technologies is not without challenges. Ethical considerations arise regarding data privacy and the potential for AI systems to reinforce or exacerbate existing biases. Novawan et al. (2024) caution that overreliance on AI-driven assessments could lead to pigeonholing students based on initial performance, potentially limiting their growth opportunities. Therefore, it is crucial for educators to maintain a critical perspective, using AI as a tool to augment rather than replace human judgment in addressing diverse learning needs. Moreover, the effectiveness of AI in supporting learners with disabilities and learning differences heavily depends on the quality and diversity of the data used to train these systems. Ensuring that AI models are trained on datasets that represent a wide range of learner profiles is essential for creating truly inclusive technologies. This underscores the importance of collaborative efforts between educators, researchers, and AI developers to create more comprehensive and representative AI systems for language education.

Building on these ideas, it can be helpful to examine how these AI technologies can be practically implemented in diverse language learning contexts. While the potential of AI to support learners with disabilities and learning differences is significant, the actual application of these tools in the classroom requires careful consideration and adaptation to specific linguistic and cultural environments. To illustrate this, let us consider two hypothetical scenarios that demonstrate how existing AI technologies could be thoughtfully integrated into language classrooms, addressing the unique challenges and opportunities presented by different target languages and learner populations. These examples, focusing on Farsi and Xhosa as foreign language classes, are constructed based on currently available AI tools and pedagogical best practices. They serve to bridge the gap between theoretical possibilities and practical implementation, showcasing how educators might leverage AI to create more inclusive and effective learning environments. It is important to note that while these scenarios are hypothetical, they are grounded in the real capabilities of existing AI technologies and the genuine needs of diverse language learners.

In a hypothetical Farsi as a foreign language class, instructors could integrate mobile speech recognition technology similar to that studied by Liakin et al. (2015) in their research on French pronunciation. While their study focused on the French /y/ sound, the principle of using mobile speech recognizers for pronunciation practice could be applied to Farsi phonemes that are challenging for non-native speakers. This technology would be particularly beneficial for students with auditory processing difficulties or speech impairments, allowing them to practice speaking at their own pace and receive personalized guidance. Additionally, the course could utilize adaptive learning algorithms similar to those employed by Duolingo. According to Duolingo's designers(2022), their AI system personalizes lesson difficulty and content sequencing based on individual user performance. In a Farsi class, this could help maintain engagement for students with attention deficit disorders or those requiring more structured learning approaches, as the system adapts to each learner's pace and areas of difficulty.

In a hypothetical Xhosa language program, educators could implement Microsoft's Translator, which includes real-time transcription and translation features. As described on Microsoft Translator's education page (2024), this tool can support students with hearing impairments by providing live transcriptions of spoken language. In a Xhosa class, this could allow students to read transcriptions of the instructor's speech and their peers' responses, making the spoken language more accessible. The program could also employ AI-powered writing assistants to support students with dyslexia or other learning differences affecting written expression. While not specific to Xhosa, the principles of AI-assisted writing tools could be applied to help students improve their written Xhosa, offering real-time suggestions for grammar and spelling.

In both hypothetical cases, these AI tools would serve as supplements to, rather than replacements for, traditional teaching methods. Instructors would need to use these technologies judiciously, always considering the specific needs of individual students and the unique challenges presented by each language. By thoughtfully integrating AI-powered tools, language programs could take significant steps towards creating more inclusive and adaptive learning environments that accommodate a wide range of learner profiles and needs. Additionally, the use cases of these applications outlined above align with the findings of Shadiev et al. (2017), who reviewed research on mobile language learning in authentic environments. They highlighted the potential of mobile technologies to provide personalized, context-aware language learning experiences, which could be particularly beneficial for learners with diverse needs.

Cultural Sensitivity, Algorithmic Bias, and AI Tools

The integration of AI tools in language education brings to the forefront critical issues of cultural sensitivity and algorithmic bias. These concerns, while not unique to language learning, take on particular significance in a field inherently tied to cultural exchange and understanding. As AI systems become more prevalent in language classrooms, educators must grapple with the potential for these tools to perpetuate or even amplify cultural biases and misrepresentations. Above, I introduced the notion of algorithmic bias. As a reminder, algorithmic bias in AI language tools can manifest in various ways, from skewed language models that favor certain dialects or registers to translation systems that perpetuate gender stereotypes or cultural misconceptions. For instance, Bender et al. (2021) highlight how large language models, trained predominantly on Western, English-language data, can propagate a narrow worldview that fails to capture the nuances of diverse cultural contexts. This bias becomes particularly problematic in language learning environments, where exposure to authentic, culturally diverse content is crucial.

The challenge of ensuring cultural sensitivity in AI-enhanced language education extends beyond mere representation. It involves a deep consideration of how language and culture are intertwined and how AI systems interpret and reproduce cultural norms. Blodgett et al. (2020) argue that addressing bias in natural language processing systems requires not just technical solutions but a fundamental rethinking of how we conceptualize and operationalize concepts like bias and fairness in cross-cultural contexts. For language educators, this means adopting a critical stance towards the AI tools they employ in their classrooms. It requires an ongoing process of evaluation and adaptation, ensuring that these technologies enhance rather than detract from the goal of fostering intercultural competence. Chapelle and Sauro (2017) emphasize the importance of developing digital literacies that enable both teachers and learners to critically engage with AI technologies, questioning their outputs and understanding their limitations.

Moreover, the pursuit of cultural sensitivity in AI-enhanced language learning necessitates a collaborative approach. Educators, AI developers, and cultural experts must work together to create more inclusive and representative systems. This collaboration could involve diversifying the data sets used to train AI models, incorporating feedback mechanisms that allow for continuous refinement based on user experiences, and developing AI systems that are explicitly designed to support cultural learning objectives. In addressing these challenges, it is crucial for language educators and researchers and AI developers to recognize that AI tools, despite their limitations, also offer unique opportunities for promoting cultural understanding. When thoughtfully implemented, they can expose learners to a wider range of cultural perspectives and linguistic variations than might be possible in traditional classroom settings. The key lies in leveraging these technologies as tools for cultural exploration and critical thinking, rather than as definitive sources of cultural knowledge.

Ultimately, addressing issues of cultural sensitivity and algorithmic bias in AI-enhanced language education is an ongoing process. It requires vigilance, adaptability, and a commitment to the core values of linguistic and cultural diversity that underpin the field of language education. By approaching these challenges with a critical and collaborative mindset, educators can work towards creating AI-enhanced learning environments that not only avoid perpetuating biases but actively contribute to fostering greater intercultural understanding and appreciation.

Tech Equity and Equal Access to AI-enhanced Learning

Finally, and perhaps increasingly salient in modern education is the issue of tech equity. Said more simply, we cannot assume that all learners have equal access to technological resources. They may have limited compute capabilities – c.f., a Chromebook vs. a high-powered gaming rig – or limited network capabilities – c.f., a limited satellite connection vs. a dedicated gigabit fiber connection. Therefore, the issue of tech equity and equal access to AI-enhanced learning is a critical concern in the rapidly evolving landscape of language education. As AI technologies become increasingly integrated into language learning environments, there is a growing risk of exacerbating existing educational disparities. This section explores strategies for promoting equitable access to AI-enhanced learning opportunities, acknowledging that the digital divide extends beyond mere access to devices and internet connectivity.

At its core, tech equity in AI-enhanced language learning involves ensuring that all students, regardless of their socioeconomic background, geographic location, or personal circumstances, have the opportunity to benefit from these advanced educational tools. However, as Reich and Ito (2017) point out in their seminal work on educational technology and equity, simply providing access to technology is insufficient. True equity requires addressing a complex web of factors including digital literacy, cultural relevance, and the quality of implementation. One key strategy for promoting equal access is the development of AI-enhanced learning tools that are adaptable to a wide range of devices and internet speeds. Warschauer and Matuchniak (2010) emphasize the importance of creating educational technologies that are accessible on low-cost smartphones and in areas with limited bandwidth. This approach ensures that students in resource-constrained environments can still participate in AI-enhanced learning experiences.

Another crucial aspect is the provision of comprehensive digital literacy training for both students and educators. As Selwyn (2020) argues, the ability to effectively use and critically engage with AI technologies is becoming an essential skill in modern education. Language programs must incorporate digital literacy components that specifically address AI tools, ensuring that all learners have the skills to navigate and benefit from these technologies. Furthermore, and closely related to driving AI literacy skills, is promoting equal access requires addressing the linguistic and cultural biases often embedded in AI systems. Bender (2019) highlights the importance of developing AI language models that represent a diverse range of languages and dialects, rather than prioritizing dominant languages. This approach not only enhances the effectiveness of AI-enhanced learning for linguistically diverse students but also promotes a more inclusive educational environment. To address these issues, collaboration between educational institutions, tech companies, and policymakers is essential in addressing the infrastructure and resource gaps that hinder equal access. Initiatives like the ones described by Resta and Laferrière (2015) demonstrate how partnerships can lead to innovative solutions for providing technology access in underserved communities.

By implementing these strategies, language educators and institutions can work towards creating a more equitable landscape in AI-enhanced language learning. The goal is not merely to provide access to AI technologies but to ensure that these tools are effectively leveraged to enhance learning outcomes for all students, regardless of their backgrounds or circumstances. This requires a holistic understanding of equity that goes beyond technological access, encompassing cultural relevance, linguistic diversity, and pedagogical effectiveness. Achieving this goal necessitates ongoing collaboration between educators, technologists, policymakers, and students themselves. Developing truly inclusive digital learning environments demands a participatory approach that values diverse perspectives and experiences. This collaborative effort should focus on creating AI-enhanced language learning tools that are not only accessible but also culturally responsive and pedagogically sound. Additionally, addressing equity in AI-enhanced language learning involves a continuous process of evaluation and adaptation. Educators must regularly assess the impact of these technologies on different student populations, with particular attention to potentially marginalized groups. This assessment should consider not only academic outcomes but also factors such as student engagement, cultural competence, and long-term language retention.

Applied AI Ethics in Language Teaching and Learning

Up to this point, I have focused our attention on some of the ethical issues that crop up when integrating AI technologies into language teaching and learning contexts. While having offered a few example of what these issues look like in the classroom, and how to attempt to address them, it does raise a very important question to address, what does AI ethics look like in language teaching and learning? In this section, we will explore the specific ethical considerations that arise when integrating AI technologies into language teaching and learning environments, focusing on three key areas: transparency in AI decision-making processes, addressing potential biases in AI algorithms, and ethical considerations in AI-assisted assessment and feedback.

Transparency in AI decision-making processes is fundamental to ethical AI use in language education. As Holmes and Bi (2023) and Zanzotto (2019) argue, educators must be clear about when and how AI is being used in their teaching, ensuring that students understand the role of these technologies in their learning process. This transparency extends to the limitations and potential biases of AI systems, fostering critical thinking and digital literacy among learners. For instance, when using AI-powered writing assistants, educators should explicitly discuss how these tools generate suggestions and the importance of human judgment in accepting or rejecting them. Beyond creating the space for students to be transparent about their AI use, language educators must also practice this transparency *with* their students regarding their own AI use, further modeling this ethical behavior early and often.

Here, again, we return to the issue of algorithmic bias, which speaks to its importance and saliency. Addressing potential biases in AI algorithms is crucial in language education, where cultural and linguistic diversity is paramount. Sennrich (2016) highlights the risk of bias in machine translation and other language technologies, particularly for less-resourced languages (see also Cotton et al., 2023). Educators must critically examine the AI tools they employ for potential biases that might disadvantage certain groups of learners or perpetuate stereotypes. This involves not only selecting tools carefully but also teaching students to recognize and critique potential biases in AI outputs.

Ethical considerations in AI-assisted assessment and feedback are particularly salient in language teaching. While AI can offer efficient and objective evaluation of certain language skills, Chapelle and Voss (2016) caution against over-relying on automated assessments, particularly for high-stakes decisions. Similarly, Coeckelbergh (2023) underscores the need for a balanced approach, where AI is used to enhance rather than replace human judgment in evaluating language proficiency. Ethical use of AI in assessment involves ensuring the validity and reliability of AI-based tools, as well as considering their impact on learner motivation and self-perception. Educators must strike a balance, using AI to enhance rather than replace human judgment in evaluating language proficiency. Moreover, as Laufer and Nation (2012) suggest, the use of AI in vocabulary assessment and feedback can provide valuable insights into learner progress, but it must be implemented with careful consideration of individual learning contexts and goals. Educators should be transparent about how AI-generated feedback is produced and encourage students to engage critically with this feedback rather than accepting it unquestioningly.

By addressing these ethical dimensions, language educators can work towards a responsible and beneficial integration of AI technologies in their practice. This approach ensures that these powerful tools serve to enhance, rather than compromise, the core values and objectives of language education, while preparing students to engage critically with AI technologies in their future language use contexts. In the remainder of this section, I will offer language education practitioners and researchers with illustrations of the different forms that these ethical principles can take as well as examples of how they can deploy them in their professional practice. Understand that these are not *the* form that these ethical principles *must* take but are, rather, options that professionals should adapt to their institutional and professional realities before their adoption.

AI Transparency in Language Teaching, Learning, and Research

At its core, *transparency* is all about setting and maintaining expectations about AI use disclosure. It attempts to account for how people use technological tools while also requiring individuals to self-disclose how they used these tools to support, instead of replace, human effort and intelligence. Said more simply, it is about creating value around the idea of being forthcoming about how we collaborate with AI agents to navigate the world around us. Admittedly, the form that this transparency takes will vary based on class context and the population at questions – students, teachers, researchers, etc. But the honesty and accountability that being transparent about AI use can create is an important part of working collaborative *with* AI tools in a manner that facilitates lifelong learning and professional development while also creating an environment of trust that further supports these highly negotiated and social processes.

Transparency in AI decision-making processes, when applied to language classrooms, involves openly communicating with students about the presence, purpose, and functioning of AI tools in their learning environment. This principle supports learners by demystifying AI technologies, fostering critical engagement with these tools, and empowering students to make informed decisions about their use. By being transparent about AI's role, capabilities, and limitations, educators can cultivate digital literacy skills that are crucial in an increasingly AI-influenced world. Moreover, this approach helps maintain the integrity of the language learning process by ensuring that students understand how AI suggestions are generated and the importance of their own judgment in language production. The following example illustrates how an instructor might implement this principle of transparency in a university-level Spanish as a foreign language course.

In our hypothetical university-level advanced Spanish writing course, the instructor decides to integrate an AI-powered writing assistant to help students improve their L2 writing products. At the beginning of the semester, the instructor dedicates a class session to introducing the AI tool. They explain its functionality, including how it generates suggestions based on patterns in large language datasets. The instructor emphasizes that while the tool can provide helpful feedback on grammar, vocabulary, and style, it is not infallible and may not always understand the nuances of context or creative expression. From there, the instructor then demonstrates the tool's use in real-time, showing students how to access it, input their text, and interpret the suggestions. They also model the critical thinking process of evaluating the AI's recommendations, sometimes accepting them and other times rejecting them based on the specific context or intended meaning. Additionally, to foster digital literacy, the instructor guides students through the tool's documentation, pointing out sections that describe its limitations and potential biases. They discuss how the AI might perform differently with various Spanish dialects or struggle with colloquial expressions.

The instructor establishes clear guidelines for the tool's use in the course, introducing a comprehensive "AI Use Reflection Table" (see Figure 6.1, below, for an example) as a mandatory component of each writing assignment. This table requires students to document their interaction with AI tools throughout their writing process in detail. For each stage of writing (brainstorming, drafting, revising, and editing), students must record:

1. Which specific AI tool(s) they used (e.g., grammar checker, style suggester, translation aid)
2. The purpose for which they employed the tool
3. Examples of AI suggestions they received
4. Whether they accepted, modified, or rejected each suggestion, and their reasoning for this decision
5. Their perception of how the AI tool influenced their final output

Additionally, students are asked to provide a brief overall reflection on how the AI tools impacted their writing process and final product. They might consider questions such as: Did the AI help them express their ideas more clearly? Did it introduce any errors or misunderstandings? How did using AI affect their confidence in their language skills?

Figure 6.1 Example AI Use Table from Student Assignment

Appendix A: AI Assistance Statement and Reflection

In the spirit of professionalism and academic integrity, I hereby assert that I used the following AI agents to assist in drafting, revising, and editing this paper. The core ideas of this paper and the synthesis of evidence to support key ideas and an analysis of how that support functions are original to me. However, I did deploy AI agents during the following stages for specific purposes, as outlined in the table below.

Stage of writing	AI Used	Purpose of usage	Impact on Writing
Research	GPT-3.5	I used GPT to understand more about machine learning models and how they work, but I did not use any of the information it generated.	This increased my writing skills and allowed me to provide more detailed information. It supports research by providing information on machine learning models and malware.
Drafting	-----	As this assignment did not allow for AI usage during drafting, I hereby assert that the actual text of this paper was generated totally by me and without the assistance of AI in any way.	Bandlapalli Saketh
Editing	Grammarly Basic	I used Grammarly Basics in my work to help me with effective grammar and syntax choices.	This created more professional work and helped me in finding and fixing grammar mistakes.

To further encourage critical engagement, the instructor requires students to highlight or annotate their final essays, indicating sections where AI suggestions were incorporated. This visual representation helps both the student, and the instructor understand the extent of AI influence on the work. This work is then expanded upon through peer review. During peer review sessions, students are encouraged to discuss their AI use experiences, comparing notes on how they navigated AI suggestions and what they learned about their own writing process through this documentation.

This comprehensive approach provides instructors with a wealth of data to assess AI's impact on student learning and writing development. Through AI Use Reflection Tables and annotated essays, instructors can gather insights into patterns of AI tool usage, types of language features students frequently seek assistance with, and how students engage with AI suggestions. This data allows for both quantitative and qualitative analyses, offering a nuanced understanding of AI's role in the language learning process. Quantitatively, instructors can track the frequency of AI use throughout the semester, identifying trends in student reliance on these tools. By comparing AI use patterns with student performance, they can explore potential correlations between AI assistance and language proficiency development. This analysis might reveal common areas where students consistently accept or reject AI suggestions, potentially highlighting gaps in language instruction that require additional focus. Meanwhile, qualitatively examining students' reflections on AI use can provide valuable insights into their decision-making processes and metacognitive awareness. Instructors can identify misconceptions about language use that may be reinforced or challenged by AI tools, and assess the development of students' critical thinking skills in relation to AI use over time.

Armed with these insights, instructors can tailor their teaching practices and assessment strategies. They might adjust lesson plans to address areas where students heavily rely on AI, ensuring these language aspects receive more focused instruction. Targeted exercises can be developed to challenge students to apply language skills in contexts where AI tools struggle, promoting a deeper understanding of the language. Furthermore, this approach allows instructors to refine assessment criteria to account for and evaluate students' critical engagement with AI tools. It provides a foundation for creating meaningful class discussions or workshops that address common themes or issues emerging from students' AI use reflections. Perhaps most importantly, this data enables instructors to monitor the ethical use of AI in the classroom, ensuring that students are using these tools as learning aids rather than shortcuts. It offers an opportunity to identify students who may be over-relying on AI and provide them with additional support or guidance.

By transforming AI use into a subject of study itself, this approach not only addresses ethical concerns but also enriches the language learning experience. It fosters critical digital literacy skills that are increasingly crucial in an AI-augmented world, preparing students to be thoughtful and discerning users of AI technologies in their future language endeavors. To facilitate this further, throughout the semester, the instructor can regularly check in with students about their experiences with the AI tool, encouraging open discussion about its benefits and limitations. They use these conversations to reinforce the importance of maintaining human agency in the writing process and to address any emerging ethical concerns. By implementing transparency in this way, the instructor not only ensures ethical use of AI in the classroom but also equips students with valuable skills in critical thinking and digital literacy that extend beyond the language learning context.

Transparency in AI decision-making processes extends beyond student use to encompass instructors' own engagement with AI tools in their teaching practice. This principle of instructor transparency supports the educational environment by modeling ethical AI use, demystifying the role of AI in education, and fostering open dialogue about the benefits and limitations of these technologies. By being transparent about their own AI use, instructors can cultivate a culture of critical engagement with AI tools and demonstrate the importance of human judgment in educational contexts.

Consider a hypothetical scenario in a graduate-level Teaching English to Speakers of Other Languages (TESOL) teacher education program, where an instructor incorporates various AI tools into their course design and delivery. At the beginning of the semester, the instructor dedicates a portion of the first class to discussing their use of AI in course preparation and management. They explain how they employ AI tools for tasks such as generating initial lesson plan ideas, creating sample language exercises, and providing preliminary feedback on student assignments. The instructor demonstrates these tools in real-time, showing how they interact with AI to brainstorm lesson concepts or generate exercise templates. They emphasize that while AI provides valuable assistance, all content undergoes critical review and often significant modification to ensure its appropriateness and effectiveness for the specific learning context. Then, to foster a deeper understanding of AI's role in their teaching process, the instructor introduces an "Instructor AI Use Log" as part of the CMS content platform (see Figure 6.2). This log, shared with students at regular intervals throughout the semester, documents:

1. The specific AI tools used in course preparation and delivery
2. The purposes for which each tool was employed
3. Examples of AI-generated content or suggestions
4. How the AI output was evaluated, modified, or incorporated into the course
5. Reflections on the impact of AI use on the teaching process and learning outcomes
6. How students can learn from the teacher's AI use challenges and opportunities to improve their own, future, practice.

Figure 6.2 Sample of an Instructor AI Use Log

Instructor AI Use Log

Date	AI Tool Used	Purpose	AI-Generated Content	Evaluation & Modification	Instructor Reflection	Student Learning Application
Week 1	ChatGPT	Generating initial lesson plan ideas	Lesson plan outline on teaching modal verbs	Reviewed AI suggestions, modified examples to fit student proficiency levels	AI provided a creative starting point, but significant customization was needed to match course objectives	Encourage students to critically assess AI outputs in their own lesson planning.
Week 2	QuillBot	Refining language exercises	Reworded practice sentences for clarity	Fine-tuned exercises to better align with course terminology	The AI helped streamline content creation, though human oversight ensured accuracy	Students can use AI tools to enhance clarity in their written communication
Week 3	Grammarly	Preliminary feedback on student essays	Automated grammar and style suggestions	Used AI feedback as a baseline, added personalized comments	AI feedback saved time, but it lacked contextual understanding—human feedback was crucial	Highlight the importance of supplementing AI feedback with personal insight
Week 4	DALL-E	Creating visual aids for vocabulary	Generated images representing different emotions	Selected and modified images to culturally suit student demographics	AI visuals sparked engagement, but cultural appropriateness needed careful consideration	Encourage students to critically evaluate AI-generated media for cultural relevance
Week 5	ChatGPT & Google Translate	Translating course materials	Translations of key terms into students' L1	Reviewed and corrected inaccuracies in the AI translation	AI offered a quick translation, but errors highlighted the need for bilingual verification	Students should learn to spot-check AI translations and rely on their linguistic knowledge

The instructor uses this log as a basis for ongoing discussions about AI in education, encouraging students to critically analyze the choices made in AI integration and to consider how they might approach similar decisions in their future teaching careers. By foregrounding their own critical reflections on AI use, the instructor further reinforces the spirit of transparency and collaboration necessary for effective and ethical AI integration into language teaching practice, from which their own students can further learn. Then, to promote more extensive transparency and critical engagement, the instructor includes annotations in course materials, such as lesson plans and assignment instructions, indicating where AI tools influenced the content. This visual representation helps students understand the extent of AI's role in course development and encourages them to question and discuss these choices.

Throughout the semester, the instructor dedicates time in class to reflect on their AI use, sharing insights, challenges, and ethical considerations that arise. They discuss instances where AI suggestions were particularly helpful or problematic, explaining their decision-making process in each case. This ongoing dialogue serves to model critical thinking about AI use and reinforces the importance of human expertise in educational contexts.

This approach to instructor transparency provides valuable learning opportunities for students in the TESOL program. It offers insights into the practical application of AI in language teaching, demonstrates the critical evaluation of AI-generated content, and highlights the ethical considerations involved in integrating these technologies into educational practice. By modeling transparency in their own AI use, instructors not only address ethical concerns but also prepare future educators to navigate the complexities of AI integration in their own careers. This approach fosters a nuanced understanding of AI's potential and limitations in language education, encouraging students to develop a balanced and critical perspective on these emerging technologies. Here, it should be noted that as AI tools continue to evolve and become more prevalent in educational settings, this practice of instructor transparency will become increasingly crucial. It serves as a foundation for ongoing discussions about the role of AI in education, helping to ensure that future language educators are well-equipped to use these tools ethically and effectively in their own teaching practice.

Transparency in AI decision-making processes is equally crucial in the realm of language education research, particularly when researchers employ AI tools for data analytics. This principle of research transparency supports the integrity of the scientific process by clearly communicating the role of AI in data analysis, acknowledging its capabilities and limitations, and enabling other researchers to critically evaluate and potentially replicate the findings. By being transparent about AI use in research, scholars can foster trust in their results and contribute to the responsible advancement of AI-assisted research methodologies in the field of language education.

Consider a hypothetical scenario where a team of researchers is conducting a large-scale study on the effectiveness of various online language learning platforms. The study involves analyzing vast amounts of user data, including learning patterns, engagement metrics, and language proficiency outcomes. To manage and analyze this complex dataset, the researchers decide to incorporate AI-powered data analytics tools into their research process. At the outset of the study, the research team develops a comprehensive "AI Use in Research Protocol." This protocol, which will be included in the methodology section of their final paper and any related presentations, outlines:

1. The specific AI tools and algorithms used for data analysis
2. The rationale for choosing these particular AI tools
3. The types of data inputted into the AI systems
4. The parameters and settings used in the AI analysis
5. The process for validating and interpreting AI-generated results
6. Potential limitations or biases of the AI tools that may affect the analysis

Throughout the research process, the team maintains a detailed log of their interactions with the AI tools. This log includes:

1. Dates and specific instances of AI use
2. Any adjustments made to the AI parameters during the study

3. Unexpected results or anomalies produced by the AI analysis
4. Human interventions in the AI-driven analysis process
5. Reflections on how AI-generated insights influenced research directions or conclusions

To ensure transparency and enable critical evaluation of their methods, the researchers make this log available as supplementary material with their published findings. Additionally, In their data analysis section, the researchers clearly delineate between results directly produced by AI tools and those derived from human interpretation of AI outputs. They provide a thorough explanation of how they integrated AI-generated insights with traditional statistical methods and qualitative analysis. Furthermore, the researchers also dedicate a section of their paper to discussing the ethical implications of using AI in their research process. They reflect on potential biases in the AI algorithms, how these might have affected the results, and the steps taken to mitigate these effects. This discussion includes considerations of data privacy and the ethical use of learner data in AI-powered analysis. By doing so, the team ensures that during conference presentations and peer review processes, they are prepared to answer detailed questions about their AI use.

This commitment to transparency in AI use extends to the researchers' data sharing practices. They provide clear documentation on how AI tools were used in data preprocessing and analysis, enabling other researchers to understand the full context of the data and potentially replicate the study. By adopting this transparent approach to AI use in research, the team not only ensures the integrity of their own study but also contributes to the broader discourse on ethical AI use in language education research. Their practices serve as a model for other researchers, promoting a culture of openness and critical engagement with AI tools in the field.

As AI continues to play an increasingly significant role in research methodologies, this level of transparency will become essential. It will help the research community collectively navigate the complexities of AI-assisted analysis, ensuring that the benefits of these powerful tools are realized while maintaining the highest standards of research ethics and integrity. While not explicitly discussed thus far, increased transparency around AI tool use also creates space for us to address our next ethical component, which is directly addressing and mitigating potential algorithmic biases that might exist in our tools and have negative impacts on our professional practice and our students' learning. In the next section, we turn our attention to just this issue, with more examples of how language teaching and research professional can begin to address them.

Addressing Potential Algorithmic Biases

Here, we return to an idea we have already examined in the context of planning for AI integration; namely, *algorithmic* bias. Algorithmic bias in language education refers to the systematic and repeatable errors in AI systems that create unfair outcomes, such as privileging one group of language learners over others. This issue is particularly pertinent in language learning contexts, where cultural and linguistic diversity are inherent to the field. Because of the nature of training AI systems on massive amounts of existing data, over time AI models tend to take on many of the biases inherent in the society of their designers unless concerted actions are taken to mitigate said biases (see Christian, 2021; Pasquale, 2020). Therefore, as AI tools become increasingly integrated into language teaching and learning processes, understanding and addressing these biases is crucial for ensuring equitable educational experiences.

Sennrich (2017) provides a salient example of some of the risks and challenges of AI, NLP, and ML technologies in the language classroom. He highlights the risk of bias in machine translation and other language technologies, particularly for less-resourced languages. This bias can manifest in various ways, from inaccurate translations that misrepresent cultural nuances to writing assistance tools that favor certain linguistic styles over others. Cotton et al. (2023) further emphasize that these biases can have far-reaching consequences, potentially reinforcing existing inequalities in language education and limiting opportunities for learners from diverse backgrounds, in part by failing to adequately challenge dominant discourses that tend to advantage certain groups at the expense of others (see also Paiz, 2020).

To illustrate this concept, consider a popular language learning app that uses AI to generate conversation practice scenarios. The app might consistently present dialogues set in Western, urban contexts, featuring characters with Anglo-Saxon names engaging in activities typical of middle-class lifestyles. This bias, while perhaps unintentional, could alienate learners from different cultural backgrounds or socioeconomic statuses, making the learning content less relatable and potentially less effective for a significant portion of users. Consider it from this perspective, from applied linguistics to engineering education, we know that students must see themselves represented in our instructional materials to be able to imagine future success. When AI models default to advantaging metropolitan contextual settings and their concomitant sociolinguistic trappings, it reinforces the notion for the learners that if they are not from these dominant, privileged groups they are less likely to succeed in learning. This reality has been shown to significantly contribute to attrition across educational contexts (c.f., Litzler & Young, 2012; Norton & Toohey, 2004).

Because of this it is important for any ethical framework for AI integration into language teaching and learning to also equip practitioners to be able to identify common types of biases. Some of the common types of algorithmic bias that tend to appear in many AI models used in language technologies include:

1. Representation bias: When certain languages, dialects, or cultural contexts are overrepresented in the AI's training data, leading to better performance for some groups of learners than others
2. Linguistic bias: The tendency of AI systems to favor standard or prestige varieties of a language, potentially dismissing or misinterpreting valid linguistic variations
3. Cultural bias: When AI tools make assumptions or generate content based on specific cultural norms, which may not be universally applicable
4. Gender bias: The perpetuation of gender stereotypes or unequal representation in language examples and translations

These biases can be observed across various language learning tools. For instance, in translation tools, idiomatic expressions from less commonly taught languages might be consistently mistranslated, failing to capture their cultural significance. Writing assistance tools may suggest corrections that standardize language use, potentially erasing important dialectal features. In language assessment, AI-powered speaking tests might struggle to accurately evaluate accents or pronunciations that deviate from what the system was primarily trained on.

The impact of these biases on diverse learner populations can be significant. Consider a case where an AI-powered speaking assessment tool is used in a university's English language program. The tool, trained primarily on North American English accents, consistently underscores students from West African countries, despite their grammatical and lexical proficiency. This bias not only affects these students' scores but could also impact their confidence and future academic opportunities. And, this is far from an imagined threat, as early work on AI detectors have consistently shown that they are biased against multilingual writers from non-North American contexts (see Liang et al., 2023; Myers, 2023).

Addressing algorithmic biases requires a multifaceted approach from educators. First and foremost, critical evaluation of AI tools before implementation is crucial. This involves researching the tool's development process, understanding its training data, and testing it with diverse language samples to identify potential biases. From there, ongoing monitoring and assessment of AI tool outputs is equally important. Educators should regularly review the content and feedback generated by AI tools, looking for patterns that might indicate bias. This could involve comparing AI-generated feedback across different student demographics or analyzing translation outputs for consistent cultural misrepresentations.

Additionally, mitigation will require the thoughtful complementing of AI tools with diverse, human-curated resources is an effective strategy to mitigate bias. For example, an educator teaching Spanish might supplement an AI-powered vocabulary tool with authentic materials from various Spanish-speaking countries, ensuring a more comprehensive representation of the language's diversity. In keeping with the themes of collaborative AI discussed throughout book, educators and other language practitioners will also have to continually partner with students and research participants to develop their awareness and critical thinking about AI biases, as this represents another key mitigation strategy. Educators, for instance, can incorporate discussions about AI limitations and biases into their curriculum, encouraging students to question and critically evaluate AI-generated content. A practical example of addressing bias in the classroom might involve a Japanese language instructor using an AI writing assistant. Upon noticing that the tool consistently suggests formal language regardless of context, the instructor could turn this into a teachable moment. They might ask students to compare the AI suggestions with examples from authentic Japanese texts, discussing the importance of register and context in language use.

From the preceding discussion addressing algorithmic bias in language education is an ongoing process that requires vigilance, critical thinking, and a commitment to equity. By implementing engaging with these challenges head on, educators can harness the benefits of AI tools while mitigating their potential biases, ensuring a more inclusive and effective language learning experience for all students. However, given the emergent nature of this area of student and professional development, there is, admittedly, much need for vetted, reliable materials and skilled trainers to help guide practitioners and researchers as they continue to pivot for an AI-rich future. Next, we turn our attention away from general discussions of AI ethics and to an issue that strikes at the very core of the educational mission of applied linguists and language educators – academic integrity.

Reimaging Academic Integrity in the Age of AI

The integration of AI into language education has ushered in a new era of opportunities and challenges, particularly in the realm of academic integrity. As AI technologies become increasingly sophisticated and accessible, they are fundamentally altering the landscape of teaching, learning, and assessment in language classrooms worldwide (Shannon & Chapelle, 2017). This transformation necessitates a reevaluation of traditional concepts of academic honesty and a thoughtful consideration of how to maintain the integrity of language education in an AI-enhanced environment. This reimaging of academic integrity is necessary now because, historically, academic integrity in language learning has grappled with issues such as plagiarism, unauthorized collaboration, and the use of translation tools (Pecorari, 2013). However, the advent of advanced AI, particularly generative AI systems like ChatGPT, Claude, and other large language models, has introduced a new dimension to these challenges. These tools can produce human-like text, translate with increasing accuracy, exhibit growing reasoning capabilities, and even mimic different writing styles, blurring the lines between authentic student work and AI-generated content (Susnjak & McIntosh, 2024).

The implications of this technological shift are profound. On one hand, AI tools offer unprecedented support for language learners, providing instant feedback, personalized practice, and access to vast linguistic resources (Settles et al., 2018). On the other hand, they raise serious questions about the nature of language proficiency, the validity of traditional assessment methods, and the very essence of what it means to learn a language in the twenty-first century. Therefore as educators and researchers in the field of language education, we find ourselves at a critical juncture. We must navigate the delicate balance between harnessing the potential of AI to enhance language learning and preserving the fundamental principles of academic integrity that underpin educational systems (Kumar et al., 2024). This challenge is not merely about policing the use of new technologies; it is about reimagining our approach to language education in a world where AI is an integral part of the linguistic landscape.

In this section, we will explore the multifaceted challenges posed by generative AI tools in language education, discuss strategies for maintaining academic integrity in this new context, and consider approaches to educating students on the ethical use of AI in their studies. My goal, here, is not to present AI as an adversary to academic integrity, but rather to provide a framework for integrating these powerful tools into language education in ways that are ethical, effective, and aligned with the core values of academic honesty and authentic learning (Coghlan et al., 2023). Throughout this discussion, it is crucial to remember that the landscape of AI in education is rapidly evolving. The strategies and approaches discussed in this section will need to be continuously reassessed and adapted as technologies advance and our understanding of their implications deepen. By engaging critically with these issues now, we can help shape a future where AI enhances rather than undermines the integrity and value of language education (Wang et al., 2024). One of the first steps in critically engaging with this discussion is to acknowledge the new, or some cases *re*newed challenges that language educators and practitioners now face in terms of academic integrity. These challenges are multifaceted, affecting various aspects of language learning, assessment, and the overall educational process.

One of the primary concerns is the ease with which AI can generate human-like text. Large language models like GPT-4o and its successors can produce coherent, contextually appropriate writing that is increasingly difficult to distinguish from human-authored content (Brown et al., 2020), and as discussed previously even AI detectors are no remedy because of considerable concerns around algorithmic bias. Therefore, this capability raises significant questions about the authenticity of student work, particularly in written assignments and essays, and perhaps even more critical questions about instructors' abilities to accurately and effectively uncover such lapses in academic integrity. As Susnjak and McIntosh (2024) point out, these AI models can generate essays, answer open-ended questions, and even mimic different writing styles, making it challenging for educators to determine whether a submission is the student's original work or AI-generated. This challenge is then compounded if students take the time to do more than just copy and paste the response – if they take the time to at all modify that response to sound more like them it is even more difficult to spot.

Moving away from compositional writing, consider language translation, where AI tools have made remarkable progress. Neural machine translation systems now offer translations of unprecedented quality, often approaching human-level performance for certain language pairs (Popel et al., 2020). While these tools can be valuable learning aids, they also present challenges in assessing a student's true language proficiency. The line between using translation tools as a learning support and relying on them to complete assignments becomes increasingly blurred, complicating the evaluation of a student's actual language skills. And in programs that culminate in a professional certification, this can degrade the quality and marketability of not only the program but the certification as well.

Moreover, AI's impact extends beyond text generation and translation. Advanced language models can now engage in complex reasoning tasks, answer follow-up questions, and provide explanations for their outputs (Chowdhery, 2022). This capability raises concerns about the integrity of homework assignments, problem-solving tasks, and even some forms of exams. Students might be tempted to use AI not just for generating text, but for working through entire problem sets or analytical tasks, potentially bypassing the learning process these assignments are designed to facilitate.

Another significant challenge lies in the area of personalized learning and adaptive technologies. While these AI-driven systems offer tremendous potential for tailoring education to individual needs, they also raise questions of equity and fairness. More specifically, unequal access to advanced AI tools could create disparities in educational outcomes, with some students having access to powerful AI assistants while others do not. This inequity could extend to the realm of academic integrity, where students with access to more sophisticated AI tools might have an unfair advantage in completing assignments or preparing for assessments by flaunting AI use limitations because their instructors, who may only be familiar with the lower quality output of free-tier models simply are not equipped to identify the oftentimes more complex, more robust output of paid-tier models (e.g., Claude 3 Haiku vs. Claude 3.5 Sonnet or ChatGPT 3.5 vs. ChaptGPT4o).

The use of AI in research and information synthesis presents yet another challenge. AI tools can rapidly analyze vast amounts of information, generate literature reviews, and even propose research questions (Cao et al., 2023). While this capability can greatly enhance the research process, it also raises questions about originality and attribution. How do we ensure that students develop critical research skills when AI can seemingly do much of the work? How do we attribute ideas or insights generated by AI systems? Moreover, how do we ensure that both researchers and reviewers are making appropriate use of AI tools to support what is often an underfunded, or completely gratis, part of the work of the research active language professional? We have, in computer science, already begun to see the damning impacts of AI use during the review process, as even in computer sciences and engineering, reviewing for a journal is free labor (see Lee, 2024).

As we navigate these challenges, it is crucial to remember that the goal is not to entirely prevent the use of AI in education, but rather to find ways to integrate these powerful tools ethically and effectively.

This brings us quite naturally to the question of what does academic integrity look like in an AI-rich world? Is it time to redefine or reconceptualize this term that has been a core part of instructional practice from day one, for many of us that have been trained in a Western academic tradition?

From the discussion on challenges above, our traditional understanding of academic integrity needs to evolve. In this new reality, academic integrity is not merely about avoiding plagiarism or unauthorized assistance; it is about fostering a deeper engagement with learning, critical thinking, and ethical use of technology. To navigate this AI-rich world and maintain our relevance to our learners, I propose that academic integrity should be redefined around the following key principles:

1. Transparency and Disclosure: Academic integrity now includes being open and honest about AI use in one's work. Rather than trying to detect and punish AI use, we should encourage students to disclose when and how they have used AI tools, fostering a culture of transparency.
2. Critical Evaluation and Synthesis: Integrity in an AI-enhanced world means developing the skills to critically evaluate AI-generated content, synthesize information from multiple sources (including AI), and form independent conclusions.
3. Process-Oriented Learning: The focus shifts from the final product to the learning process. Academic integrity involves engaging meaningfully with the subject matter, using AI as a tool for exploration and learning rather than a shortcut to completion.
4. Ethical AI Usage: Students demonstrate integrity by using AI tools responsibly and ethically, understanding their capabilities and limitations, and recognizing when reliance on AI might compromise their learning.
5. Originality of Thought: While AI can generate content, true academic integrity lies in contributing original ideas, perspectives, and analyses that go beyond what AI can produce.
6. Collaborative Intelligence: Integrity in an AI world involves learning to work effectively with AI tools, much like collaborating with human peers, while maintaining one's own intellectual contribution.
7. Digital Literacy and AI Awareness: Academic integrity now encompasses a strong understanding of AI technologies, their implications, and the ability to navigate an AI-enhanced academic environment responsibly.

Under this new paradigm, academic integrity is less about policing student behavior and more about empowering students to be ethical, critical, and innovative users of technology in their learning journey. It acknowledges that AI is an integral part of the modern world and focuses on preparing students to interact with these technologies in ways that enhance rather than undermine their education. Additionally, this redefinition challenges traditional assessment methods and requires a reimagining of how we evaluate student learning and achievement. It calls for new forms of assessment that can gauge a student's ability to work with AI productively while still demonstrating their own understanding and skills. Ultimately, this new concept of academic integrity in the age of AI aims to cultivate learners who are not just consumers of information or users of technology, but critical thinkers, ethical tech users, and innovative problem solvers. It prepares students not just for academic success, but for a future where AI is an integral part of professional and personal life.

While I will be the first to admit that applying such a framework can be challenging, especially in larger institutional settings, there is one place where the language practitioner often has some greater degree of control – namely, their own classroom. To that end, I will now turn our attention to an example of what applying this framework can look like in the language classroom. Here, again, I am providing you this thought experiment as an opportunity to think through an emergent issue in a slightly more structured manner. So, I would encourage you to consider what might be applicable to your own practices and what might require some degree of modification.

In our imagined university-level advanced Uyghur language course, the instructor embraces a version of the redefined principles of academic integrity outlined above to create an AI-inclusive learning environment. The class begins with the introduction of an "AI Use Log," a tool designed to promote transparency and disclosure. Students are encouraged to document their interactions with AI tools during assignments, such as when using AI translators to assist with Uyghur script. They record which phrases they translated and explain how they verified or modified the AI's output, fostering a culture of openness about technology use. From there, they work to develop critical evaluation and synthesis skills, the instructor assigns comparative analysis tasks. Students examine AI-generated translations of Uyghur texts alongside human translations, critically analyzing the differences and discussing cultural nuances that AI might overlook. This exercise not only sharpens their language skills but also hones their ability to critically evaluate AI outputs.

Shifting focus to process-oriented learning, the instructor implements a "writing portfolio" system. Rather than grading solely on final compositions, students showcase their drafts, including AI-assisted versions, and reflect on how they refined the AI-generated content to improve their language skills. This approach emphasizes the learning journey and encourages students to engage meaningfully with the subject matter. Students' new collaborative AI-infused writing processes are further scaffolded through explicit discussions about appropriate use. This is done using the language of Ethical AI usage and exploring more and less appropriate AI use scenarios with students. The class explores situations where AI might be beneficial, such as initial brainstorming, versus instances where it could hinder learning, like generating entire conversations without understanding. Through these discussions, students collaboratively develop guidelines for ethical AI use in their Uyghur studies.

To promote originality of thought, cultural and experiential projects are designed to push students beyond AI-generated information. While they may use AI to gather basic facts about Uyghur traditions, students are required to contribute original analyses. This might involve interviewing Uyghur speakers in their community and comparing these firsthand accounts with AI-generated information, encouraging deeper, more authentic cultural understanding. This helps to reinforce both communicative and collaborative skills, as they will need to build new knowledge and understanding by deploying technological, social, and academic resources in tandem to successfully tackle this new assignment type. It also creates space for additional in-class collaboration, feeding into the notion of collaborative intelligence. This concept is further explored through group projects. Students are encouraged to view AI tools as a "team member" in their creative process. For instance, they might use an AI writing assistant to help draft a script for a Uyghur language skit. However, the emphasis is on collaborative refinement, where students work together to enhance the language, add cultural authenticity, and ultimately perform the skit, demonstrating their ability to work effectively with AI while maintaining their own intellectual contributions.

Digital literacy and AI awareness are, importantly, woven throughout the curriculum. The instructor incorporates lessons on the mechanics of AI language models, their current limitations in processing less-common languages like Uyghur, and potential biases. Students engage in research projects exploring the challenges of developing AI tools for minority languages, presenting their findings to the class. This can even take the form of a service learning project to create a guide to using AI for Uyghur community members with targeted advice about how to get publicly available AI tools more aligned with the values and needs of the community despite the fact that they were likely under-represented in the original training data.

By implementing these practices, the Uyghur language class transforms into a space where AI is not just a tool, but a subject of study and critical engagement. Students develop a nuanced understanding of how to leverage AI in their language learning journey while maintaining the integrity of their academic pursuits. This approach acknowledges the reality of AI's presence in education while ensuring that the unique cultural and linguistic aspects of Uyghur language learning are preserved and enhanced. Through this holistic integration of AI, students are prepared not just for language proficiency, but for ethical and critical engagement with technology in their academic and professional futures.

Building on our exploration of redefining academic integrity and its practical application in language classrooms, we now turn our attention to the broader context of responsibly implementing AI in CALL. While the potential benefits of AI in language education are substantial, their integration must be approached with careful consideration and ethical awareness. In the next section, we will examine three crucial aspects of responsible AI implementation in CALL:

1. Transparency: Ensuring clear communication about when and how AI is being used in language learning processes
2. Purposeful Integration: Incorporating AI tools with clear pedagogical objectives, avoiding technology use for its own sake
3. Scaffolded Approach: Developing a framework that values and prioritizes human expertise while gradually introducing AI support

By addressing these areas, we can create a foundation for the thoughtful and responsible incorporation of AI technologies in language teaching and learning. This approach ensures that we harness AI's potential while maintaining the integrity of our educational practices and the centrality of human interaction in language acquisition across diverse linguistic and technological environments.

On Responsible Implementation

In navigating our new AI-rich reality and purposefully managing the integration of AI technologies into CALL context, it is crucial to approach this process with careful consideration and ethical awareness. The potential benefits of AI in language education are substantial, but they must be balanced against the need to maintain the integrity of the learning process and the centrality of human interaction in language acquisition. Indeed, all that we do must be service to two primary goals: (1) driving student learning and success and (2) ensuring that human expertise is valued above thoughtless generative AI outputs deployed uncritically and without human intervention. This section explores three key aspects of responsible AI implementation in CALL: transparency, purposeful integration, and a scaffolded approach.

Transparency in AI Integration

Transparency is fundamental to the ethical use of AI in language learning environments. It involves clear communication about when and how AI is being used in the learning process. This openness helps build trust between educators, learners, and the technology itself. Its importance to building a collaborative approach to AI integration in language teaching and learning should be readily apparent at this point as it has been a recurrent theme throughout much of the book, beginning with my own attempts to be transparent about my use of generative AI while preparing this text.

In practice, transparency can be achieved through several means. First, learning materials and activities should clearly indicate when AI is involved. For instance, if an AI-powered chatbot is used for conversation practice, students should be explicitly informed that they are interacting with an AI, not a human tutor. Similarly, if AI-generated content is used in teaching resources, this should be disclosed to both educators and learners. Beyond this, learners should be equipped with the tools and critical AI literacy skills to understand how AI impacts their own learning and to be transparent about their own uses. This way we can move away from a deficit-view of the learner than encourages the policing of behavior and towards an environment of collaboration and support. For researchers, this means being transparent about AI's role in review, protocol planning, and data analysis. Again, to create an environment where AI serves as just one more tool in the language professional's quiver, and not a crutch and sign of weakness.

Additionally, this transparency extends to how we talk about AI's capabilities with stakeholders in the language teaching, learning, and research process – working to avoid the scourge of "over-promise/under-deliver" that has defined so much of AI development since the 1950s (see Crawford, 2021; Pasquale, 2020). This then means that explaining AI's role and limitations is equally important. Learners should understand what the AI can and cannot do, preventing unrealistic expectations and encouraging critical engagement with the technology. For example, when introducing an AI writing assistant, educators should clarify that while it can help with grammar and vocabulary suggestions, it may not understand context-specific nuances or cultural references.

Beyond this, as practitioners and researchers, we must work to make AI decision-making processes understandable to students and research participants, as this is another crucial aspect of transparency. While the technical details may be complex, providing simple explanations of how AI generates responses or evaluates language can help users engage more critically with the technology. This might involve basic explanations of concepts like pattern recognition or statistical analysis in language processing.

Purposeful Integration of AI Tools

The integration of AI in CALL should always be driven by clear pedagogical objectives, avoiding the pitfall of using technology merely for its novelty. Each implementation of AI should be justified based on its potential to enhance specific aspects of language learning. This begins when first considering AI tools and the potential place in our professional practice. Educators should first identify the language learning objectives they aim to address. For instance, if the goal is to improve learners' pronunciation, an AI-powered speech recognition tool might be appropriate. However, if the objective is to enhance cultural understanding through conversation, human interaction might be more suitable than an AI chatbot.

A case study can illustrate this principle: In an advanced English writing course, an instructor implements an AI writing assistant. The tool is not used indiscriminately, but specifically to help students with sentence-level grammar and vocabulary choices. The instructor carefully designs assignments that require students to use the AI tool for initial drafting but then engage in peer review and self-reflection to critically evaluate and refine the AI-suggested content. This approach ensures that the AI serves as a scaffold for learning, not a shortcut that bypasses the development of writing skills.

Scaffolded Approach to AI Implementation

A scaffolded approach to AI implementation recognizes the irreplaceable value of human expertise in language instruction while gradually introducing AI tools to support the learning process. This approach ensures that AI enhances rather than replaces human-led instruction. The foundation of this approach is prioritizing human expertise. AI tools should be introduced as supplements to, not substitutes for, human teaching. For example, in a beginner Spanish class, an AI pronunciation coach might be used to provide additional practice outside of class, but it doesn't replace the nuanced feedback and cultural insights a human instructor can provide.

Gradual introduction of AI tools allows both educators and learners to adapt to new technologies without overwhelming the learning process. This might involve starting with simple AI-powered vocabulary flashcards and progressively moving to more complex applications like AI writing assistants or conversational agents. Balancing AI assistance with opportunities for independent language production is crucial. While AI can provide valuable support, learners must also have ample opportunities to use the language without technological aids. This balance helps prevent over-reliance on AI and ensures that learners develop genuine language skills. For instance, a course might use AI-powered grammar checking tools for homework assignments but require students to produce in-class writing samples without any AI assistance.

In conclusion, responsible implementation of AI in CALL requires a thoughtful approach that prioritizes transparency, purposeful integration, and scaffolded implementation. By adhering to these principles, we can harness the potential of AI to enhance language learning while maintaining the integrity of the educational process and the essential role of human interaction in language acquisition. As we continue to explore and expand the use of AI in language education, these guiding principles will help ensure that our approach remains ethical, effective, and centered on the needs of learners.

From Ethics in Action to Purposeful Policy Making

As we have explored throughout this chapter, the integration of AI in language teaching and learning presents both unprecedented opportunities and significant ethical challenges. From data privacy and security concerns to issues of digital equity and inclusivity, from addressing algorithmic biases to reimagining academic integrity, the landscape of AI in education is complex and rapidly evolving.

The ethical considerations we have discussed – transparency, purposeful integration, and a scaffolded approach to AI implementation – serve as guiding principles for navigating this new terrain. These principles underscore the importance of maintaining human expertise at the center of language education while leveraging AI as a powerful tool to enhance learning experiences. Throughout this discussion, I have worked to make clear how transparency in AI use can foster trust and critical engagement among learners, how purposeful integration ensures that AI serves clear pedagogical objectives rather than being employed for its own sake, and how a scaffolded approach can gradually introduce AI tools without overwhelming learners or diminishing the role of human instruction. This extended, quite naturally, into considerations around academic integrity, considering the instructional role in which many language practitioners find themselves. Moreover, this exploration of academic integrity in the age of AI highlights the need for a paradigm shift in how we conceptualize and promote ethical academic practices. By focusing on transparency, critical evaluation, process-oriented learning, and collaborative intelligence, we can cultivate learners who are not just consumers of AI-generated content, but critical thinkers and ethical users of technology.

As we move forward, it is crucial to remember that the ethical integration of AI in language education is an ongoing process that requires continuous reflection, adaptation, and collaboration among educators, learners, researchers, and technology developers. The examples and strategies provided in this chapter serve as starting points for this ongoing conversation and adaptation.

In the next chapter, we will build upon these ethical foundations to explore the practical aspects of crafting classroom and institutional policies that embrace a collaborative AI approach. This will involve translating the principles discussed here into concrete guidelines and practices that can be implemented across various educational contexts. By continuing to engage critically and creatively with AI technologies, we can work towards a future where AI enhances language education in ways that are equitable, inclusive, and aligned with our highest educational ideals. The journey ahead is challenging, but it also offers exciting possibilities for reimagining language teaching and learning in the digital age.

7

Towards Collaborative AI: Classroom and Institutional Policy Considerations

Introduction

AI continues to have growing impacts on language education, there is an urgent need for comprehensive policies that guide its integration at both classroom and institutional levels. However, it is crucial to acknowledge that our policy responses in this domain have largely been emergent, piecemeal, and not well-studied. Indeed, in some contexts policy decisions have been left entirely up to individual instructors, leading to a confusing environment for our learners to navigate as they move through the institution. This reality, along with the more substantial research focus on pedagogical considerations and ethical implications of AI in education, means that the development of cohesive policy frameworks, particularly in language education, has lagged behind our efforts to understand AI's implications for our professional practice and our students' learning.

This gap is understandable given the rapid pace of AI development and its relatively recent widespread integration into educational contexts. Nevertheless, it underscores the pressing need for a concerted move towards a more thoughtful, proactive policymaking that can address the unique challenges and opportunities presented by AI in language teaching and learning. Additionally, it speaks to the real and perceived needs of our learners. During my time working as an AI in Education specialist in Bahrain, the number one request from students was for clarity and support from their teachers and their learning institutions to help them become effective and ethical learners. This concern was echoed by my own students at George Washington University who expressed frustration at the university's varied response to AI in the classroom – with one student mentioning that they had one professor who actively taught about AI because it was an important workplace skill and yet another in the same subject area who denounced it as vociferously as they did traditional academic integrity violations.

Therefore, comprehensive AI policies are essential for several reasons. At the classroom level, they provide clear guidelines for both educators and students, ensuring fair and ethical use of AI tools in language learning activities and assessments. They help maintain academic integrity while harnessing the potential of AI to enhance language acquisition. At the institutional level, such policies ensure consistency across departments, protect student data, align AI use with broader educational goals, and provide a framework for addressing emerging ethical concerns.

In response to the current policy vacuum, I propose a collaborative AI integration approach. This approach recognizes AI not as a replacement for human expertise, but as a powerful tool that can augment and enhance language teaching and learning when used thoughtfully and ethically. While much of this chapter will focus on local (read: classroom-level) and institutional policy making considerations, I will begin by summarizing what a collaborative AI approach looks like in regards to policymaking. In later sections, I will expand on these ideas with salient examples and actionable recommendations for practitioners and administrators.

The collaborative AI integration approach advocated for herein is characterized by:

1. Transparency: Open communication about when and how AI is being used in the educational process
2. Inclusivity: Involving all stakeholders – educators, students, administrators, and technologists – in the policymaking process
3. Flexibility: Creating policies that can adapt to rapidly evolving AI technologies and emerging best practices
4. Ethical considerations: Prioritizing fairness, privacy, and the promotion of genuine language learning
5. Pedagogical focus: Ensuring that AI integration always serves clear educational objectives rather than being implemented for its own sake

By adopting this collaborative approach, I aim to create a framework for policies that foster an environment where AI enhances rather than diminishes the human aspects of language education. These policies should empower educators to innovate with AI tools while providing clear boundaries that protect educational integrity and student interests.

In the following sections, I will explore how to develop and implement such policies at both the classroom and institutional levels. While we may not have a wealth of language education-specific research to draw upon, I will extrapolate from related fields, consider the unique aspects of language learning, and propose novel approaches based on our understanding of the challenges and opportunities AI presents in this context. My goal is to provide a starting point for educators and institutions to develop robust, flexible policies that can evolve alongside AI technology, ensuring that language education remains effective, ethical, and deeply human in an increasingly AI-augmented world.

Developing Classroom Policies for Collaborative AI Integration

As most of us are active educators, the classroom is where we can exert the most control and influence. To that end, it often serves as the primary environment in which we can attempt to exert any meaningful influence over the integration of AI in language education. As educators, our role is to create thoughtful, comprehensive policies that guide AI use in ways that enhance learning while upholding educational integrity. This process requires a delicate balance of embracing technological advancements and preserving the essential human elements of language acquisition. Beyond this, however, it also requires us to partner with the stakeholders that are part of our educational contexts. This may, variably, include co-teachers, administrators, and parents in different settings. But it will always include our learners, who are eager for meaningful and transparent direction that will facilitate their learning while preparing them for an uncertain future.

This, therefore, means that establishing clear guidelines for AI use is a critical part of our approach to integrating AI in language education. The process of developing these guidelines for assignments and assessments begins with a thorough evaluation of your course structure and learning objectives. This reflective process should involve not only personal consideration but also input from students and, where possible, colleagues or educational technologists. By engaging in collaborative discussions about the potential benefits and drawbacks of AI tools in various aspects of your course, you create a foundation of shared understanding and purpose.

However, it is important to recognize that this collaborative process may reveal a disparity of views among stakeholders. Students, for instance, might advocate for more liberal use of AI tools, seeing them as valuable aids in their learning process. Conversely, some colleagues or administrators might express concerns about academic integrity or the potential dilution of traditional language learning methods. Educational technologists might push for cutting-edge AI integration, while you, as the instructor, must balance these perspectives with your pedagogical goals and ethical considerations. Naturally, navigating these diverse viewpoints requires a nuanced approach. Begin by creating a space for open dialogue where all stakeholders feel heard and valued. This could take the form of focus group discussions, anonymous surveys, or a series of one-on-one conversations. The key is to gather a comprehensive understanding of the various perspectives at play. Next, work towards finding common ground. While stakeholders may disagree on specific implementations, they likely share overarching goals such as effective language acquisition, preparation for real-world language use, and maintaining academic integrity. Use these shared objectives as a foundation for building consensus.

When faced with conflicting viewpoints, consider adopting a phased or experimental approach. For example, if there is disagreement about the extent of AI use in writing assignments, you might implement a trial period where different levels of AI assistance are allowed for different assignments. This allows for data collection and evaluation of outcomes, which can inform more permanent policy decisions. It is also crucial to educate all stakeholders about the capabilities and limitations of AI in language learning. Misconceptions or unrealistic expectations often fuel resistance or overenthusiasm. By providing clear, factual information about what AI can and cannot do, you create a more informed basis for policy discussions. It can be helpful to remember that the goal is not necessarily to achieve unanimous agreement, but rather to create policies that are well-reasoned, ethically sound, and pedagogically effective. Be prepared to make difficult decisions, always prioritizing student learning outcomes and ethical considerations. By acknowledging and thoughtfully addressing the disparity of views among stakeholders, you can create more robust, well-rounded AI policies that take into account diverse perspectives while still maintaining a clear focus on educational goals. This inclusive approach not only leads to better policies but also fosters a sense of community and shared purpose in navigating the complex landscape of AI in language education.

Having established the importance of collaborative policymaking and addressing diverse stakeholder viewpoints, let us now turn our attention to the specific components that should be included in a comprehensive classroom AI policy. These concrete elements will form the backbone of your approach to AI integration, providing clear guidance for both you and your students. A well-crafted AI policy should begin with a clear statement of purpose. This introduction should articulate the rationale behind AI integration in your language course, emphasizing how it aligns with learning objectives and prepares students for real-world language use. For instance, you might state: "This policy aims to harness the potential of AI tools to enhance our language learning experience while maintaining the integrity of the learning process and developing critical AI literacy skills."

Next, specify the AI tools permitted in your course. Be as precise as possible, naming specific applications or types of AI assistants allowed. For example: "Students may use Grammarly for grammar and spell-checking, and DeepL for initial translation attempts. The use of ChatGPT or similar large language models for generating original text is not permitted unless explicitly stated in the assignment guidelines." This clarity helps prevent misunderstandings and ensures all students are on equal footing. Additionally, when working with older learners it can be wise to make clear not only what the policy is, but why it is in place. So, if your policy is going to limit tools or stages of work where AI tools can be deployed, it can be helpful to the learner to clearly state why by connecting the rationale back to their learning.

Documentation requirements should form another crucial component of your policy, as this helps to facilitate the transparency necessary for a collaborative approach to AI integration in language teaching and learning. This means that either your course policies or individual assignments will need to outline how students should record and report their AI use. This might involve creating an "AI use log" for each assignment, where students note which tools they used, for what purpose, and how they critically engaged with the AI output. For instance: "For each written assignment, students must submit an AI use log detailing any AI tools used in the writing process, including specific examples of AI suggestions and how these were evaluated and incorporated or discarded." Or it may mean creating a follow up reflective assignment or in-class discussion that centers around AI use and its impacts on their learning.

Addressing the ethical use of AI is paramount. Include guidelines on how students should approach AI-generated content, emphasizing the importance of critical evaluation and original thought. You might state: "While AI tools can assist in the writing process, all submitted work must reflect the student's own analysis, synthesis, and language skills. Directly submitting AI-generated text without substantial revision and critical engagement is considered a violation of academic integrity." It is important to note, here, the detecting AI generated text is far from a certain science. Even AI detectors fail at it with shocking regularity (Sadasivan et al., 2023).

It is also important to outline the consequences for policy violations. These should be clear, fair, and proportionate to the offense. For example: "First-time violations of the AI use policy will result in a mandatory revision of the assignment and a one-on-one meeting to discuss appropriate AI use. Repeated violations may lead to a reduced grade or, in severe cases, course failure." Beyond this, to ensure a robust policy for your classroom, you may want to consider including a section on exceptions and special circumstances. There may be instances where more extensive AI use is permitted or even encouraged as part of a specific learning activity. In doing so, you will want to be sure to clarify how these exceptions will be communicated and managed.

Finally, include a statement on policy evolution; this can be a helpful inclusion because of the emergent nature of AI capabilities and our understanding of how to effectively use these tools to support our learners. The rapid pace of AI development means that what is cutting-edge today may be obsolete tomorrow, and new ethical considerations may arise as technologies advance. Moreover, our pedagogical understanding of how to best integrate AI into language learning is continually evolving based on research and practical experience. So, it is wise to note that the policy may be subject to change. This acknowledgment serves multiple purposes. It prepares students for potential adjustments, demonstrates the instructor's commitment to staying current with technological advancements, and creates a sense of flexibility that can facilitate ongoing dialogue about AI use.

For instance, your policy might state: "This AI use policy will be reviewed and potentially revised at the end of each semester to ensure it remains relevant and effective in light of technological advancements and emerging best practices. Students will be actively involved in this review process through surveys and focus group discussions. Any changes to the policy will be clearly communicated at the beginning of each new semester, with a summary of updates and their rationale provided." Furthermore, consider including a mechanism for mid-semester adjustments if significant developments occur. You might add: "In the event of major AI advancements or newly identified ethical concerns during the semester, interim policy updates may be implemented. These will be discussed in class and require student acknowledgment before taking effect." This approach to policy evolution not only addresses the practical need for keeping guidelines current but also serves as a learning opportunity for students. It models adaptability and critical engagement with technological change, skills that will serve them well in their future careers and personal lives where AI is likely to play an increasingly significant role.

Remember, the goal of these policy components is not to restrict learning, but to create a framework that allows for innovative AI integration while maintaining the integrity of language education. By providing clear guidelines, you empower students to explore AI's potential responsibly and ethically, fostering a learning environment that balances technological assistance with genuine language acquisition and critical thinking skills.

Having outlined the key components of a comprehensive classroom AI policy, including the importance of a statement on policy evolution, we now turn our attention to the crucial task of implementation. Even the most well-crafted policy will have limited impact if not effectively introduced and consistently enforced in the classroom setting. The strategies we employ to communicate and integrate these policies can significantly influence their reception, understanding, and adherence by students. Building on the idea of policy evolution mentioned earlier, it is important to frame the implementation process as an ongoing, adaptive endeavor rather than a one-time announcement. This approach aligns with the dynamic nature of AI technology and our evolving understanding of its role in language education.

Begin by introducing the AI policy at the outset of your course. Dedicate a significant portion of your first class session to discussing the policy, its rationale, and its implications for student learning. This initial introduction should be more than a mere reading of rules; it is an opportunity to engage students in a dialogue about the role of AI in language learning and their future careers. Consider using interactive activities to make this introduction more engaging. For instance, you might present scenarios involving AI use in language learning and ask students to discuss the ethical implications, or have them brainstorm potential benefits and drawbacks of AI in language acquisition. Additionally, and to help ensure thorough understanding, provide the policy in multiple formats. A written document in your syllabus or course management system is essential, but consider also creating a visually appealing infographic or short video explanation. These varied formats can cater to different learning styles and increase retention of the policy details. Moreover, it can be helpful to integrate policy awareness into daily classroom activities. This ongoing reinforcement helps cement the policy's importance and keeps it at the forefront of students' minds. For example, when introducing a new assignment, explicitly discuss how AI tools can and cannot be used. You might say, "For this essay, you are welcome to use Grammarly for initial proofreading, but remember to document this in your AI use log. The use of AI for generating content ideas is not permitted for this particular assignment." To further aid in this, consider implementing a system of "AI check-ins" throughout the semester. These could be brief discussions at the start of class where students share their recent experiences with AI tools, challenges they have encountered, or insights they have gained. This not only reinforces policy awareness but also provides valuable feedback on how students are interacting with AI in their learning process.

Enforcement of the policy should be consistent but educational rather than punitive. When violations occur, use them as teaching moments. Schedule one-on-one meetings with students who have misused AI tools to discuss their understanding of the policy and explore any underlying issues that led to the violation. This approach can help prevent future infractions while deepening students' understanding of ethical AI use. Additionally, consider creating assignments that explicitly engage with AI ethics and policy. This can help not only to reinforce the AI policy in force in your classes, but also to challenge some of the punitive attitudes that students may bring to the classroom with them. For instance, you might assign a reflective essay where students analyze the course AI policy, compare it with policies from other courses or institutions, and propose potential improvements. This not only reinforces policy awareness but also develops critical thinking skills about AI use in education. Finally, be prepared to model proper AI use yourself. When you use AI tools in lesson preparation or demonstration, be transparent about it. Explain to students how you are using the tool, why you chose it, and how you are critically evaluating its output. This modeling reinforces the policy guidelines and demonstrates that ethical AI use is a skill relevant to all language users, not just students. Remember, the goal of implementation is not just compliance, but fostering a classroom culture where ethical and effective AI use becomes second nature. By consistently reinforcing and engaging with the policy, you create an environment where students do not just follow rules, but develop a nuanced understanding of AI's role in language learning and use.

As we implement AI policies in our language classrooms, it is crucial to regularly assess their effectiveness and make necessary adjustments. This ongoing evaluation process ensures that our policies remain relevant, achieve their intended goals, and continue to serve our students' best interests in an ever-evolving technological landscape. To begin the evaluation process, clearly define the goals of your AI policy. These might include promoting ethical AI use, enhancing language learning outcomes, developing critical AI literacy, or maintaining academic integrity. Having well-defined objectives will provide a framework for your assessment.

From there, it can be beneficial to attempt to implement both quantitative and qualitative methods to gather comprehensive data on policy effectiveness. Quantitative measures might include tracking the frequency and types of AI tools used, analyzing changes in assignment scores or language proficiency metrics, or monitoring the number of policy violations over time. Qualitative data can be collected through student surveys, focus group discussions, and individual interviews. These methods can provide invaluable insights into students' experiences with the policy and its impact on their learning process. For example, you can consider creating a rubric for evaluating AI use in assignments. This rubric could assess factors such as the appropriateness of AI tool selection, the critical evaluation of AI-generated content, and the depth of reflection in AI use logs. By systematically applying this rubric across assignments, you can track trends in how students engage with AI tools over the course of the semester. Additional qualitative insights can be gained through touching base with our learners. The regular check-ins with students, mentioned earlier, can serve a dual purpose of reinforcing policy awareness and gathering feedback. Use these sessions to ask pointed questions about the policy's impact on their learning experience. For example: "How has the AI policy influenced your approach to writing assignments?" or "What challenges have you encountered in adhering to the policy?"

That being said, we must be open to the fact that our policy interventions may have unintended consequences, and that these could have negative impacts on learners' experiences in our classes. For instance, has the policy inadvertently created barriers for certain groups of students? Are there signs that the policy is stifling creativity or critical thinking rather than enhancing it? These observations can guide policy refinements. For example, we may choose to impose specific limits on which AI tools can be used by the class – for example, only publicly available, free models can be used by all students and paid models are expressly forbidden. The goal behind this would be to attempt to create a more equal playing field for all learners.

At the end of each semester, conduct a comprehensive review of your policy. Analyze the data you've collected, revisit your initial goals, and assess to what extent they have been met. This review should culminate in a report that outlines successes, challenges, and proposed modifications to the policy. Importantly, involve students in this review process. Consider forming a student advisory group that can provide input on policy revisions. This not only ensures that student perspectives are central to policy development but also models collaborative decision-making – a valuable skill in the AI era.

Remember that policy evaluation is not about achieving perfection, but about continuous improvement. Be transparent with your students about this process. Share the results of your evaluations and the rationale behind any policy changes. This transparency can increase buy-in and reinforce the idea that adapting to technological change is an ongoing, collaborative process. By systematically evaluating and refining your AI policy, you create a dynamic, responsive framework that evolves alongside AI technology and our understanding of its role in language education. This approach ensures that your policy remains a living document, continually aligned with your pedagogical goals and the needs of your students in an AI-enhanced learning environment.

From Classrooms to Institutions

As we conclude our exploration of classroom-level AI policies, it is important to recognize that these localized efforts, while crucial, exist within broader institutional contexts. The insights and practices developed at the classroom level can serve as valuable building blocks for more comprehensive, institution-wide AI policies. This transition from micro to macro policymaking is essential for creating a coherent and effective approach to AI integration across an entire educational institution.

The classroom serves as a vital laboratory for AI policy development. The strategies, guidelines, and evaluation methods we have discussed can be scaled up to inform institutional policies. For instance, the concept of AI use logs, which proved effective in individual classrooms, might be adapted into a standardized reporting system across all language courses in an institution. Similarly, the collaborative policymaking approach involving students could be expanded to include representatives from various departments and student bodies in crafting institution-wide guidelines. However, scaling up is not simply a matter of applying classroom policies wholesale to the entire institution. It requires careful consideration of how these practices can be adapted to serve a more diverse set of stakeholders and a broader range of educational contexts. What works in a small, advanced language class may need significant modification to be effective in large, introductory courses or across different disciplines.

In the next section, we will begin to outline a collaborative AI view of institutional AI policymaking. But, first, I must acknowledge that moving from classroom to institutional policies presents unique challenges. One significant hurdle is achieving consensus among diverse faculty members, each with their own teaching philosophies and varying levels of comfort with AI technology. Institutions must navigate these differing perspectives to create policies that are flexible enough to accommodate various teaching styles while maintaining consistency in core principles. Another challenge lies in ensuring equitable access to AI tools across the institution. While individual instructors might curate AI resources for their specific courses, institutions need to consider how to provide and support AI tools on a larger scale, addressing issues of licensing, technical support, and training. Additionally, data privacy and security concerns also become more complex at the institutional level. While classroom policies might focus on ethical use of AI, institutional policies must grapple with larger questions of data storage, sharing, and compliance with legal regulations like FERPA or GDPR. Furthermore, institutions must consider how AI policies align with existing academic integrity frameworks, assessment practices, and learning outcome metrics. This may require revisiting and potentially revising long-standing institutional policies to accommodate the realities of AI in education.

As we transition to discussing institutional policies in the next section, we'll explore how to address these challenges and develop comprehensive frameworks for AI integration. We'll examine strategies for aligning AI policies with broader institutional goals and values, establishing robust data privacy and security protocols, defining ethical guidelines that can apply across diverse departments, and creating flexible frameworks for AI-enhanced pedagogy that can serve the entire institution. By building on the foundations laid in classroom policy development and thoughtfully addressing the complexities of institution-wide implementation, we can create AI policies that not only enhance language education but contribute to a forward-thinking, technologically adept educational environment across all disciplines.

Collaborative AI and Institutional Policy Making

Aligning AI policies with institutional goals and values is a critical first step in developing a comprehensive approach to AI integration in higher education. This alignment ensures that the adoption of AI technologies serves the broader mission of the institution while addressing the unique challenges and opportunities presented by these emerging tools. The process begins with a thorough institutional AI readiness assessment, which serves as a foundation for informed policymaking and strategic planning.

This assessment involves a multifaceted evaluation of the institution's current technological infrastructure, the AI literacy levels of faculty and staff, and the identification of potential barriers to AI integration. By gauging the existing technological capabilities, institutions can determine what upgrades or investments may be necessary to support AI initiatives effectively. Similarly, assessing the AI literacy of faculty and staff helps identify knowledge gaps and informs the development of training programs. Recognizing potential barriers, whether they be technological, financial, or cultural, allows institutions to proactively address these challenges in their policy development process. Before moving on, however, I want to draw our collective attention to why a coherent institutional policy stance on AI is so vital. At the University of Bahrain, both faculty and students expressed discontent with the slow approach the institution was taking to providing AI policy guidance. The policy vacuum created a sense of uncertainty for students and a feeling of being unsupported by faculty. However, a reactionary approach can lead to similar feelings amongst community members. At The George Washington University, they took a reactive and polyvocal approach – providing faculty with three options for policy alignment ranging from complete prohibition to complete integration. While faculty felt empowered because they could take institution policy and implement it in their classes in a way that they felt supported their learners, students felt confused because each and every class they stepped into, even in the same department, had a different approach to AI integration and they were left to navigate these disparities with little understanding for why they existed in the first place. So, a coherent and collaborative approach to institutional AI integration policy is certainly needed.

That is not to say that this will be a simple task. So to guide this complex process of policy development and implementation, the establishment and empowerment of an agile AI steering committee is crucial. This committee should be diverse and interdisciplinary, comprising administrators, faculty representatives from various departments, IT specialists, legal counsel, and importantly, student representatives. In regard to the composition of this committee, the inclusion of students in this process ensures that their perspectives and concerns are considered, fostering a sense of ownership and engagement in the AI integration process. Beyond this, they should be working off agile development principles to encourage continuous development and deployment of policy stances. This committee bears the responsibility of developing policies, overseeing their implementation, and conducting ongoing evaluations to ensure the policies remain effective and relevant in the face of rapidly evolving AI technologies.

A key task for the AI steering committee is to articulate AI-specific institutional goals that align with and enhance the broader mission of the institution. These goals might include leveraging AI to enhance student learning outcomes, promoting digital literacy and AI competency among students and faculty, maintaining academic integrity in an AI-augmented environment, and preparing students for careers in a world increasingly influenced by AI technologies. By clearly defining these goals, institutions can ensure that their AI policies are purposeful and aligned with their educational mission. However, it is important to recognize that these new AI policies do not exist in isolation. They must be carefully integrated with existing institutional frameworks to ensure coherence and avoid conflicts. This integration involves aligning AI policies with the institution's mission statements and strategic plans, harmonizing them with existing academic integrity policies, and coordinating them with IT and data governance policies. This holistic approach ensures that AI integration enhances rather than disrupts the institution's core values and operational frameworks.

The process of aligning AI policies with institutional goals and values is inherently collaborative and iterative, reflecting the dynamic nature of both AI technology and higher education. This approach recognizes that effective policymaking in this rapidly evolving field cannot be a one-time event, but must instead be an ongoing process of dialogue, assessment, and refinement. Central to this process is the cultivation of ongoing dialogue between various stakeholders. This dialogue should extend beyond the AI steering committee to include regular town halls, departmental meetings, and student forums. For instance, a university might organize semi-annual AI policy symposiums where faculty, students, administrators, and even industry partners come together to discuss the impact of current policies and propose adjustments. These events can serve as a platform for sharing experiences, addressing concerns, and collectively envisioning the future of AI in education.

Regular reassessment of goals in light of technological advancements is another crucial aspect of this iterative process. The rapid pace of AI development means that what seems cutting-edge today may be obsolete tomorrow. Institutions must therefore establish mechanisms for staying abreast of AI advancements and regularly evaluating their implications for educational goals. This might involve partnering with tech companies for early access to emerging AI tools, or creating an AI watchdog group within the institution to monitor and report on significant developments in the field. Moreover, institutions must cultivate a willingness to adapt policies as new challenges and opportunities emerge. This adaptability is key to maintaining relevant and effective AI policies. For example, if a new AI tool gains popularity among students for language learning, the institution should be prepared to quickly assess its potential benefits and risks, and adjust policies accordingly. This might involve creating sandbox environments where new AI tools can be tested and evaluated before being integrated into broader institutional policies.

By approaching policy development in this collaborative and iterative manner, institutions can create a flexible yet robust framework for AI integration. This framework should be designed to evolve alongside technological advancements while remaining firmly grounded in the institution's core educational mission. For instance, a policy framework might include regular review cycles, clear procedures for proposing and implementing changes, and built-in flexibility to accommodate emerging technologies. Such a framework serves the dual purpose of enhancing current educational practices and preparing students for a future where AI plays an increasingly significant role. It allows institutions to leverage AI to improve learning outcomes, streamline administrative processes, and enhance research capabilities. At the same time, it ensures that students gain hands-on experience with AI tools and develop the critical thinking skills necessary to navigate an AI-augmented world.

For example, a language department might use the policy framework to implement an AI-assisted writing program that helps students improve their composition skills while also teaching them to critically evaluate AI-generated text. Meanwhile, the career services department could use the same framework to develop programs that prepare students for AI's impact on various industries, ensuring that graduates are well-equipped for the job market of the future.

In essence, the collaborative and iterative approach to AI policy development creates a living document that reflects the institution's commitment to innovation, ethical technology use, and student success. It acknowledges that the integration of AI in higher education is not a destination but a journey – one that requires constant vigilance, open dialogue, and a willingness to adapt and evolve. As we move forward in developing institutional AI policies, it is crucial to remember that the goal is not to implement AI for its own sake, but to harness its potential to enhance teaching, learning, and research in ways that align with the institution's core values and objectives. This alignment sets the stage for the development of more specific policies around data privacy, ethics, and pedagogy, which we will explore in the following sections.

Establishing robust data privacy and security protocols is a critical component of any institutional AI policy framework. As AI technologies become more deeply integrated into educational processes, they inevitably interact with vast amounts of sensitive student and institutional data. This intersection of AI and data presents both unprecedented opportunities for enhancing learning experiences and significant challenges in maintaining privacy and security. Therefore, institutions must approach this task with utmost diligence and foresight.

The foundation of effective data privacy and security protocols lies in conducting a comprehensive data audit. This audit serves as a crucial first step, providing a clear picture of the types of data collected and processed by AI tools within the institution. It involves methodically cataloging all data touchpoints, from student information systems and learning management platforms to AI-powered tutoring tools and research databases. Beyond mere identification, the audit should map out how data flows within the institution, tracing its path from collection to storage, processing, and potential sharing or deletion. For instance, a language learning department might use AI-powered speech recognition tools to assess student pronunciation. The data audit would need to track not only the audio recordings themselves but also any derived data (such as pronunciation scores), metadata (like timestamps or user IDs), and how this information interfaces with other systems (such as grade books or student profiles). This granular understanding of data flows is essential for identifying potential vulnerabilities and ensuring comprehensive protection.

Armed with insights from the data audit, institutions can then develop AI-specific data protection policies. These policies must ensure compliance with relevant regulations such as the Family Educational Rights and Privacy Act (FERPA) in the United States or the GDPR in the European Union. However, given the unique capabilities of AI to process and analyze data in novel ways, institutions should strive to go beyond mere regulatory compliance. This means establishing clear protocols for data retention and deletion that account for the persistent nature of machine learning models. For example, if an AI system is trained on student writing samples, how can the institution ensure that a student's right to be forgotten is upheld when their data is so intricately woven into the model's parameters? Institutions might consider implementing regular retraining schedules with updated datasets or developing techniques for selective forgetting in AI models. Moreover, data anonymization and pseudonymization techniques should be employed wherever possible. This could involve creating synthetic datasets for AI training purposes or using differential privacy techniques to add noise to datasets in ways that preserve overall patterns while protecting individual privacy. The goal is to maximize the utility of data for AI-driven educational improvements while minimizing the risk of individual identification.

Parallel to these protective measures, institutions must also create guidelines for ethical AI data use. These guidelines should clearly define appropriate uses of student data for AI training and analysis. For instance, is it acceptable to use anonymized student essays to train an AI writing assistant? If so, under what conditions? Establishing clear consent protocols for data collection and use is crucial, ensuring that students (and faculty) understand how their data might be used and have the opportunity to opt out if desired. The implementation of robust cybersecurity measures forms another critical layer of data protection. This includes not only encrypting AI-processed data both in transit and at rest but also regularly updating AI systems to address newly discovered security vulnerabilities. Given the complex and often opaque nature of AI systems, institutions should consider implementing advanced security measures such as federated learning techniques that allow AI models to be trained without raw data ever leaving secure local environments.

Crucially, the human element must not be overlooked in these technical considerations. Comprehensive training programs should be developed to educate staff and faculty on AI-related security best practices. This might include guidance on secure data handling, recognizing potential AI-related phishing attempts, and understanding the implications of sharing certain types of data with AI systems. It is important to note that establishing data privacy and security protocols is not a one-time task but an ongoing process. The rapidly evolving nature of AI technologies means that new data privacy and security challenges will continually emerge. Institutions must therefore establish mechanisms for regular policy reviews and updates, perhaps through a dedicated AI governance committee that works in close collaboration with IT security teams and legal counsel. By taking a proactive and comprehensive approach to data privacy and security, institutions can create an environment where AI can be leveraged to its full potential in education while maintaining the trust and privacy of all stakeholders. This careful balancing act sets the stage for ethical and responsible AI use across all departments, a topic we will explore in the next section.

Defining ethical guidelines for AI use across departments is a critical component of institutional AI policy that requires careful consideration and broad stakeholder engagement. As AI technologies become increasingly integrated into various aspects of higher education, from admissions processes to research methodologies, institutions must grapple with complex ethical questions that often outpace existing regulatory frameworks. The goal is to create a set of principles and practices that ensure AI is used in ways that align with the institution's values, promote fairness and inclusivity, and uphold the highest standards of academic integrity.

A foundational step in this process is the establishment of an AI ethics review board. This board should be diverse in its composition, bringing together ethicists, technologists, educators, and student representatives. The inclusion of multiple perspectives is crucial, as ethical considerations in AI often involve nuanced trade-offs that benefit from varied viewpoints. For instance, an AI system that promises to increase efficiency in grading might be viewed favorably by administrators but raise concerns among educators about the nuances of assessment or among students about the fairness of automated evaluations. The AI ethics review board's responsibilities should extend beyond simply approving or rejecting AI implementations. It should play an active role in shaping the institution's approach to AI, reviewing proposed AI systems not just for technical functionality but for alignment with ethical principles. This might involve developing assessment frameworks that consider factors such as algorithmic bias, transparency, and the potential for unintended consequences.

Building on the work of the ethics review board, institutions should develop a comprehensive AI ethics framework. This framework should articulate core ethical principles that will guide all AI implementations across the institution. These principles might include fairness, transparency, accountability, privacy, and human-centeredness. However, it is crucial that these aren't just lofty ideals but are translated into actionable guidelines. For example, a principle of fairness might be operationalized through requirements for regular bias audits of AI systems, particularly those involved in high-stakes decisions like admissions or scholarship allocations. Transparency could be enforced through mandates for explainable AI, where the reasoning behind AI-driven decisions can be articulated in understandable terms. Accountability might involve creating clear lines of responsibility for AI systems, ensuring that there is always a "human in the loop" for critical decisions. The ethics framework should also address the thorny issue of AI-generated content, a particularly relevant concern in academic settings. Clear guidelines need to be established for when and how AI-generated content can be used in academic work, taking into account discipline-specific norms and the educational goals of different courses. These guidelines should be flexible enough to accommodate the rapid evolution of AI capabilities while maintaining the integrity of academic work.

Implementing these ethical guidelines requires more than just policy documents; it necessitates a culture shift within the institution. To this end, AI ethics training programs should be developed and made mandatory for faculty and staff who will be using or overseeing AI tools. These programs should go beyond simple do's and do nots, fostering a deep understanding of the ethical implications of AI in education. Moreover, AI ethics should not be confined to training programs but should be integrated into the curriculum across disciplines. This could involve developing new courses specifically focused on AI ethics, as well as incorporating ethical considerations into existing courses that touch on AI. For instance, a computer science course on machine learning could include modules on algorithmic bias, while a business course might explore the ethical implications of AI in marketing and customer analytics.

Creating mechanisms for ethical oversight and accountability is another crucial aspect of this process. This could involve establishing clear reporting systems for AI-related ethical concerns, allowing students, faculty, and staff to flag potential issues without fear of reprisal. Regular ethical audits of AI systems and practices should also be conducted, perhaps on an annual basis, to ensure ongoing compliance with ethical guidelines and to identify areas for improvement. It is important to note that ethical guidelines for AI use cannot be static. As AI technologies evolve and new ethical challenges emerge, these guidelines must be regularly reviewed and updated. This might involve annual ethics symposiums where stakeholders from across the institution come together to discuss emerging ethical issues and propose updates to the guidelines. Furthermore, institutions should consider how their AI ethics guidelines interface with broader societal discussions about AI ethics. This could involve participating in inter-institutional collaborations on AI ethics, engaging with policymakers on AI regulation, or partnering with industry to develop ethical AI solutions for education.

By thoughtfully defining and implementing ethical guidelines for AI use across departments, institutions can create an environment where AI enhances rather than compromises educational values. These guidelines serve as a compass, helping navigate the complex ethical terrain of AI in education while fostering a culture of responsible innovation. As we move forward, these ethical considerations will inform the development of frameworks for AI-enhanced pedagogy, which we will explore in the next section.

Creating frameworks for AI-enhanced pedagogy represents the culmination of institutional efforts to integrate AI technologies into the educational landscape. This process involves not just the adoption of new tools, but a fundamental rethinking of teaching and learning practices in light of AI's capabilities. The goal is to harness AI's potential to enhance educational experiences while maintaining the core values and objectives of higher education.

Developing institutional guidelines for AI integration in teaching is a crucial first step. These guidelines should define appropriate uses of AI across different disciplines, recognizing that what works in a computer science course may not be suitable for a literature seminar. For instance, in a language learning course, AI-powered chatbots might be used to provide students with conversational practice, while in a physics course, AI simulations could help students visualize complex phenomena. The key is to ensure that AI tools are used to augment, not replace, the critical thinking and creativity that are hallmarks of higher education. These guidelines should also establish best practices for AI-enhanced instruction and assessment. This might include protocols for using AI in grading, ensuring that automated assessments are fair, transparent, and aligned with learning objectives. It is crucial to strike a balance between the efficiency AI can offer and the nuanced understanding that human educators bring to the assessment process.

Implementing AI competency standards for educators is another vital component of this framework. As AI becomes more prevalent in educational settings, it is essential that faculty and staff are equipped with the knowledge and skills to use these tools effectively and ethically. This could involve creating AI literacy programs that cover not just the technical aspects of AI but also its pedagogical applications and ethical implications. These programs should be tailored to different levels of expertise and comfort with technology. For some faculty, this might mean introductory workshops on AI basics and their potential applications in education. For others, it could involve more advanced training on developing AI-enhanced curricula or even creating custom AI tools for their courses. Establishing mentorship programs can also be valuable, pairing AI-savvy educators with those looking to integrate AI into their teaching for the first time.

Fostering innovation in AI-enhanced pedagogy should be a key focus of these frameworks. Institutions might consider creating grants or incentives for AI-enhanced course development, encouraging faculty to experiment with new AI tools and pedagogical approaches. This could lead to the development of novel teaching methods that leverage AI's capabilities in ways we have yet to imagine. Establishing centers for AI in education research and development can further drive innovation. These centers could serve as hubs for interdisciplinary collaboration, bringing together educators, computer scientists, and learning scientists to explore the frontiers of AI in education. They could also partner with ed-tech companies to pilot new AI tools and provide valuable feedback from an educational perspective. Developing support structures for AI-enhanced learning is crucial for the success of these initiatives. This might involve creating AI-specific learning resource centers where students can get help with AI tools used in their courses. Training teaching assistants and tutors in AI-enhanced pedagogy ensures that support is available at all levels of the educational experience.

Establishing assessment frameworks for AI-enhanced courses is essential to ensure that these new approaches are actually improving learning outcomes. This involves developing guidelines for AI-aware assignment design, creating protocols for evaluating the effectiveness of AI integration in courses, and establishing methods for gathering and analyzing data on student engagement and performance in AI-enhanced learning environments. It is important to note that these assessment frameworks should go beyond traditional metrics. They should consider how AI tools are impacting students' critical thinking skills, creativity, and ability to apply knowledge in real-world contexts. This might involve developing new types of assessments that can capture these more nuanced aspects of learning.

Facilitating cross-departmental collaboration on AI integration is another crucial aspect of these frameworks. AI's potential in education cuts across disciplinary boundaries, and there is much to be gained from sharing experiences and best practices. Organizing interdisciplinary workshops and conferences on AI in education can foster this kind of collaboration. Creating platforms for sharing AI-enhanced teaching practices across departments can help spread innovative ideas and prevent duplication of efforts. As with all aspects of AI integration in education, creating frameworks for AI-enhanced pedagogy should be an iterative process. Regular review and refinement of these frameworks are necessary to keep pace with rapidly evolving AI technologies and our growing understanding of their educational impacts. Moreover, it is crucial that these frameworks maintain a focus on the human aspects of education. While AI can offer powerful tools for enhancing learning, it should not come at the cost of the personal interactions and mentorship that are at the heart of the educational experience. The goal should be to use AI to free up educators to focus more on these high-value, uniquely human aspects of teaching.

By thoughtfully creating and implementing frameworks for AI-enhanced pedagogy, institutions can position themselves at the forefront of educational innovation. These frameworks provide a structure for leveraging AI's potential while maintaining the core values and objectives of higher education. As we look to the future, it is clear that AI will play an increasingly significant role in education. By proactively developing these frameworks, institutions can shape that future in ways that benefit all learners.

While creating robust institutional policy guidance provides the structural foundation for integrating AI into educational practices, the success of these initiatives ultimately depends on the culture within which they are implemented. Even the most well-crafted policies and innovative frameworks can fall short if they are not embraced and actively supported by the entire institutional community. This brings us to a crucial aspect of institutional AI integration: fostering a collaborative AI culture.

A collaborative AI culture goes beyond mere policy implementation; it involves cultivating an environment where AI is seen not as a threat or a panacea, but as a powerful tool to be explored, understood, and leveraged collectively for the benefit of all. This culture is characterized by open dialogue, shared learning experiences, and a collective commitment to responsible AI use. In the following section, we will explore how institutions can promote transparency in AI use, encourage cross-departmental collaboration and knowledge sharing, and create robust support systems for AI-enhanced teaching and learning. These elements are essential for transforming AI policies and frameworks from abstract guidelines into living, breathing aspects of institutional culture.

Fostering a Culture of Collaborative AI

Fostering a culture of collaborative AI represents the crucial next step in the journey of AI integration within higher education institutions. While robust policies and frameworks provide the necessary structure for AI adoption, it is the cultivation of a supportive, inclusive, and innovative culture that breathes life into these initiatives. This cultural shift is not merely about accepting AI as a new tool in the educational toolkit; rather, it is about embracing AI as a collaborative partner in the pursuit of educational excellence, one that requires ongoing dialogue, ethical consideration, and collective engagement from all members of the institutional community.

In this section, we explore the multifaceted approach required to nurture such a culture. From promoting transparency in AI use and encouraging cross-departmental collaboration to creating comprehensive support systems and ensuring ethical, inclusive AI practices, each aspect plays a vital role. By fostering a culture of collaborative

AI, institutions can create an environment where AI enhances rather than replaces human expertise, where innovation flourishes alongside critical reflection, and where the benefits of AI are equitably distributed across the educational landscape. This cultural foundation is essential not only for the successful implementation of AI technologies but also for preparing students, faculty, and staff to thrive in an increasingly AI-driven world.

Promoting transparency in AI use at all levels is a cornerstone of fostering a culture of collaborative AI within educational institutions. Transparency not only builds trust among stakeholders but also facilitates informed decision-making, encourages responsible AI use, and promotes a shared understanding of AI's role in the educational ecosystem. As AI systems become more prevalent and complex, the need for clear, accessible information about their use becomes increasingly critical.

Developing a comprehensive AI transparency policy is the first step in this process. This policy should clearly define what information about AI use should be disclosed, to whom, and through what channels. For instance, it might mandate that any use of AI in grading or assessment be explicitly communicated to students, or that all AI-assisted research be clearly labeled as such in publications. The policy should also establish regular channels for AI-related communications, such as dedicated sections in institutional newsletters or regular email updates about new AI implementations. To operationalize this transparency, institutions should consider creating and maintaining AI inventories and usage reports. A public catalog of AI tools used across the institution can serve as a valuable resource for students, faculty, and staff, allowing them to understand what AI technologies are available and how they are being used. This catalog might include brief descriptions of each tool, its intended use, and any potential implications for learning or assessment. Additionally, producing annual reports on AI integration and its impacts can provide a broader view of the institution's AI journey, highlighting successes, challenges, and future directions.

Implementing explainable AI practices is another crucial aspect of transparency. While some AI models, particularly deep learning systems, can be notoriously opaque, efforts should be made to use interpretable AI models where possible, especially in high-stakes educational contexts. When black-box models are necessary, institutions should develop guidelines for explaining AI-driven decisions to stakeholders in clear, non-technical language. For example, if an AI system is used to flag students at risk of academic failure, there should be clear protocols for explaining to students and advisors what factors contributed to this assessment.

Facilitating open dialogue about AI is perhaps the most dynamic aspect of promoting transparency. Regular town halls and forums on AI use in the institution can provide opportunities for stakeholders to ask questions, express concerns, and share ideas about AI implementation. These events should not be mere presentations of decisions already made, but genuine opportunities for collaborative discussion and problem-solving. Creating multiple channels for feedback and concerns about AI implementation – such as dedicated email addresses, online forums, or AI ombudspersons – ensures that transparency is not just about information flowing outward, but also about actively listening to and addressing stakeholder perspectives.

It is important to note that promoting transparency in AI use is not without challenges. There may be concerns about intellectual property or competitive advantage that limit how much detail can be shared about certain AI systems. Additionally, the complexity of some AI technologies can make true transparency difficult to achieve without oversimplification. Institutions must navigate these challenges carefully, always striving for the highest degree of transparency possible while respecting other important considerations. Moreover, transparency should not be seen as an end in itself, but as a means to foster understanding, engagement, and responsible use of AI. As such, transparency efforts should be coupled with education initiatives that help stakeholders interpret and act on the information provided. For instance, alongside the catalog of AI tools, the institution might offer workshops on how to critically evaluate AI systems or integrate them effectively into teaching and learning practices. By prioritizing transparency in AI use at all levels, institutions lay the groundwork for a culture where AI is not a mysterious force operating behind the scenes, but a well-understood, collaboratively managed tool for enhancing education. This transparency sets the stage for the cross-departmental collaboration and knowledge sharing that we will explore in the next section, as a well-informed institutional community is better equipped to work together in leveraging AI's potential.

Encouraging cross-departmental collaboration and knowledge sharing is a vital component in fostering a culture of collaborative AI within educational institutions. The multidisciplinary nature of AI and its wide-ranging applications across various fields of study make it imperative that institutions break down traditional silos and create avenues for shared learning and cooperative innovation. This collaborative approach not only maximizes the potential of AI integration but also ensures a more holistic and balanced implementation that considers diverse perspectives and needs.

Establishing AI working groups and communities of practice serves as a foundational step in this process. These interdisciplinary teams bring together faculty, staff, and students from different departments to tackle AI-related challenges collectively. For instance, a working group might be formed to explore the ethical implications of AI use in research, drawing expertise from computer science, philosophy, and various applied fields. Communities of practice, on the other hand, can provide more informal platforms for sharing AI best practices across departments. These could take the form of regular meetups, online forums, or collaborative workspaces where individuals can share experiences, ask questions, and collaboratively solve problems related to AI integration in their respective areas.

Organizing cross-departmental AI events and workshops further reinforces this collaborative culture. AI symposiums can serve as a showcase for innovative AI applications across different disciplines, inspiring new ideas and potential collaborations. Hackathons focused on solving institutional challenges using AI can bring together diverse teams, fostering creativity and cross-pollination of ideas. Department exchanges centered on AI applications provide opportunities for in-depth exploration of how AI is being used in different academic contexts. For example, a workshop where the English department shares its experiences with AI-powered writing assistants could spark ideas for similar tools in other language-based disciplines.

Developing an institutional AI knowledge base is crucial for sustaining and scaling collaborative efforts. This centralized repository of AI resources, case studies, and best practices serves as a living document of the institution's collective AI wisdom. It might include technical guides, ethical frameworks, success stories, and lessons learned from AI implementations across different departments. Importantly, this knowledge base should be dynamic, with systems in place for continuous updates and contributions from across the institution. This could be achieved through a wiki-style platform or regular submission processes, ensuring that the knowledge base remains current and relevant.

Fostering AI champions across departments is another effective strategy for promoting collaboration and knowledge sharing. These individuals serve as bridges between their departments and the broader institutional AI initiatives. AI champions can be faculty members who have successfully integrated AI into their teaching or research, or staff members who have leveraged AI to improve administrative processes. By identifying and supporting these champions, institutions create a network of AI expertise distributed across departments. An AI mentor program can further spread this expertise, pairing AI-savvy individuals with those looking to integrate AI into their work.

It is important to note that encouraging cross-departmental collaboration in AI is not without its challenges. Different disciplines may have varying levels of AI readiness or divergent views on the role of AI in their field. There may also be concerns about resource allocation or credit for collaborative work. Institutions must be prepared to address these challenges proactively, perhaps by establishing clear guidelines for collaborative AI projects or creating incentive structures that reward cross-departmental cooperation. Moreover, collaboration should not be pursued at the expense of disciplinary depth. The goal is to complement specialized knowledge with interdisciplinary insights, not to homogenize approaches to AI across the institution. Each department should be encouraged to explore how AI can best serve their specific needs and objectives, while also contributing to and drawing from the collective AI knowledge of the institution.

By fostering robust cross-departmental collaboration and knowledge sharing, institutions can create a rich ecosystem of AI innovation and learning. This collaborative environment not only enhances the quality and scope of AI integration but also prepares students for a world where interdisciplinary AI literacy is increasingly valuable. As we move forward, this culture of collaboration sets the stage for creating comprehensive support systems for AI-enhanced teaching and learning, which we will explore in the next section.

Creating robust support systems for AI-enhanced teaching and learning is a critical component in fostering a culture of collaborative AI within educational institutions. As AI technologies become more prevalent in educational settings, it is essential to ensure that all stakeholders – faculty, staff, and students – have access to the resources, knowledge, and assistance they need to effectively leverage these tools. Well-designed support systems not only facilitate the adoption of AI technologies but also promote innovation, ensure responsible use, and help maximize the educational benefits of AI integration. To this end, establishing AI support centers serves as a cornerstone of these support systems. These dedicated spaces act as hubs for AI experimentation, learning, and problem-solving. They can be physical locations equipped with the latest AI technologies, as well as virtual platforms accessible to the entire institutional community. These centers should offer a range of services, from hands-on workshops with AI tools to one-on-one consultations on integrating AI into curricula. For instance, a language professor looking to incorporate an AI-powered conversation partner into their course could visit the center to explore available tools, discuss pedagogical approaches, and receive technical assistance in implementation.

Developing comprehensive AI training programs is crucial for building institutional capacity in AI-enhanced education. These programs should offer tiered learning pathways to accommodate different levels of AI proficiency and diverse needs across the institution. For beginners, introductory courses might cover AI basics, ethical considerations, and foundational applications in education. More advanced tracks could explore topics like designing AI-enhanced curricula, data analysis for personalized learning, or even programming custom AI tools for specific educational needs. Regular workshops on emerging AI tools and techniques ensure that the institution stays at the forefront of educational AI innovation.

Implementing AI-enhanced learning analytics represents a powerful application of AI in supporting teaching and learning. By leveraging AI to analyze educational data, institutions can provide personalized learning support at scale. This might involve AI systems that identify students at risk of falling behind and suggest targeted interventions, or tools that analyze patterns in student engagement to help instructors optimize their teaching strategies. Developing user-friendly dashboards for tracking AI's impact on learning outcomes allows educators to make data-informed decisions about their teaching practices and helps administrators assess the effectiveness of AI initiatives.

Creating AI-focused educational technology teams is essential for providing specialized, ongoing support for AI integration. These teams should comprise a mix of technologists, instructional designers, and educators who can bridge the gap between AI capabilities and pedagogical needs. They can assist in selecting appropriate AI tools for different educational contexts, provide technical support for AI-enhanced teaching initiatives, and help troubleshoot issues as they arise. Moreover, these teams can play a crucial role in evaluating new AI technologies and their potential applications in the institution's specific educational context.

It is important to note that creating support systems for AI-enhanced teaching and learning is not just about providing technical assistance. It also involves cultivating a mindset of continuous learning and adaptation. As AI technologies evolve rapidly, support systems must be flexible and responsive to changing needs. This might involve regular reassessment of support offerings, gathering feedback from users, and staying abreast of developments in the field of AI in education. Furthermore, these support systems should be designed with inclusivity in mind. They must cater to a diverse range of users with varying levels of technological proficiency, different disciplinary backgrounds, and diverse learning needs. This might involve offering support in multiple languages, ensuring accessibility for users with disabilities, and providing options for both synchronous and asynchronous assistance.

The creation of these support systems should also be seen as an opportunity for collaborative learning and innovation. For example, students in computer science or education programs might be involved in developing and maintaining these support systems as part of their coursework or research projects. This not only provides valuable real-world experience for students but also brings fresh perspectives to the support offerings. By creating comprehensive support systems for AI-enhanced teaching and learning, institutions demonstrate their commitment to making AI an integral and accessible part of the educational experience. These systems empower educators to innovate in their teaching, enable students to engage more deeply with AI tools, and foster a culture where AI is seen as a collaborative partner in the educational process. As we move forward, this supportive environment sets the stage for cultivating an ethical AI mindset.

Cultivating an ethical AI mindset is a crucial component in fostering a culture of collaborative AI within educational institutions. As AI technologies become more deeply integrated into various aspects of academic life, from admissions processes to research methodologies, it is imperative that all stakeholders approach AI with a keen awareness of its ethical implications. This ethical mindset goes beyond mere compliance with rules; it involves developing a nuanced understanding of AI's potential impacts and a commitment to using AI in ways that align with the institution's values and broader societal good. Integrating AI ethics into the institutional culture forms the foundation of this effort. This integration should be visible at all levels, from the institution's mission statement to its day-to-day operations. For instance, an institution might revise its values statement to explicitly mention responsible and ethical AI use. Regular communications about AI initiatives should consistently highlight ethical considerations, normalizing the practice of ethical reflection in AI-related decision-making. This could involve featuring "AI ethics moments" in institutional newsletters or social media posts, where brief scenarios or questions prompt the community to consider ethical aspects of AI use.

Developing AI ethics training for all stakeholders is essential for building this ethical mindset across the institution. For students, mandatory AI ethics courses can be integrated into the core curriculum, ensuring that every graduate has a foundational understanding of AI ethics regardless of their major. These courses should cover topics such as algorithmic bias, privacy concerns, the societal impacts of AI, and frameworks for ethical decision-making in AI contexts. For faculty and staff, ongoing ethics training can take the form of workshops, seminars, or online modules. These should be tailored to different roles and departments, addressing the specific ethical challenges that might arise in various academic and administrative contexts.

Establishing AI ethics consultation services provides a valuable resource for the institutional community. This service could offer easy access to ethics experts who can provide guidance on AI-related ethical questions. For example, a researcher considering using an AI tool for data analysis could consult with an ethics expert to discuss potential biases in the AI model and strategies for mitigating them. Additionally, offering ethical review services for AI projects, similar to Institutional Review Boards for human subjects research, ensures that ethical considerations are systematically addressed in AI implementations across the institution. These consultation services can help to foster a critical approach to AI integration by encouraging critical thinking about AI, which is crucial for developing a truly ethical AI mindset. This involves creating spaces for open dialogue and debate about the societal impacts of AI. Institutions might organize regular panel discussions or debates on controversial AI topics, inviting experts from various fields to provide diverse perspectives. Integrating AI ethics case studies into courses across disciplines helps students apply ethical reasoning to real-world scenarios. For instance, a business course might examine the ethical implications of using AI in hiring processes, while a healthcare course could explore the ethical considerations of AI-assisted diagnoses.

It is important to recognize that cultivating an ethical AI mindset is not about prescribing a single "correct" ethical stance on AI issues. Rather, it is about equipping the institutional community with the tools to engage in thoughtful ethical reasoning and to navigate the complex ethical landscape of AI. This involves fostering an environment where ethical questions are welcomed and where there is an understanding that many AI ethics issues involve balancing competing values and considerations. Moreover, the ethical AI mindset should extend beyond considering the direct impacts of AI use within the institution. It should also encompass reflection on the broader societal implications of the AI technologies being developed or studied within the academic community. This might involve discussions about the potential dual-use nature of AI research or the long-term consequences of advancing certain types of AI technologies.

Institutions should also consider how to assess and reinforce the ethical AI mindset over time. This could involve incorporating ethical considerations into the evaluation criteria for AI-related projects or creating awards that recognize exemplary ethical practices in AI use or development. Regular surveys or focus groups could help gauge the prevalence and depth of ethical thinking about AI across the institution, informing ongoing efforts to cultivate this mindset. By cultivating an ethical AI mindset, institutions not only promote responsible AI use within their own communities but also prepare students to be ethically conscious AI practitioners and citizens in their future careers. This ethical foundation is crucial for ensuring that the power of AI is harnessed in ways that benefit society and align with human values. As we move forward, this ethical mindset sets the stage for fostering innovation and experimentation with AI.

Fostering innovation and experimentation with AI is a critical aspect of cultivating a culture of collaborative AI within educational institutions. This approach not only drives the development of novel AI applications in education but also creates an environment where creativity flourishes, and where the full potential of AI can be explored and realized. By encouraging innovation, institutions can position themselves at the forefront of AI-enhanced education, continuously improving their practices and preparing students for a rapidly evolving technological landscape. The first part of facilitating the creativity of instructional faculty and staff is to ensure that such efforts are appropriately recognized and receive necessary fiscal support.

To meet this need, creating AI innovation grants and challenges can be an effective way to stimulate creative thinking and practical application of AI in educational contexts. Institutions can offer funding for novel AI applications in education, encouraging faculty, staff, and students to propose innovative ideas that leverage AI to enhance teaching, learning, or administrative processes. These grants could range from small seed funding for early-stage ideas to larger awards for more developed projects. Additionally, organizing competitions to solve institutional problems using AI can engage the community in collaborative problem-solving. For instance, a challenge might focus on using AI to improve student engagement in online courses or to enhance accessibility for students with disabilities. This challenge can be further supported by establishing AI sandboxes and testbeds for development and practice. These spaces provide safe environments for experimenting with new AI tools and methodologies. These controlled spaces allow innovators to trial AI applications without risking disruption to core educational processes. For example, a sandbox environment might be set up to test an AI-powered adaptive learning system before deploying it in actual courses. These sandboxes should be equipped with representative datasets and simulated scenarios that mirror real-world educational contexts. Furthermore, facilitating pilot programs for AI-enhanced teaching methods allows for controlled, real-world testing of promising innovations. These pilots should be carefully designed with clear objectives, evaluation criteria, and feedback mechanisms to ensure that insights gained can inform broader implementation decisions.

Partnering with AI companies and researchers can significantly accelerate an institution's AI innovation efforts. Collaborations with industry partners can provide access to cutting-edge AI technologies and real-world perspectives on AI applications. These partnerships might involve co-developing educational AI tools, participating in beta testing of new AI products, or creating internship opportunities for students in AI-related roles. Equally important is participation in academic research networks focused on AI in education. These collaborations can foster the exchange of ideas, methodologies, and findings across institutions, contributing to the broader advancement of AI in education.

Moreover, celebrating AI success stories is crucial for maintaining momentum and enthusiasm for AI innovation. Much of the innovative practices that practitioners develop go un- or under-recognized. Therefore, institutions should actively recognize and publicize innovative uses of AI across departments. This could involve featuring AI projects in institutional publications, organizing showcase events where innovators can present their work, or creating awards for exceptional AI initiatives. Sharing detailed case studies of successful AI integrations not only provides recognition but also offers valuable insights and inspiration for others in the institutional community.

It is important to note that fostering innovation and experimentation with AI should be balanced with responsible practices and ethical considerations. Innovators should be encouraged to consider the ethical implications of their AI projects from the outset, perhaps by incorporating ethical review processes into innovation grant applications or sandbox testing protocols. Moreover, the institution should provide resources and guidance on responsible AI development practices, ensuring that innovation efforts align with the institution's values and ethical standards. Moreover, Institutions should also consider how to make AI innovation inclusive and accessible to all members of the community. This might involve providing extra support or mentorship for those less experienced with AI technologies, or ensuring that innovation initiatives span a wide range of disciplines and application areas. Encouraging interdisciplinary collaboration in AI projects can lead to particularly innovative outcomes, as diverse perspectives often spark creative solutions. Furthermore, fostering a culture of constructive failure is essential in innovation efforts. Not all AI experiments will succeed, and it is important to frame these experiences as valuable learning opportunities rather than setbacks. Institutions might consider creating "failure forums" where innovators can share lessons learned from unsuccessful AI projects, fostering a community of practice that values iteration and continuous improvement.

By actively fostering innovation and experimentation with AI, institutions create a dynamic environment where the boundaries of AI in education are constantly being pushed. This not only leads to tangible improvements in educational practices but also instills a spirit of innovation in students, preparing them to be creative problem-solvers in an AI-driven world. These habits of minds and work skills will be vital to helping future-proof our learners as they enter a rapidly evolving labor market (McKinsey and Company, 2023). As we move forward, this culture of innovation sets the stage for ensuring inclusivity in AI implementation, which we will explore in the next section.

Ensuring inclusivity in AI implementation is a critical component of fostering a truly collaborative AI culture within educational institutions. As AI technologies become more prevalent in educational settings, it is essential to ensure that these tools and practices are accessible, equitable, and beneficial to all members of the institutional community, regardless of their background, abilities, or level of technological expertise. This commitment to inclusivity not only aligns with broader educational equity goals but also enhances the effectiveness and reach of AI initiatives. Therefore, addressing AI accessibility issues should be a primary concern in any AI implementation. This involves ensuring that AI tools and platforms are usable by students, faculty, and staff with diverse needs, including those with disabilities. For instance, AI-powered learning platforms should be compatible with screen readers for visually impaired users, and voice-activated AI assistants should have alternatives for users with speech impairments. Developing guidelines for inclusive AI design can help standardize these practices across the institution. These guidelines might include principles such as providing multiple means of engagement with AI tools, ensuring that AI-generated content is accessible in various formats, and regularly testing AI systems with diverse user groups.

Mitigating AI-related biases is another crucial aspect of ensuring inclusivity. AI systems can inadvertently perpetuate or even amplify existing societal biases, particularly when trained on historical data that may reflect past inequities. Institutions should implement regular bias audits of AI systems, examining them for potential discriminatory outcomes across different demographic groups. This might involve analyzing the performance of AI-powered admissions screening tools across various ethnicities, genders, and socioeconomic backgrounds, or assessing whether AI-generated course recommendations show any systematic biases. Creating diverse teams for AI development and implementation can help catch potential biases early in the process, as team members from different backgrounds can offer varied perspectives on how AI systems might impact different groups.

Bridging the AI divide is essential for ensuring that all members of the institutional community can benefit from AI advancements. This involves providing resources to ensure equal access to AI tools, which might include lending programs for necessary hardware, ensuring campus-wide access to high-speed internet, or providing cloud computing resources for AI projects. Additionally, offering additional support for students less familiar with AI technologies is crucial. This could take the form of introductory AI workshops, peer mentoring programs, or AI help desks staffed by knowledgeable students or staff. The goal is to create an environment where lack of prior exposure to AI doesn't become a barrier to academic success or participation in AI-enhanced learning experiences.

Promoting diverse perspectives in AI decision-making is vital for creating inclusive AI policies and practices. This involves ensuring representation from various groups in AI committees and working groups. For instance, when forming an AI ethics board, institutions should strive to include members from different academic disciplines, cultural backgrounds, and levels of the organization, including student representatives. Actively seeking input from underrepresented groups on AI initiatives can uncover potential issues or opportunities that might otherwise be overlooked. This could involve holding focus groups with diverse student populations to gather feedback on proposed AI tools, or creating channels for ongoing input from faculty and staff across all departments and roles. It is important to recognize that ensuring inclusivity in AI implementation is an ongoing process that requires continuous attention and adaptation. As AI technologies evolve and new applications emerge, new inclusivity challenges may arise. Institutions should establish mechanisms for regularly assessing the inclusivity of their AI practices, perhaps through annual equity audits or by incorporating inclusivity metrics into their overall AI strategy evaluation.

Moreover, fostering inclusivity in AI implementation extends beyond just providing access and mitigating biases. It also involves empowering all members of the institutional community to be active participants in shaping the AI landscape. This might involve creating opportunities for students from all disciplines to engage in AI projects, not just those in technical fields. It could also mean providing resources and support for faculty from diverse backgrounds to incorporate AI into their teaching and research, ensuring that AI applications in education reflect a wide range of perspectives and needs. Additionally, institutions should also consider the global implications of their AI practices, particularly if they have international student populations or global partnerships. This might involve ensuring that AI tools can function effectively across different languages and cultural contexts, or considering how AI implementation might impact students from regions with different levels of technological infrastructure.

By prioritizing inclusivity in AI implementation, institutions can create an environment where AI enhances educational opportunities for all, rather than exacerbating existing inequalities. This inclusive approach not only aligns with the fundamental values of higher education but also enriches the AI ecosystem with diverse perspectives and experiences. As we conclude this chapter on fostering a culture of collaborative AI, it is clear that inclusivity is not just an add-on consideration, but a core principle that should inform every aspect of AI integration in educational settings.

Policy Requires a Foundation of a Well-trained Community

As we have explored throughout this chapter, the integration of AI in educational settings presents both significant opportunities and complex challenges. The development of comprehensive, collaborative AI policies at both classroom and institutional levels is crucial for harnessing the potential of AI while maintaining the integrity and human-centeredness of education. By adopting a transparent, inclusive, and flexible approach to AI integration, institutions can create an environment where AI enhances rather than diminishes the educational experience. Key to this process is the fostering of a collaborative AI culture that extends beyond mere policy implementation. This culture encourages innovation, promotes ethical considerations, and ensures inclusivity in AI use across all levels of the institution. It requires ongoing dialogue, continuous learning, and a willingness to adapt as AI technologies and our understanding of their educational impacts evolve. And as we look to the future of AI in education, it becomes increasingly clear that the success of these initiatives will largely depend on the preparedness of our educators. The policies and frameworks we have discussed provide a crucial foundation, but their effective implementation relies on teachers who are well-equipped to navigate this new landscape. This brings us to our next critical area of focus: teacher education.

In the following chapter, we will explore how teacher education programs can be designed to prepare educators for collaboration with AI systems. We will examine strategies for equipping teachers with the knowledge, skills, and mindsets necessary to create effective and functional AI-enhanced learning environments. By bridging the gap between policy and practice, we can ensure that the potential of AI in education is fully realized, benefiting learners and educators alike in this rapidly evolving digital age.

8

Teacher Professional Development for AI Integration

The rapid advancement of AI in education has created an urgent need for comprehensive professional development programs focused on AI integration in language teaching. As AI tools become increasingly prevalent in educational settings, language educators must be equipped not only with technical knowledge but also with the critical skills to evaluate, implement, and adapt these technologies effectively. This chapter draws on firsthand experiences from AI-focused teacher training initiatives conducted in Bahrain through the US Department of State's English Language Programs Office, offering insights that bridge theory and practice.

While generative AI's advent may feel at once all-too-recent and mostly historical fact at this point, relatively little work has been done on effective teacher education strategies to prepare educators for an AI-rich world. Some of the more recent studies have highlighted the growing importance of AI literacy among educators. Zhai et al. (2021) emphasize that teachers' understanding of AI significantly impacts its successful integration into classroom practices. However, as Chen et al. (2020) point out, many educators still feel underprepared to use AI tools effectively, often experiencing anxiety or skepticism towards these technologies. This refrain is echoed by the contributors to Searson et al.'s (2024) edited collection on teacher education in an age of AI, but with a more hopeful note by connecting recent AI innovations and skill demands to those that had to be mastered by teachers in the past when the computer first entered the classroom in the late 1980s/early 1990s and then when the internet arrived in the 2000s.

Here, my work with university teacher educators at the University of Bahrain and K-12 English teachers at the Ministry of Education revealed several key principles for effective AI-focused professional development. First, addressing educators' AI anxiety is crucial for fostering openness to new technologies. Second, hands-on experimentation with various AI tools is essential for developing critical AI literacy. Lastly, understanding how different AI models perform and recognizing potential algorithmic biases are fundamental skills for responsible AI integration. This chapter will explore these principles in depth, providing a framework for designing and implementing AI-focused professional development programs that empower language educators to harness the potential of AI while maintaining pedagogical integrity and ethical considerations.

Creating Space for AI Anxiety

The integration of AI in education often evokes a range of emotions among teachers, with anxiety being a predominant response. This anxiety can stem from various sources: fear of being replaced, uncertainty about one's technological competence, or concerns about the ethical implications of AI in education. Recognizing and addressing this anxiety is crucial for the successful implementation of AI in language teaching. During my professional development sessions in Bahrain, for Example, I observed that many educators, regardless of their experience level, exhibited signs of AI anxiety. This aligns with findings from recent studies. For instance, Wang et al. (2021) found that a majority of surveyed teachers expressed some level of anxiety about integrating emerging technologies into their classrooms. Similarly, Zawacki-Richter et al. (2019) noted that teacher anxiety was a significant barrier to AI adoption in educational settings.

To address this anxiety effectively, I implemented a three-pronged approach in my training sessions. First, I focused on creating safe spaces for discussion. Each session began by acknowledging the legitimacy of AI-related concerns. By openly discussing fears and reservations, I created an environment where educators felt heard and understood. This approach aligns with recommendations by Opps (2024), who emphasize the importance of emotional support in technology-focused professional development. More specifically, I used techniques such as anonymous polling and small group discussions to encourage educators to share their concerns without fear of judgment. Common anxieties included fear of job obsolescence, concerns about the reliability and accuracy of AI tools, ethical considerations regarding student data privacy, and uncertainty about maintaining classroom control with AI integration.

The second prong of my approach involved demystifying AI through education. Much of the anxiety surrounding AI stems from misconceptions and lack of understanding. I dedicated significant time to explaining AI basics, its capabilities, and limitations in language education contexts. This included clear explanations of what AI can and cannot do in language teaching, real-world examples of successful AI integration in classrooms, and discussions on the complementary role of AI to human teaching, rather than as a replacement. This educational approach helped reduce anxiety by providing educators with a realistic understanding of AI's current state in education. As noted by Holmes et al. (2022), increased knowledge about AI technologies correlates with reduced anxiety and increased willingness to adopt these tools.

The third and perhaps most effective strategy in alleviating AI anxiety was providing educators with opportunities for guided, hands-on experimentation with AI tools. I set up workshops where teachers could explore various AI applications relevant to language teaching, such as language models, translation tools, and AI-powered writing assistants. These practical sessions allowed educators to gain firsthand experience with AI tools in a low-stakes environment, discover the potential benefits of AI in enhancing their teaching practices, and identify limitations and potential issues with AI tools, fostering critical evaluation skills. The effectiveness of this approach is supported by Kong et al. (2024), who found that teachers who participated in hands-on AI workshops reported significantly lower levels of technology anxiety and higher levels of self-efficacy in using AI tools.

By addressing AI anxiety through open discussion, education, and practical experience, I observed a notable shift in educators' attitudes. Many participants moved from apprehension to cautious optimism about AI's role in language education. This change in mindset is crucial for the successful integration of AI in teaching practices. As we progress through the remainder of this chapter, I will explore how this foundation of reduced anxiety and increased openness sets the stage for developing critical AI literacy and implementing AI tools effectively in language classrooms.

Fostering Critical AI Literacy as Teacher Education

The development of critical AI literacy among language educators is paramount in the age of rapidly advancing AI technologies. This literacy goes beyond mere technical proficiency; it encompasses the ability to critically evaluate AI tools, understand their implications for language teaching and learning, and apply them ethically and effectively in educational contexts. My experiences in Bahrain underscored the importance of fostering this multifaceted literacy as a cornerstone of teacher education, a perspective I have explored in previous work

(Paiz, 2024a). Critical AI literacy for language educators can be understood as a synthesis of technical knowledge, pedagogical application, and ethical consideration. It involves not only understanding how AI works but also critically examining its role in language education, its potential biases, and its broader societal implications. This aligns with the perspective of Holmes and Tuomi (2022), who argue that AI literacy in education must encompass both technical and ethical dimensions.

In designing the professional development program for educators in Bahrain, I structured the fostering of critical AI literacy around three key components: technical understanding, pedagogical integration, and ethical awareness. This approach builds on the framework I proposed in *Artificial Intelligence and Teacher Education: An AI Handbook for Bahrain Teachers College* (Paiz, 2024b). Here, technical understanding forms the foundation of critical AI literacy. It involves comprehending the basic principles of how AI systems function, their capabilities, and their limitations. During the training sessions, I introduced educators to fundamental concepts such as machine learning, natural language processing, and neural networks. We explored how these technologies power various AI tools relevant to language teaching, such as automated writing assistants, language models, and translation software.

However, technical knowledge alone is insufficient. The pedagogical integration component focused on how AI can be meaningfully incorporated into language teaching practices. This aspect of literacy involves understanding how AI tools can enhance rather than replace traditional teaching methods. We examined case studies of successful AI integration in language classrooms, discussing how these tools can support differentiated instruction, provide personalized feedback, and create more engaging learning experiences. In the Bahraini training sessions, for instance, we explored how AI-powered writing assistants could be used not just for error correction, but as tools for teaching the writing process itself. Educators learned to guide students in critically evaluating AI suggestions, thus turning the use of these tools into a learning opportunity. This approach aligns with the findings of Kohnke et al. (2023), who emphasize the importance of using AI as a catalyst for critical thinking in language learning.

The ethical awareness component of critical AI literacy is perhaps the most crucial. It involves understanding the ethical implications of AI use in education, including issues of privacy, bias, and equity. We probed into discussions about the potential biases in AI systems, particularly those that might affect language learners from diverse backgrounds. Educators were encouraged to critically examine AI outputs for potential cultural or linguistic biases, a practice that Bender et al.

(2021) argue is essential for responsible AI use in language contexts. Moreover, we addressed the ethical considerations surrounding data privacy and student autonomy. Educators learned about the importance of transparency in AI use, the need for informed consent when using student data, and the potential risks of over-reliance on AI tools. These discussions were grounded in real-world scenarios, prompting educators to grapple with complex ethical dilemmas they might face in their classrooms, an approach I have advocated for in previous work (Paiz et al., 2025).

Throughout the training, I emphasized that critical AI literacy is not a static skill but an ongoing process of learning and adaptation. As AI technologies continue to evolve, educators must cultivate a mindset of continuous inquiry and critical evaluation. This aligns with the perspective of Crawford (2021), who argues that understanding AI is not just about mastering current technologies but about developing the capacity to critically engage with future developments. To reinforce this dynamic understanding of AI literacy, I incorporated hands-on activities that required educators to apply their evolving literacy skills. For example, participants were tasked with evaluating different AI language tools, comparing their outputs, and discussing the implications for language teaching. They also developed lesson plans that incorporated AI tools, with a focus on fostering critical thinking skills among their students. The outcomes of this approach were encouraging. Educators who participated in the training reported feeling more confident in their ability to critically evaluate and integrate AI tools in their teaching. Many expressed a newfound appreciation for the complexities of AI in education and the importance of maintaining a critical perspective.

However, fostering critical AI literacy is not without challenges. The rapid pace of AI development means that educators must continually update their knowledge and skills. Additionally, the complex nature of AI systems can sometimes be daunting, particularly for educators with limited technical backgrounds. To address these challenges, I emphasized the importance of creating supportive professional learning communities where educators can share experiences, discuss challenges, and collaboratively explore new AI developments.

As we move forward in integrating AI into language education, fostering critical AI literacy among educators will remain a crucial task. It is not just about equipping teachers with new tools, but about empowering them to be informed, critical, and ethical users and shapers of AI in education. By cultivating this literacy, we can ensure that AI enhances rather than diminishes the rich, complex process of language teaching and learning.

Experiential Learning with AI Tools

Building upon the foundation of reduced anxiety and critical AI literacy, the next crucial step in preparing language educators for AI integration is providing hands-on, experiential learning opportunities. This approach aligns with Kolb's (1984) experiential learning theory, which emphasizes the importance of concrete experiences in the learning process. Additionally, this experiential approach has been shown to be key in helping to reduce resistance to integrating new technologies into teaching and learning (see Ertmer & Ottenbreit-Leftwich, 2010; Tondeur et al., 2017), in part because it helps to demystify the technology in question and can underscore for practitioners its actual potential value. This hands-on experience allows educators to cut through marketing hype and imagine real possibilities for their own classrooms. In the context of AI, this approach is particularly crucial given the often-inflated claims about the capabilities of the technology, the lack of AI literacy amongst the general public, and understandable anxieties surrounding these technologies that are often exacerbated by corporate media (Holmes et al., 2022). In the context of AI in language education, experiential learning allows teachers to move beyond theoretical understanding to practical application and critical evaluation of AI tools.

During my work in Bahrain, I found that experiential learning was particularly effective in helping educators bridge the gap between conceptual knowledge and practical implementation. This approach not only reinforced their understanding of AI but also boosted their confidence in using these tools in their classrooms. As noted in my previous work (Paiz, 2024b; Paiz et al., in press), the hands-on experience was often the turning point for many educators, transforming their perception of AI from an abstract, potentially threatening concept to a tangible, manageable tool for enhancing language instruction. With both the Bahraini Ministry of Education and the Teachers College of the University of Bahrain, the experiential learning component of our professional development program was structured around three key areas: structured exploration sessions, practical application workshops, and exercises in identifying and addressing algorithmic bias. Each of these components was designed to provide educators with a comprehensive, hands-on understanding of AI in language education.

The structured exploration sessions served as a guided introduction to various AI models and tools relevant to language teaching. These sessions were designed to provide educators with firsthand experience of different AI applications, allowing them to understand their functionalities, strengths, and limitations. Moreover, incorporating such sessions into the trainings allowed the educators to develop their critical AI literacy (see chapter 4, above; Paiz et al. in press) by creating space for the to learn not just about AI tools, but also how they operate so that they could make professional informed decisions about when to use and when to restrict the use of such tools in their classroom spaces.

We began with guided tours of AI models and tools, carefully selected for their potential relevance to language education and how likely our students were to make use of them. These included large language models like OpenAI's GPT model, Anthropic's Claude model, and Mistral's Nemo – popular for its multilingual training and fine-tuning – as well as AI-powered writing assistants such as Grammarly and Hemingway APP, and language learning platforms like Duolingo. During these tours, I demonstrated the basic functionalities of each tool, explaining how they work and their potential applications in language teaching. For instance, when exploring the GPT, we engaged in interactive demonstrations where educators could input prompts and observe, evaluate, and critique the AI's responses. This hands-on approach allowed teachers to see firsthand the model's capabilities and limitations. For example, many pointed to the formulaic nature of the responses or the repetitious structural properties of the generated text, while others praised the model's reasoning or creativity. We then discussed how such a tool could be used to generate writing prompts, create example sentences, or even simulate conversations in the target language by continuing to practice different styles of prompting (e.g., chain-of-though/reasoning, multi-shot prompting, etc.) before talking through how we thought we would need to modify the system outputs to better fit the needs and expectations of our learner and institutional contexts.

A crucial aspect of these sessions was the comparative analysis of outputs on the same prompt by different AI models. Here, educators were encouraged to test the same prompts or tasks across different AI tools and compare the outputs. This exercise was particularly enlightening, as it highlighted the variability in AI performance and the importance of critical evaluation. For example, instructors were impressed with how hard a model like Claude worked to not tell a falsehood (read: hallucinate in AI parlance) but were correct in noting the marked reduction in creativity. Meanwhile, they appreciated the increased flexibility and creativity on the GPT model, but worried about the impacts of it, then-frequent, hallucinations. In another session, we compared the translations of a complex idiomatic expression across several AI translation tools (e.g., Google Translate, ChatGPT, DeepL). The varying results sparked a rich discussion about the nuances of language that AI might miss and the continued importance of human expertise in language instruction. This activity aligns with the findings of Kohnke et al. (2023), who emphasize the value of comparing AI outputs as a means of developing critical thinking skills in language education.

Throughout these exploration sessions, I encouraged educators to maintain a critical perspective. We discussed not only what the AI tools could do, but also what they could not do, and the potential risks of overreliance on AI in language teaching. This approach helped to reinforce the idea of AI as a tool to augment, rather than replace, human teaching. Moreover, it directly speaks to a key component of critical AI literacy (Paiz et al. in press), namely that we must increasingly know not only how to use AI tools, or which tools to use for which tasks, but also be able to make sound judgements about whether or not AI tools are appropriate for a specific use case in the first place.

Here, the participants in the training sessions really dove into oft-spirited debates allowing them to voice and address their concerns about AIED. This means that the structured exploration sessions also provided an opportunity to address specific concerns or questions that educators had about AI. By allowing teachers to interact directly with the tools in a supportive environment, we were able to demystify AI and build confidence in its use. As one participant noted, "Seeing these tools in action and being able to test them myself made AI feel much less intimidating and more like something I could actually use in my classroom." These sessions laid the groundwork for the more in-depth practical applications that would follow, providing educators with a solid foundation of hands-on experience with AI tools. The insights gained during these explorations would prove invaluable as we moved into designing AI-enhanced lesson plans and addressing more complex issues like algorithmic bias.

Building upon the insights gained from the structured exploration sessions, the next phase of our experiential learning program focused on practical application. These workshops were designed to bridge the gap between theoretical understanding and classroom implementation, allowing educators to develop concrete strategies for integrating AI into their language teaching practices. The workshops centered around two main activities: designing AI-enhanced lesson plans and integrating AI tools into existing curricula. Throughout these sessions, I emphasized the importance of maintaining a pedagogical focus, ensuring that AI was used to enhance, rather than replace, effective teaching practices.

In designing AI-enhanced lesson plans, educators worked in small groups to create lessons that meaningfully incorporated AI tools. For example, one group developed a lesson on persuasive writing for advanced English learners, using a model of their choosing available on the freely available HuggingChat platform, to generate example texts of varying quality. Students would then analyze these texts, identifying strengths and weaknesses, before crafting their own persuasive essays. This approach not only provided students with diverse examples but also encouraged critical thinking about AI-generated content. Another group designed a lesson utilizing AI-powered pronunciation feedback tools like ELSA Speak. They created a series of speaking activities where students would receive immediate, personalized feedback on their pronunciation, followed by targeted practice sessions. This lesson plan demonstrated how AI could provide individualized support at a scale that would be challenging for a single teacher to achieve. These exercises in lesson planning sparked discussions about the pedagogical implications of AI integration. Educators grappled with questions such as: How does the use of AI tools affect student motivation and engagement? How can we ensure that AI enhances rather than hinders language acquisition? These conversations echoed the findings of Paiz et al. (2025), who highlight the importance of critical reflection in AI integration.

The second focus of our workshops was on integrating AI tools into existing curricula. This approach recognized that wholesale changes to teaching materials are often impractical, and that effective AI integration often involves enhancing rather than overhauling current practices. Participants brought their existing lesson plans and worked on identifying opportunities for AI integration. For instance, one teacher adapted a traditional reading comprehension lesson by incorporating an AI tool that generated follow-up questions based on students' responses. This not only provided more personalized practice but also freed the teacher to focus on students who needed additional support. Another educator enhanced a vocabulary lesson by using an AI-powered image generation tool to create custom flashcards, making abstract terms more concrete and memorable for students. This creative application demonstrated how AI could be used to address specific pedagogical challenges in language teaching. Throughout these exercises, I encouraged educators to maintain a critical perspective, constantly evaluating the benefits and potential drawbacks of each AI integration. We discussed the importance of maintaining a balance between AI-assisted and traditional teaching methods, ensuring that students still had ample opportunities for human interaction and authentic language use.

The workshops also addressed practical considerations such as technology access, tech equity, and student privacy. We discussed strategies for implementing AI tools in contexts with limited resources, acknowledging the digital divide that exists both between and within countries. Educators brainstormed creative solutions, such as using AI tools for lesson preparation even when students could not access them directly, or implementing a rotation system for shared devices. Naturally, students' right to privacy and the protected nature of much educational data came up. This, then, led to discussions about the ethical implications of AI use, particularly regarding data privacy and consent in educational settings. Participants developed guidelines for transparently communicating with students and parents about AI use in the classroom, ensuring informed consent and building trust in the educational community. By the end of these practical application workshops, participants had not only created tangible, AI-enhanced teaching materials but had also developed a more nuanced understanding of how to thoughtfully integrate AI into their teaching practice. As one participant reflected, "I now see AI not as a replacement for my teaching, but as a powerful tool that, when used judiciously, can help me better meet my students' needs."

This hands-on experience in designing and adapting AI-enhanced lessons proved invaluable in building educators' confidence and competence in AI integration. It also laid the groundwork for addressing more complex issues, such as algorithmic bias, which we would explore in subsequent sessions. This exploration was facilitated by the fact that as educators became more comfortable with AI tools, their own concerns started to shift away from integration issues towards preemptively addressing the linguistic and cultural bias that may be reflected in the outputs of generative AI models. To that end, the final component of our experiential learning program focused on equipping participants with the skills to identify potential biases in AI outputs and strategies to mitigate their impact in the classroom.

We began by exploring the concept of algorithmic bias, discussing how AI systems can inadvertently perpetuate or amplify existing societal biases. Drawing on the work of Bender et al. (2021), we examined how language models trained on internet data can reflect and reproduce problematic patterns of language use, including racial, gender, and cultural biases. To make this concept tangible, we conducted a series of exercises in detecting bias in AI outputs. For instance, participants used various AI writing assistants to generate descriptions of professionals in different fields, then analyzed the results for gender or racial stereotypes. In another exercise, we used AI image generation tool to create visual aids for a lesson on afterschool routines and were surprised at how often the models (e.g., DALL-E, Midjourney) would default to produce white, male children with blonde hair doing things like playing video games or making peanut butter and jelly sandwiches.

These exercises proved eye-opening for many participants. As one educator noted, "I hadn't realized how subtle, or in some cases pervasive, these biases could be. It has made me much more cautious about using AI-generated content without careful review." This speaks to the need both for language teaching professionals and researchers to develop strong AI literacy skills, but also for our students to be equipped with them early and often as well. By building on these insights, we developed strategies for mitigating bias in the classroom that we felt were appropriate for the cultural and professional contexts in which the participants worked. These included:

1. Cross-referencing AI outputs: We practiced using multiple AI tools for the same task and comparing results to identify potential biases or inconsistencies
2. Human-in-the-loop approaches: Participants designed lesson plans that used AI as a starting point but incorporated human oversight and curation of AI-generated content
3. Diverse input prompts: We explored how varying the phrasing or context of prompts given to AI tools could help generate more inclusive and diverse outputs
4. Critical analysis activities: Educators developed classroom activities that encouraged students to critically evaluate AI-generated content, fostering digital literacy skills
5. Supplementing with diverse sources: We discussed the importance of complementing AI tools with a wide range of human-curated, culturally diverse materials

Throughout these exercises, we emphasized that addressing algorithmic bias wasn't just about improving the accuracy of AI tools but about promoting equity and inclusion in the classroom. As Crawford (2021) argues, understanding and mitigating AI bias is crucial for ensuring that these technologies do not exacerbate existing inequalities. We also explored the potential of AI bias as a teaching tool in itself. Participants designed lessons where students could analyze biased AI outputs, using them as a springboard for discussions about language, culture, and social justice. This approach aligned with the critical pedagogy advocated by a number of applied linguists and language researchers including Crookes (2022), Paiz (2020), and Pennycook (2001). Specifically, participants coalesced around the idea of using technology not just as a tool for language instruction, but as a means of developing critical thinking and social awareness.

The workshop concluded with a collaborative session where participants developed a set of guidelines for ethical AI use in their institutions. These guidelines included protocols for vetting AI tools, strategies for transparently communicating about AI use with students and parents, and commitments to ongoing professional development in this rapidly evolving field. By the end of this section, educators had not only developed practical skills in identifying and addressing algorithmic bias, but had also deepened their understanding of the broader ethical implications of AI in education.

This focus on algorithmic bias and ethical considerations provided a crucial capstone to our experiential learning program, ensuring that participants were prepared to be not just users of AI, but informed, critical, and responsible champions of AI integration in language education. Beyond these insights, the workshop series as a whole, repeated across multiple weeks and venues with different educators from diverse professional backgrounds and institutional contexts highlights quite saliently that addressing AI integration and language teacher professional development would not be a one-off affair. Indeed, it underscored the very real need for continuous professional development and support for language practitioners to feel empower to create collaborative classroom environments that included AI and traditional tools and pedagogies.

Continuous Professional Development and Support

What was abundantly clear not only from the Bahraini training workshops, but also from numerous conversations I have with stakeholders across my home institution is that meaningfully addressing AI in education necessitates an approach to professional development that extends beyond one-time workshops or training sessions. As observed during my work in Bahrain and echoed by researchers like Opps (2024), continuous learning and support are crucial for educators to effectively integrate AI into their teaching practices over time. This section outlines strategies for fostering ongoing professional growth and support in AI integration for language educators.

One of the most effective ways to support continuous professional development is through the establishment of communities of practice. These collaborative groups allow educators to share experiences, discuss challenges, and collectively explore new AI developments in language teaching. During our program in Bahrain, we laid the groundwork for several such communities, both within individual institutions and across the broader educational landscape. These communities took various forms, including:

1. Regular meetups: Monthly or bi-monthly gatherings where educators shared their experiences with AI integration, discussed new tools, and collaboratively solved problems
2. Online forums: Dedicated digital spaces where teachers could ask questions, share resources, and engage in ongoing discussions about AI in language education
3. Peer mentoring programs: Pairing AI-enthusiastic educators with those less comfortable with the technology, fostering knowledge sharing and mutual support

The rationale for these communities aligns with findings from Searson et al. (2024), who highlight the value of peer support in technology integration. They draw attention to how it can lower resistance to new technologies and facilitate contextually aware integration attempts that support student learning in ways that align with institutional mission or requirements from central educational planning authorities (e.g., local school districts or national ministries of education).

A recurrent theme for educators was concern over how quickly everything seems to be changing in education – and with AI both as a tool and a pedagogical instrument. This is an understandable sentiment when, given the rapid pace of AI development, staying current with new technologies and their potential applications in language teaching is a significant challenge. To address this, we set up several strategies that our Bahraini partners could adapt to fit their needs/capabilities in their specific institutions or school buildings:

1. Tech watch teams: Groups of educators tasked with monitoring new AI developments and reporting back to the larger community
2. Partnerships with tech companies: Collaborations with AI developers to provide educators with early access to new tools and features relevant to language teaching
3. Regular update sessions: Quarterly workshops focused on introducing new AI technologies and discussing their potential applications in the classroom

These approaches helped educators feel more confident in their ability to adapt to new technologies, reducing the anxiety often associated with rapid technological change (Chen et al., 2020). Moreover, they create value around the notion that education specialists should have a voice in the room with (ed) tech companies who are designing and marketing tools that can impact the learning process. By positioning ourselves as experts in language education with functional knowledge of AI and its pedagogical implications, we are better positioned to make our voices heard in industry and to demand attention so that future versions of these tools are more aligned with our professional values and needs.

Finally a recognizing that educators have diverse needs and preferences for professional development, we also emphasized the importance of self-directed learning. We curated a range of resources to support individual exploration of AI in language education:

1. Online course library: A collection of vetted online courses covering various aspects of AI in education, from technical fundamentals to pedagogical applications
2. AI sandbox environments: Safe, controlled spaces where educators could experiment with new AI tools without risking student data or classroom disruption. This often relied on using tools like GPT4All to run open source LLMs on the participant's local device.
3. Curated reading lists: Regularly updated compilations of articles, research papers, and books on AI in language education, catering to different levels of expertise and interest
4. Reflection journals: Structured templates for educators to document their AI integration journey, promoting metacognition and self-assessment

This multifaceted approach to continuous professional development ensures that educators have ongoing support as they navigate the complex and rapidly changing world of AI in language education. By fostering communities of practice, facilitating access to evolving technologies, and providing resources for self-directed learning, we can empower educators to become lifelong learners and innovators in AI-enhanced language teaching. AIED, collaborative AI, and AI integration are certainly moving targets, and we find ourselves in a highly fluid professional moment. However, by committing to continuous professional development and support, we can ensure that educators are well-equipped to harness AI's potential AI while maintaining the critical, ethical, and pedagogical foundations that are essential to effective language teaching.

Conclusion

Reflecting on the discussion thus far, several key takeaways emerge for effective AI-focused professional development. First and foremost, addressing AI anxiety through open dialogue and hands-on experience is crucial for fostering educator buy-in. By creating safe spaces for discussion and providing opportunities for guided experimentation, we can transform apprehension into cautious optimism. Secondly, the development of critical AI literacy among educators is paramount. This multifaceted literacy, encompassing technical understanding, pedagogical integration, and ethical awareness, empowers teachers to become informed, critical, and responsible users of AI in education. The emphasis on experiential learning, as demonstrated in the Bahrain workshops, proves invaluable in bridging the gap between theoretical knowledge and practical application. Moreover, continuous professional development and support are essential in this rapidly evolving field. The establishment of communities of practice, regular update sessions, and resources for self-directed learning ensure that educators can keep pace with technological advancements and their pedagogical implications.

Looking to the future, several directions for research and practice emerge. There is a need for longitudinal studies examining the long-term impact of AI integration on language learning outcomes. Additionally, research into culturally responsive AI integration in diverse educational contexts could provide valuable insights for global implementation. In practice, the development of AI-enhanced curricula that balance technological innovation with sound pedagogical principles presents an exciting frontier. Moreover, the creation of ethical guidelines for AI use in education, particularly addressing issues of data privacy and algorithmic bias, will be crucial as AI becomes more prevalent in classrooms. As we move forward, the potential of AI to transform and enhance language teaching and learning is increasingly clear. However, realizing this potential will require a collaborative approach that values human expertise alongside technological innovation. The next chapter will explore this future in greater depth, examining emerging trends and technologies that promise to further alter the field of language teaching.

9

Looking Ahead: AI, ELT, and Human Expertise

As we reach the conclusion of our exploration into artificial intelligence and language learning, it is fitting to reflect on the journey we have taken and look ahead to the possibilities that may await us, although this is admittedly challenging given how rapidly the capabilities of generative AI tools have evolved. For example, when I started drafting this book back in January 2023, GPT models struggled with basic math. As I finished drafting in September 2024 the newer GPT models could outperform math Olympiads and reasons at the level of PhD students in the natural sciences. Despite this, this book has done its best to remain tool-agnostic and provide actionable recommendations to language practitioners and researchers alike. Our discussion has taken us from the fundamental concepts of AI to its practical applications in education, assessment, and ethical considerations. We have explored frameworks for pedagogical approaches, institutional policies, and interrogated the crucial role of teacher professional development in this rapidly evolving landscape. In this final chapter, I will turn our attention to the horizon, envisioning the transformative potential of AI in shaping the future of CALL. Here, we'll explore emerging trends and technologies, consider their potential impacts, reaffirm the enduring importance of human expertise, and contemplate a future where humans and AI collaborate seamlessly in the realm of language education. As we embark on this forward-looking discussion, we invite you to imagine the possibilities and challenges that lie ahead in the dynamic world of AI-enhanced language learning.

Emerging Trends and Technologies in AI for CALL

AI in CALL is evolving at a breathtaking pace, with new technologies and methodologies continually reshaping our approach to language acquisition. Let us examine some of the most promising trends that are likely to define the future of CALL. This is far from an exhaustive exploration, and more of a teaser of things that may be coming just around the corner.

As we move forward, we can expect to see significant advancements in Natural Language Processing (NLP) technologies that cater to multilingual and multicultural contexts. These systems will become increasingly sophisticated in understanding and generating language across a diverse range of linguistic structures, idioms, and cultural nuances. Imagine AI systems that can seamlessly switch between languages, providing learners with real-time translation, interpretation, and cross-linguistic comparisons with native-like competency regardless of target language. Most models now offer uneven performance across different languages, and (at best) sound like highly proficient second language users. These advanced NLP models will be able to analyze a learner's speech patterns, grammar usage, and vocabulary choices across multiple languages, offering personalized insights into their language development and areas for improvement.

Furthermore, we may see the emergence of AI-powered language learning platforms that can adapt to regional dialects and sociolinguistic variations, ensuring that learners are exposed to authentic language use in various cultural contexts. This level of linguistic flexibility and cultural awareness in AI systems will revolutionize how we approach multilingual education and intercultural communication. Importantly, models that can do so without replicating biases or stereotypes could go a long way towards empowering language professionals and students a like to create more inclusive instructional environments.

The future of CALL will likely see a growing shift towards hyper-personalized learning experiences driven by sophisticated AI algorithms. These systems will go beyond simple adaptive learning paths, evolving into comprehensive personal language coaches that understand each learner's unique cognitive style, motivation, and learning preferences. These AI tutors will analyze vast amounts of data from a learner's interactions, including speech patterns, writing samples, reading speed, and even physiological responses (such as eye movements or stress levels) to create truly tailored learning experiences. They might adjust the difficulty of tasks in real-time, select the most effective teaching methods for each individual, and even predict potential challenges a learner might face before they occur. Moreover, these systems could integrate with a learner's daily life, suggesting relevant language practice opportunities based on their schedule, interests, and current environment. For instance, if a learner has an upcoming business trip to

Japan, the AI might prioritize business Japanese and cultural etiquette in the weeks leading up to the trip.

As our world becomes increasingly interconnected, the demand for multilingual competence is growing. Future AI systems in CALL will likely place a greater emphasis on facilitating cross-linguistic transfer and supporting multilingual education. These AI tools will be adept at identifying similarities and differences between languages, helping learners leverage their knowledge of one language to accelerate their acquisition of others. For example, an AI system might help a Spanish speaker learning Italian by highlighting cognates, similar grammatical structures, and shared Latin roots. Furthermore, we may see the development of AI-powered platforms that support simultaneous or sequential learning of multiple languages, adapting to each learner's unique linguistic repertoire. These systems could create custom learning paths that maximize the benefits of positive transfer while mitigating negative interference between languages.

Potential Impacts on Computer-Assisted Language Learning

The integration of advanced AI technologies into CALL is poised to bring about significant changes in how we approach language learning and teaching. One of the most promising aspects of AI in CALL is its potential to revolutionize differentiated instruction. As AI systems become more sophisticated in understanding individual learner needs, they will be able to offer truly personalized learning experiences that cater to diverse linguistic and cultural backgrounds. These AI-powered systems will be capable of analyzing a learner's proficiency level, learning style, cultural background, and even their emotional state to deliver customized content and activities. For instance, an AI tutor might recognize that a learner from a tonal language background is struggling with English intonation patterns and provide targeted exercises to address this specific challenge. Moreover, AI could help bridge cultural gaps in language learning by providing culturally relevant examples and explanations. This could be particularly beneficial in multicultural classrooms, where an AI system could adapt its teaching approach to align with different cultural learning styles and expectations.

The future of assessment and feedback in CALL environments is likely to be more continuous, comprehensive, and constructive, thanks to AI technologies. Traditional periodic tests may give way to ongoing, AI-powered evaluation that provides instant, detailed feedback on a learner's performance across all language skills. Imagine AI systems that can analyze a learner's speech in real-time, offering immediate feedback on pronunciation, grammar, and vocabulary use. Or consider writing assessment tools that not only correct errors but also provide context-specific suggestions for improvement and track a learner's progress over time. Furthermore, AI could revolutionize the way we approach standardized language testing. Adaptive AI-powered tests could adjust their difficulty in real-time based on a test-taker's responses, providing a more accurate assessment of their language proficiency while reducing test anxiety.

AI technologies have the potential to dramatically increase learners' exposure to authentic language use and intercultural communication opportunities. AI-powered language exchange platforms could match learners with native speakers or other learners for conversation practice, using sophisticated algorithms to ensure compatible language levels and shared interests. Virtual and augmented reality technologies, combined with AI, could transport learners to simulated real-world environments where they can practice their language skills in context. These immersive experiences could range from virtual tours of foreign cities to simulated job interviews in the target language. Moreover, AI could play a crucial role in making authentic materials more accessible to learners at various proficiency levels. AI-powered tools could automatically adapt authentic texts or videos to a learner's level, simplifying complex language while maintaining the essence of the content. This would allow learners to engage with real-world materials earlier in their language learning journey, enhancing motivation and cultural understanding.

The integration of AI in CALL is likely to foster greater learner autonomy and self-directed learning. AI tutors could act as personal learning assistants, helping learners set realistic goals, create effective study plans, and monitor their own progress. These AI systems could provide learners with insights into their learning patterns, helping them understand their strengths and areas for improvement. For example, an AI might notice that a learner consistently performs better on vocabulary exercises in the evening and suggest adjusting their study schedule accordingly. Furthermore, AI could support metacognitive skill development by prompting learners to reflect on their learning process, helping them become more aware of effective learning strategies. This could lead to more efficient, personalized learning experiences and empower learners to take greater control of their language learning journey.

As we consider these potential impacts, it is important to recognize that while AI has the power to transform CALL in numerous positive ways, its integration must be approached thoughtfully and ethically. In the next section, we'll explore why human expertise remains crucial in this AI-enhanced landscape. Doing so is central to maintaining a collaborative approach to meaningful AI integration.

The Enduring Importance of Human Expertise in CALL

No matter how performant generative AI systems become, it is crucial to recognize that human expertise remains indispensable. While AI can enhance and support language learning in numerous ways, there are fundamental aspects of language acquisition and education that continue to rely on human insight, empathy, and judgment. Indeed, much of this book has been focused on advocating for a collaborative view of AI, one which values human expertise above all else and sees AI solely as a tool to augment and supplement human cognition and abilities.

Language is deeply intertwined with culture, history, and human experience. While AI can process vast amounts of linguistic data, it lacks the nuanced understanding of cultural contexts that human teachers bring to language education. Human experts play a vital role in helping learners navigate the complex relationship between language and culture. For instance, understanding idiomatic expressions, humor, or cultural references often requires a level of critical thinking and contextual knowledge that current AI systems struggle to replicate. Human teachers can provide insights into the subtle cultural nuances of language use, explaining not just what is said, but why it is said in a particular way in a specific context. Moreover, human educators are better equipped to foster critical thinking skills in language learners. They can engage students in meaningful discussions about cultural differences, encourage them to question assumptions, and help them develop a deeper, more nuanced understanding of the target language and culture.

Learning a new language can be an emotionally charged experience, often involving feelings of vulnerability, frustration, and occasional breakthroughs of exhilaration. Human teachers bring emotional intelligence to the classroom, an ability that current AI systems cannot fully replicate. Human educators can read subtle emotional cues, provide encouragement when a student is struggling, and celebrate achievements in a way that resonates on a human level. They can adapt their teaching style in real-time based on the emotional state of individual learners or the overall mood of a class.

Furthermore, human teachers play a crucial role in motivating learners. While AI systems can use gamification and personalized goal-setting to boost motivation, human educators can inspire learners through their own passion for the language, share personal anecdotes that make the learning process more relatable, and create a supportive classroom community that encourages peer learning and motivation. While affective computing remains an active area of research and development in AI specifically, and computer science more generally, it is a nascent field of research and has yet to make many salient contributions outside of sentiment analysis, being prone to considerable bias in their outputs that limit their usefulness. Said more simply, AI is current rubbish at reading *embodied, enacted* human emotion. For this, we still need human educators.

As AI becomes more prevalent in language education, ethical considerations become increasingly important. Human expertise is crucial in making ethical decisions about how and when to integrate AI tools into the learning process. Educators and administrators need to carefully consider issues such as data privacy, algorithmic bias, and the potential for over-reliance on AI tools. They must ensure that AI integration aligns with pedagogical goals and ethical standards, and that it doesn't inadvertently disadvantage certain groups of learners.

Human experts are also essential in teaching students how to interact with AI language tools critically and ethically. As AI-powered writing assistants and translation tools become more advanced, it is crucial that learners understand both the capabilities and limitations of these tools, and develop the skills to use them responsibly. So, while AI has the potential to greatly enhance CALL, it should be seen as a powerful tool to augment human teaching rather than a replacement for human expertise. The future of language education lies not in choosing between human teachers and AI, but in finding the optimal ways to combine the strengths of both. In the next section, we'll explore how this collaborative future might unfold.

Towards a Collaborative Future: Humans and AI in CALL

Look forward, it is clear that the most effective approach will be one that harmoniously blends human expertise with AI capabilities. This collaborative model has the potential to create learning environments that are more personalized, effective, and inclusive than ever before.

The key to successful integration of AI in CALL lies in leveraging the strengths of both AI systems and human educators. AI excels at processing vast amounts of data, providing instant feedback, and adapting to individual learner needs. Human teachers, on the other hand, bring creativity, empathy, and the ability to inspire and motivate learners. In practice, this could mean using AI to handle routine tasks such as grammar checking or vocabulary practice, freeing up human teachers to focus on more complex aspects of language learning. For example, an AI system might provide a preliminary analysis of a student's writing, highlighting areas for improvement, while the human teacher uses this information to have a more in-depth discussion with the student about their ideas and how to express them more effectively.

As AI becomes more integrated into CALL, we'll need to develop new pedagogical approaches that make the most of these technologies while addressing the unique needs of diverse learning contexts. This might involve creating blended learning models that combine AI-driven self-study with human-led group discussions, or developing project-based learning approaches where AI tools support learners in completing complex, real-world language tasks. To this end, Educators will need to become adept at designing learning experiences that seamlessly integrate AI tools. This could involve creating lesson plans that use AI-powered virtual reality for immersive language practice, followed by human-led debriefing sessions to discuss cultural insights gained from these experiences.

As AI becomes more prevalent in language learning, it is crucial that both educators and learners develop AI literacy. This involves understanding the capabilities and limitations of AI systems, knowing how to interact with them effectively, and being able to critically evaluate the output of AI tools. For educators, this might mean professional development programs that not only teach them how to use AI tools but also how to integrate them effectively into their teaching practice. For learners, it could involve explicit instruction on how to use AI language tools responsibly, including understanding issues of plagiarism and the importance of developing their own language skills rather than over-relying on AI assistance.

As we develop AI systems for CALL, it is essential to ensure that these technologies are inclusive and accessible to diverse global language communities. This involves considering issues of linguistic diversity, cultural representation, and technological access. Efforts should be made to develop AI systems that can support a wide range of languages, including less commonly taught languages. Additionally, AI systems should be designed with cultural sensitivity in mind, avoiding biases and stereotypes that could alienate certain groups of learners. Furthermore, as we integrate more advanced technologies like virtual and augmented reality into CALL, we need to consider issues of accessibility. How can we ensure that learners with limited access to high-speed internet or advanced devices can still benefit from AI-enhanced language learning?

A (Hopefully) Optimistic Outlook for AI in Language Learning

The potential of AI in CALL is vast and exciting. Advanced natural language processing will allow for more nuanced understanding and production of language across diverse linguistic contexts. Immersive virtual and augmented reality environments will provide safe, engaging spaces for authentic language practice. Adaptive AI systems will offer hyper-personalized learning experiences tailored to each individual's needs and preferences. And AI-driven approaches to multilingual education will support learners in navigating an increasingly interconnected, multilingual world. These technological advancements promise to transform how we approach differentiated instruction, assessment and feedback, access to authentic language experiences, and self-directed learning. They have the potential to make language learning more accessible, efficient, and engaging for learners around the world.

However, as we embrace these exciting possibilities, we must not lose sight of the irreplaceable value of human expertise in language education. The nuanced understanding of cultural contexts, the ability to foster critical thinking, the emotional intelligence to motivate and support learners, and the ethical judgment needed to navigate the complexities of AI integration – these remain the domain of human educators.

The future of language learning lies not in choosing between human teachers and AI, but in finding the optimal ways to combine the strengths of both. By fostering a collaborative approach where AI augments and enhances human teaching, we can create learning environments that are truly transformative. This collaboration has the potential to address long-standing challenges in language education, from providing more personalized learning experiences to increasing access to quality language education on a global scale. As we move forward, it is crucial that we approach the integration of AI into CALL with thoughtfulness and care. We must prioritize the development of AI literacy among both educators and learners, ensuring that these powerful tools are used effectively and ethically. We must also remain committed to creating inclusive AI-CALL environments that serve diverse global language communities, bridging rather than exacerbating existing educational divides.

The journey ahead in AI-enhanced language learning is filled with both exciting opportunities and important challenges. By maintaining a balance between embracing innovation and preserving the human elements that are central to language learning, we can shape a future where AI and human expertise work in harmony to unlock the full potential of every language learner.

As we close this book, I would invite educators, learners, researchers, and technologists to approach this AI-enhanced future with optimism, creativity, and a commitment to harnessing these powerful tools in service of more effective, engaging, and equitable language education. The future of CALL is bright, and together, we can ensure that it benefits learners across the globe, helping to build a more connected and understanding world through the power of language. But, in the end, remember that in all things to value the human element above all else.

References

Abdous, M. (21 March 2023). How AI is shaping the future of higher ed. *Inside Higher Education*. https://www.insidehighered.com/views/2023/03/22/how-ai-shaping-future-higher-ed-opinion.

Adobe. (15 June 2023). Adobe firefly. *Adobe*. https://www.adobe.com/sensei/generative-ai/firefly.html.

Ahmad, S.F., Han, H., Alam, M.M., Rehmat, M., Irshad, M., Arraño-Muñoz, M., & Ariza-Montes, A. (2023). Impact of artificial intelligence on human loss in decision making, laziness and safety in education. *Humanities and Social Sciences Communications*, *10*(1), 1–14. https://doi.org/10.1057/s41599-023-01787-8.

Akgun, S., & Greenhow, C. (2022). Artificial intelligence in education: Addressing ethical challenges in K-12 settings. *AI and Ethics*, 2, 431–40. https://doi.org/10.1007/s43681-021-00096-7.

Alexander, J. (2008). *Literacy, sexuality, pedagogy: Theory and practice for composition studies*. Utah State University Press.

Alhalangy, A.G.I., & AbdAlgane, M. (2023). Exploring the impact of AI on the EFL context: A case study of Saudi universities. *Journal of Intercultural Communication, 23*(2), 41–9. https://doi.org/10.36923/jicc.v23.i2.125.

Amin, M.Y.M. (2023). AI and Chat GPT in language teaching: Enhancing EFL classroom support and transforming assessment techniques. *International Journal of Higher Education Pedagogies*, 4(4), 1–15. https://doi.org/10.33422/ijhep.v4i4.554.

An, X., Chai, C.S., Li, Y., Zhou, Y., & Yang, B. (2022). Modeling students' perceptions of artificial intelligence assisted language learning. *Computer Assisted Language Learning*. https://doi.org/10.1080/09588221.2023.2246519.

Anderson, J.R., Corbett, A.T., Koedinger, K.R., & Pelletier, R. (1995). Cognitive tutors: Lessons learned. *Journal of the Learning Sciences*, 4(2), 167–207. https://doi.org/10.1207/s15327809jls0402_2.

Arakawa, R., & Yakura, H. (2022). *AI for human assessment: What do professional assessors need?* arXiv: 2204.08471v3. https://doi.org/10.1145/3544549.3573849.

Ashrafimoghari, V. (2022). *Big data and education: Using big data analytics in language learning*. arXiv:2207.10572v1. https://doi.org/10.13140/RG.2.2.21946.06080.

Atkinson, D. (2002). Toward a sociocognitive approach to second language acquisition. *The Modern Language Journal, 86*(4), 525–45. https://doi.org/10.1111/1540-4781.00159.

Atkinson, D. (2014). Language learning in mindbodyworld: A sociocognitive approach to second language acquisition. *Language Teaching, 47*(4), 467–83. https://doi.org/10.1017/S0261444813000153.

Atkinson, D. (2019). Beyond the brain: Intercorporeality and co-operative action for SLA studies. *The Modern Language Journal, 103*(4), 724–38. https://doi.org/10.1111/modl.12595.

Azizah, S., & Soraya, S. (2023). A closer look on Indonesian EFL students' writing process: The application of cognitive and metacognitive strategies. *Journal of Research and Innovation in Language, 5*(2), 128–43. https://doi.org/10.31849/reila.v5i2.10687.

Barocas, S., & Selbst, A.D. (2016). Big Data's disparate impact. *California Law Review, 104*, 671–732. https://doi.org/10.2139/ssrn.2477899.

Barocas, S., Hardt, M., & Narayanan, A. (2023). *Fairness and machine learning*. MIT Press.

Barrot, J.S. (2023). Using automated written corrective feedback in the writing classrooms: Effects on L2 writing accuracy. *Computer Assisted Language Learning, 36*(4), 584–607. https://doi.org/10.1080/09588221.2021.1936071.

Baskara, R. (2023). Revolutionising EFL curriculum: A theoretical analysis of generative AI for active learning. In *Proceedings of UNNES-TEFLIN national conference* (Vol. 5, pp. 278–93). Teaching English as a Foreign Language in Indonesia Association.

Bassett, C. (2019). The computational therapeutic: Exploring Weizenbaum's ELIZA as a history of the present. AI & Society, *34*, 803–12. https://doi.org/10.1007/s00146-018-0825-9.

Becker, K., & Edalatishams, I. (2019). ELSA speak: Accent reduction [technology review]. In J. Levis, C. Nagle, & E. Todey (Eds.), *Proceedings of the 10th pronunciation in second language learning and teaching conference* (pp. 434–8). Iowa State University.

Bender, E.M. (14 November 2019). The #BenderRule: On naming the languages we study and why it matters. *The Gradient*. https://thegradient.pub/the-benderrule-on-naming-the-languages-we-study-and-why-it-matters/.

Bender, E.M. (2024). Resisting dehumanization in the age of "AI". *Current Directions in Psychological Science, 33*(2), 1–7. https://doi.org/10.1177/09637214231217286.

Bender, E.M., Gebru, T., McMillan-Major, A., & Shmitchell, S. (2021). On the dangers of stochastic parrots: Can language models be too big? In *Proceedings of the 2021 ACM conference on fairness, accountability, and transparency* (pp. 610–23).Association for Computing Machinery.

Bernacki, M.L., Greene, J.A., & Crompton, H. (2020). Mobile technology, learning, and achievement: Advances in understanding and measuring the role of mobile technology in education. *Contemporary Educational Psychology, 60*, 101827.

Bjork, C. (15 February 2023). ChatGPT threatens language diversity: More needs to be done to protect our differences in the age of AI. *Down to Earth*. https://downtoearth.org.in/blog/science-technology/chatgpt-threatens-language-diversity-more-needs-to-be-done-to-protect-our-differences-in-the-age-of-ai-87626.

Blake, R.J. (2007). New trends in using technology in the language curriculum. *Annual Review of Applied Linguistics, 27*, 76–97.

Block, D. (2003). *The social turn in second language acquisition*. Georgetown University Press.

Blodgett, S.L., Barocas, S., Daumé III, H., & Wallach, H. (2020). Language (technology) is power: A critical survey of 'bias' in NLP. In *Proceedings of the 58th annual meeting of the association for computational linguistics* (pp. 5454–76). Association for Computational Linguistics.

Boden, M. (2018). *Artificial intelligence: A very brief introduction*. Oxford University Press.

Bogost, I. (7 December 2022). ChatGPT is dumber than you think. *The Atlantic*. https://theatlantic.com/technology/archive/2022/12/chatgpt-openai-artificial-intelligence-writing-ethics/672386/.

Borrego, M.M. (2023). Towards a digital assessment: Artificial intelligence assisted error analysis in ESL. *Integrated Journal for Research in Arts and Humanities, 3*(4), 76–84. https://doi.org/10.55544/ijrah.3.4.10.

Brooke, R. (1987). Underlife and writing instruction. *College Composition and Communication, 38*(2), 141–53. https://doi.org/10.2307/357715.

Brown, J.D. (2016). Language testing and technology. In *The Routledge handbook of language learning and technology* (pp. 141–59). Routledge.

Brown, T., Mann, B., Ryder, N., Subbiah, M., Kaplan, J.D., Dhariwal, P., Neelakantan, A., Shyam, P., Sastry, G., Askell, A., Agarwal, S., Herbert-Voss, A., Krueger, G., Henighan, T., Child, R., Ramesh, A., Ziegler, D., Wu, J., Winter, C., Hesse, C., Chen, M., … Amodei, D. (2020). Language models are few-shot learners. *Advances in Neural Information Processing Systems, 33,* 1877–1901.

Bryant, J., Aeitz, C., Sanghvi, S., & Wagle, D. (2020). How artificial intelligence will impact K-12 teachers [white paper]. *McKinsey and Company.* htttps://mckinsey.com/industries/education/our-insights/how-artificial-intelligence-will-impact-k-12-teachers.

Buchanan, B. G., & Shortliffe, E. H. (eds.). (1984). *Rule-based expert systems: The MYCIN experiments of the Stanford Holistic Programming Experiments.* Addison Wesley.

Buolamwini, J. (2023). *Unmasking AI: My mission to protect what is human in a world of machines.* Random House.

Burrell, J. (2016). How the machine 'thinks': Understanding opacity in machine learning algorithms. *Big Data & Society, 3*(1), 1–12. https://doi.org/10.1177/2053951715622512.

Burston, J. (2014). MALL: The pedagogical challenges. *Computer Assisted Language Learning, 27*(4), 344–57. https://doi.org/10.1080/09588221.2014.914539.

Cao, Y., Li, S., Liu, Y., Yan, Z., Dai, Y., Yu, P.S., & Sun, L. (2023). *A comprehensive survey of AI-generated content (AIGC): A history of generative AI from GAN to ChatGPT.* arXiv:2303.04226.

Carbonell, J. (1970). *Mixed-initiative man-computer instructional dialogues* [Doctoral dissertation, Massachusetts Institute of Technology].

Celik, I., Dindar, M., Muukonen, H., & Järvelä, S. (2022). The promises and challenges of artificial intelligence for teachers: A systematic review of research. *TechTrends, 66,* 616–30. https://doi.org/10.1007/s11528-022-00715-y.

Chandel, A., Parate, A., Madathingal, M., Pant, H., Rajput, N., Ikbal, S., Deshmukh, O., & Verma, A. (2007). Sensei: Spoken language assessment for call center agents. In *2007 IEEE Workshop on Automatic Speech Recognition & Understanding (ASRU)* (pp. 711–16). IEEE.

Chapelle, C.A., & Chung, Y.-R. (2010). The promise of NLP and speech processing technologies in language assessment. *Language Testing, 27*(3), 301–15. https://doi.org/10.1177/0265532210364405.

Chapelle, C.A., & Sauro, S. (Eds.). (2017). *The handbook of technology and second language teaching and learning.* Wiley Blackwell.

Chapelle, C.A., & Voss, E. (2016). 20 years of technology and language assessment in *Language Learning & Technology. Language Learning & Technology, 20*(2), 116–28. https://doi.org/10125/44464.

Chen, B., Lewis, C.M., West, M., & Zilles, C. (2024). Plagiarism in the age of generative AI: Cheating method change and learning loss in an intro to

CS course. In *Proceedings of the eleventh ACM Conference on Learning@Scale* (pp. 75–85). Association for Computing Machinery.

Chen, B.X. (23 December 2022). How to use ChatGPT and still be a good person. *The New York Times*. https://nytimes.com/2022/12/21/technology/personaltech/how-to-use-chatgpt-ethically.html.

Chen, L., Chen, P., & Lin, Z. (2020). Artificial intelligence in education: A review. *IEEE Access, 8*, 75264–78. https://doi.org/10.1109/ACCESS.2020.2988510.

Chen, X., Zou, D., Xie, H., & Su, F. (2021). Twenty-five years of computer-assisted language learning: A topic modeling approach. *Language Learning & Technology, 25*(3), 151–85.

Chowdhery, A. (2022). *Scaling language modeling with pathways*. arXiv Preprint.

Christian, B. (2021). *The alignment problem: Machine learning and human problems*. W. W. Norton & Company.

Coeckelbergh, M. (2023). AI ethics – A review of three recent publications. *AI & Society, 39*(1), 143–64. https://doi.org/10.1007/s00146-023-01543-w.

Coghlan, S., Miller, T., & Paterson, J. (2021). Good proctor or "big brother"? Ethics of online exam supervision technologies. *Philosophy & Technology, 34*(4), 1581–606. https://doi.org/10.1007/s13347-021-00476-1.

Colby, K.M. (1975). Modeling a paranoid mind. *Behavioral and Brain Sciences, 1*(4), 470–81. https://doi.org/10.1017/S0140525X00000030.

Cotton, D., Susnjak, D., & Elkins, T. (2023). Exploring the ethical dimensions of using ChatGPT in language learning and beyond. *Languages, 8*(1), 107–12. https://doi.org/10.3390/languages8030191.

Counterpoint. (1 March 2023). Over 1 billion generative AI (genAI) smartphones to be shipped cumulatively during CY2024–2027. *Counterpoint Technology Market Research*. https://counterpointresearch.com/insights/over-1-billion-generative-ai-smartphones-to-be-shipped-cumulatively-during-cy-2024-2027/.

Crawford, K. (2021). *Atlas of AI: Power, politics, and the planetary costs of artificial intelligence*. Harvard University Press.

Crookes, G.V. (2022). Critical language pedagogy. *Language Teaching, 55*(1), 46–63. https://doi.org/10.1017/S0261444820000609.

Crowson, K., Biderman, S., Kornis, D., Stander, D., Hallahan, E., Castricato, L., & Raff, E. (2022). VQGAN-CLIP: Open domain image-generation and editing with natural language guidance. arXiv 2204.08583v2.

Cui, W., Xue, Z., & Thai, K.-P. (2018). Performance comparison of an AI-based adaptive learning system in China. In *2018 Chinese Automation Congress (CAC)* (pp. 3170–5). IEEE.

D'Agostino, S. (2023). Why professors are polarized on AI. *Inside Higher Education*. https://insidehighered.com/news/tech-innovation/artificial-intelligence/2023/09/13/why-faculty-members-are-polarized-ai#:~:text=Some%20resist%20the%20technology%20because,tech%20inappropriate%20for%20their%20discipline.

Dai, L., Jung, M. M., Postma, M., & Louwerse, M. M. (2022). A systematic review of pedagogical agent research: Similarities, differences, and unexplored aspects. *Computers and Education, 190*, https://doi.org/10.1016/j.compedu.2022.104607.

Dale, R., & Viethen, J. (2021). The automated writing assistance landscape in 2021. *Natural Language Engineering, 27*(4), 511–18. https://doi.org/10.1017/s1351324921000164.

Darling-Hammond, L., Flook, L., Cook-Harvey, C., Barron, B., & Osher, D. (2020). Implications for educational practice of the science of learning and development. *Applied Developmental Science, 24*(2), 97–140. https://doi.org/10.1080/10888691.2018.1537791.

Davie, L.E., & Wells, R. (1991). Empowering the learner through computer-mediated communication. *American Journal of Distance Education, 5*(1), 15–23. https://doi.org/10.1080/08923649109526728.

Deeva, G., Bogdanova, D., Serral, E., Snoeck, M., & De Weerdt, J. (2021). A review of automated feedback systems for learners: Classification framework, challenges and opportunities. *Computers & Education, 162*, 104094. https://doi.org/10.1016/j.compedu.2020.104094.

de Freitas, M.P., Piai, V.A., Farias, R.H., Fernandes, A.M.R., Rossetto, A.G.M., & Leithardt, V.R.Q. (2022). Artificial intelligence of things assistive technology: A systematic literature review. *Sensors, 22*, 8531. https://doi.org/10.3390/s22218531.

Denkin, R. (2024). On perception of prevalence of cheating and usage of generative AI. arXiv preprint arXiv:2405.18889.

Devlin, H. (2023). AI 'could be as transformative as the Industrial Revolution'. *The Guardian*. https://theguardian.com/technology/2023/may/03/ai-could-be-as-transformative-as-industrial-revolution-patrick-vallance.

Dhariwal, P., Jun, H., Payne, C., Kim, J.W., Radford, A., & Sutskever, I. (2020). Jukebox: A generative model for music. arXiv preprint arXiv:2005, 00341.

Diaz, M. (15 June 2023). Bing image creator vs. DALL-E 2: Which generates the best AI images? *ZDNet*. https://zdnet.com/article/bing-image-creator-vs-dall-e-2-which-generates-the-best-ai-images/.

DiCerbo, K. (2020). Assessment for learning with diverse learners in a digital world. *Educational Measurement: Issues and Practice, 39*(3), 90–3. https://doi.org/10.1111/emip.12374.

Dikli, S., & Bleyle, S. (2014). Automated essay scoring feedback for second language writers: How does it compare to instructor feedback? *Assessing Writing, 22*, 1–17. https://doi.org/10.1016/j.asw.2014.03.006.

Dizon, G. (2020). Evaluating intelligent personal assistants for L2 listening and speaking development. *Language Teaching & Technology, 24*(1), 16–26. https://doi.org/10125/44705.

Dobrin, D.N. (1990). A new grammar checker. *Computers and the Humanities, 24*, 67–80. https://doi.org/10.1007/BF00115029.

Dooly, M., & Vinagre, M. (2022). Research into practice: Virtual exchange in language teaching and learning. *Language Teaching, 55*(3), 392–406. https://doi.org/10.1017/S0261444821000069.

Doyle, W. (2013). Ecological approaches to classroom management. In C.M. Everston & C.S. Weinstein (Eds.), *Handbook of classroom management: Research, practice, and contemporary issues* (pp. 107–36). Routledge.

Drachsler, H., & Greller, W. (2016). Privacy and analytics: It is a DELICATE issue – A checklist for trusted learning analytics. In *Proceedings of the sixth international conference on learning analytics & knowledge* (pp. 89–98). ACM.

Duolingo. (15 November 2022). How we use AI to create effective language lessons. *Duolingo Blog.* https://blog.duolingo.com/how-we-use-ai-to-create-effective-language-lessons/.

Edelblut, P. (19–24 July 2020). Realizing the promise of AI-powered, adaptive, automated, instant feedback on writing for students in grades 3–8 with an IEP. In *Adaptive instructional systems: Second international conference, AIS 2020, held as part of the 22nd HCI international conference, HCII 2020, Proceedings 22* (pp. 283–92). Springer International Publishing.

Edge, D., Searle, E., Chiu, K., Zhao, J., & Landay, J.A. (2011). MicroMandarin: Mobile language learning in context. In *Proceedings of the SIGCHI conference on human factors in computing systems* (pp. 3169–78). Association for Computing Machinery.

Ellis, R. (2009). Corrective feedback and teacher development. *L2 Journal, 1*(1).

Ellis, R. (2017). Task-based language teaching. In *The Routledge handbook of instructed second language acquisition* (pp. 108–25). Routledge.

Ertmer, P.A., & Ottenbreit-Leftwich, A.T. (2010). Teacher technology change: How knowledge, confidence, beliefs, and culture intersect. *Journal of Research on Technology in Education, 42*(3), 255–84. https:/doi.org/10.1080/15391523.2010.10782551.

Eskenazi, M. (2009). An overview of spoken language technology for education. *Speech Communication, 51*(10), 832–44. https://doi.org/10.1016/j.specom.2009.04.005.

Evans, O., Cotton-Barratt, O., Finnveden, L., Bales, A., Balwit, A., Wills, P., Righetti, L., & Suanders, W. (2021). Truthful AI: Developing and governing AI that doesn't lie. arXiv preprint arXiv:2110.006674v1.

Felix, U. (2005). E-learning pedagogy in the third millennium: The need for combining social and cognitive constructivist approaches. *ReCALL, 17*(1), 85–100. https://doi.org/10.1017/S0958344005000716.

Fedders, B. (2019). The constant and expanding classroom: Surveillance in K-12 public schools. *North Carolina Law Review, 97*(6), 1673–1726.

Flasiński, M. (2016). *Introduction to artificial intelligence*. Springer.

Freire, P. (2000). *The pedagogy of the oppressed*. Continuum.

Froyd, J., & Simpson, N. (2008). Student-centered learning: Addressing faculty questions about student-centered learning. In *Course, curriculum, labor, and improvement conference* (Vol. 30, pp. 1–11). Scientific Research: An Academic Publisher.

Fu, Q.-K., Zou, D., Xie, H., & Cheng, G. (2024). A review of AWE feedback: Types, learning outcomes, and implications. *Computer Assisted Language Learning, 37*(1–2), 179–221. https://doi.org/10.1080/09588221.2022.2033787.

Gabriel, I. (2020). Artificial intelligence, values, and alignment. *Minds and Machines, 30*(3), 411–37. https://doi.org/10.1007/s11023-020-09539-2.

Gadney, G. (15 June 2022). Once upon an AI: Storytelling augmented with natural language and virtual production. *NVidia On-Demand*. https://nvidia.com/en-us/on-demand/session/gtcspring22-s41532/.

Gee, J.P. (2015). *Social linguistics and literacies: Ideology in discourses* (5th ed.). Routledge.

Georgia Tech Professional Education. (2016). Meet Jill Watson: Georgia Tech's first AI teaching assistant. *Georgia Tech Professional Education Blog*. https://pe.gatech.edu/blog/meet-jill-watson-georgia-techs-first-ai-teaching-assistant.

Ghahramani, Z. (31 May 2023). Introducing PaLM2. *The Keyword*. https://blog.google/technology/ai/google-palm-2-ai-large-language-model/.

Ghufron, M.A., & Rosyida, F. (2018). The role of Grammarly in assessing English as a foreign language (EFL) writing. *Lingua Cultura, 12*(4), 395–403. https://doi.org/10.21512/lc.v12i4.4582.

Gibbs, G., & Simpson, C. (2005). Conditions under which assessment supports students' learning. *Learning and Teaching in Higher Education, 1*, 3–31.

Godwin-Jones, R. (2022). Partnering with AI: Intelligent writing assistance and instructed language learning. *Language Learning and Technology, 26*(2), 5–24. https://doi.org/10125/73474.

Goel, A.K., & Polepeddi, L. (2018). Jill Watson: A virtual teaching assistant for online education. In C. Dede, J. Richards, & B. Saxberg (Eds.), *Learning engineering for online education: Theoretical contexts and design-based examples* (pp. 120–43). Routledge.

González, L.A., Neyem, A., Contreras-McKay, I., & Molina, D. (2022). Improving learning experiences in software engineering courses using artificial intelligence virtual assistants. *Computer Applications in Engineering Education, 30*(5), 1370–89. https://doi.org/10.1002/cae.22526.

González-Calatayud, V., Prendes-Espinosa, P., & Roig-Vila, R. (2021). Artificial intelligence for student assessment: A systematic review. *Applied Sciences, 11*(12), 5467. https://doi.org/10.3390/app11125467.

Goodfellow, I.J., Pouget-Abadie, J., Mirza, M., Bing, X., Warde-Farley, D., Ozair, S., Courville, A., & Bengio, Y. (2014). Generative adversarial nets. *Advances in Neural Information Processing Systems, 27.*

Gulson, K.N., Sellar, S., & Taylor Webb, P. (2022). *Algorithms of education: How datafication and artificial intelligence shape policy.* University of Minnesota Press.

Guo, Q., Feng, R., & Hua, Y. (2021). How effectively can EFL students use automated written corrective feedback (AWCF) in research writing? *Computer Assisted Language Learning, 35*(9), 2313–31. https://doi.org/10.1080/09588221.2021.1879161.

Gupta, M., Akiri, C., Aryal, K., Parker, E., & Praharaj, L. (2023). From ChatGPT to ThreatGPT: Impact of generative AI in cybersecurity and privacy. *IEEE Access,* 11, 80218–45. https://doi.org/10.1109/ACCESS.2023.3300381.

Han, T., & Sari, E. (2022). An investigation on the use of automated feedback in Turkish EFL students' writing classes. *Computer Assisted Language Learning, 37,* 961–85. https://doi.org/10.1080/09588221.2022.2067179.

Hao, J., von Davier, A.A., Yaneva, V., Lottridge, S., von Davier, M., & Harris, D.J. (2024). Transforming assessment: The impacts and implications of large language models and generative AI. *Educational Measurement: Issues and Practice, 43*(2), 16–29. https://doi.org/10.1111/emip.12602.

Hao, K. (2 August 2019). China has started a grand experiment in AI education. It could reshape how the world learns. *MIT Technology Review.* https://technologyreview.com/2019/08/02/131198/china-squirrel-has-started-a-grand-experiment-in-ai-education-it-could-reshape-how-the/.

Hardt, M. (26 September 2014). How big data is unfair: Understanding unintended sources of unfairness in data driven decision making. *Medium.* https://medium.com/@mrtz/how-big-data-is-unfair-9aa544d739de.

Harreis, H., Koullias, T., Roberts, R., & Te, K. (15 June 2023). *Generative AI: Unlocking the future of fashion.* McKinsey & Company. https://mckinsey.

com/industries/retail/our-insights/generative-ai-unlocking-the-future-of-fashion.

Haswell, R. (2005). Automated text-checkers: A chronology and a bibliography of commentary. *Computers and Composition Online*. https://wac.colostate.edu/docs/comppile/pd/textcheckers.pdf.

Hattie, J., & Timperley, H. (2007). The power of feedback. *Review of Educational Research, 77*(1), 81–112. https://doi.org/10.3102/003465430298487.

Hauck, M. (2005). Metacognitive knowledge, metacognitive strategies, and CALL. In *CALL research perspectives* (pp. 65–86). Lawrence Erlbaum.

Haven, J. (14 December 2022). ChatGPT and the future of trust. *Nieman Foundation*. https://niemanlab.org/2022/12/chatgpt-and-the-future-of-trust/.

Heidorn, G.E., Jensen, K., Miller, L.A., Byrd, R.J., & Chodorow, M.S. (1982). The EPISTLE text-critiquing system. *IBM Systems Journal, 21*(3), 305–26. https://doi.org/10.1147/sj.213.0305.

Hill, C., Rosehart, P., St. Helene, J., & Sadhra, S. (2020). What kind of educator does the world need today? Reimagining teacher education in post-pandemic Canada. *Journal of Education for Teaching, 46*(4), 565–75. https://doi.org/10.1080/02607476.2020.1797439.

Holmes, W., & Bi, M. (2023). Ethical principles for artificial intelligence in education (AIED). *Education and Information Technologies, 29*(3), 1124–41. https://doi.org/10.1007/s10639-022-11316-w.

Holmes, W., & Tuomi, I. (2022). State of the art and practice in AI in education. *European Journal of Education Research, Development, and Policy, 57*(4), 542-570. https://doi.org/10.1111/ejed.12533.

Holmes, W., Porayska-Pomsta, K., Holstein, K., Sutherland, E., Baker, T., Shum, S.B., Santos, O.C., Rodrigo, M.T., Cukurova, M., Bittencourt, I.I., & Koedinger, K.R. (2022). Ethics of AI in education: Towards a community-wide framework. *International Journal of Artificial Intelligence in Education, 32*, 504–26. https://doi.org/10.1007/s40593-021-00239-1.

Holstein, K., & Doroudi, S. (2022). Equity and artificial intelligence in education. In *The ethics of artificial intelligence in education* (pp. 151–73). Routledge.

hooks, b. (1994). *Teaching to transgress: Education as the practice of freedom*. Routledge.

Hoorn, J.F., Huang, I.S., Konijn, E.A., & van Buuren, L. (2021). Robot tutoring of multiplication: Over one-third learning gain for most, learning loss for some. *Robotics, 10*(1), 16. https://doi.org/10.3390/robotics10010016.

Huang, J., & Li, S. (2023). Opportunities and challenges in the application of ChatGPT in foreign language teaching. *International Journal of Education and Social Science Research*, 6(4), 75–89. https://doi.org/10.37500/IJESSR.2023.6406.

Huang, L. (2023). Ethics of artificial intelligence in education: Student privacy and data protection. *Science Insights Education Frontiers, 16*(2), 2577–87. https://doi.org/10.15354/sief.23.re202.

Huawei, S., & Aryadoust, V. (2023). A systematic review of automated writing evaluation systems. *Education and Information Technologies, 28*(1), 771–95. https://doi.org/10.1007/s10639-022-11200-7.

Huggins-Manley, A.C., Booth, B.M., & D'Mello, S.K. (2022). Toward argument-based fairness with an application to AI-enhanced educational assessments. *Journal of Educational Measurement, 59*(3), 362–88. https://doi.org/10.1111/jedm.12334.

Hussain Shah, S.J., Albishri, A.A., & Lee, Y. (2021). Deep learning framework for Internet of Things for people with disabilities. In *Proceedings of the 2021 IEEE international conference on big data* (pp. 3609–14). IEEE. https://doi.org/10.1109/BigData52589.2021.9671475.

Huth, T. (2020). *Interaction, language use, and second language teaching*. Routledge.

Hyland, K., & Hyland, F. (2006). Feedback on second language students' writing. *Language Teaching, 39*(2), 83–101. https://doi.org/10.1017/S0261444806003399.

Ifelebuegu, A. (2023). Rethinking online assessment strategies: Authenticity versus AI chatbot intervention. *Journal of Applied Learning &Teaching, 6*(2). https://doi.org/10.37074/jalt.2023.6.2.2.

Instructure. (2023). Canvas by Instructure. *Instructure*. https://instructure.com/k12/products/canvas.

Jeon, J., Lee, S., & Choi, S. (2023). A systematic review of research on speech-recognition chatbots for language learning: Implications for future directions in the era of large language models. *Interactive Learning Environments, 32*, 4613–31. https://doi.org/10.1080/10494820.2023.2204343.

Ji, H., Han, I., & Ko, Y. (2023). A systematic review of conversational AI in language education: Focusing on the collaboration with human teachers. *Journal of Research on Technology in Education, 55*(1), 48–63. https://doi.org/10.1080/15391523.2022.2142873.

Jobin, A., Ienca, M., & Vayena, E. (2019). The global landscape of AI ethics guidelines. *Nature Machine Intelligence, 1*(9), 389–99. https://doi.org/10.1038/s42256-019-0088-2.

Johnson, K. (15 July 2024). California teachers are using AI to grade papers. Who's grading the AI? *CalMatters*. https://calmatters.org/economy/technology/2024/06/teachers-ai-grading/.

Johnson, W.L. (2007). Tactical language and culture training system: Learn and author. In R. Larkin, K.R. Koedinger, & J. Greer (Eds.), *Proceedings of the 2007 conference on artificial intelligence in education: Building technology rich learning contexts* (p. 734). IOS Press.

Johnson, W.L., & Soloway, E. (1984). Intention-based diagnosis of programming errors. In *Proceedings of the AAAI conference on artificial intelligence* (pp. 162–8). AAAI Press.

Johnson, W.L., & Valente, A. (2009). Tactical language and culture training systems: Using AI to teach foreign language and cultures. *AI Magazine, 30*(2), 72–83. https://doi.org/10.1609/aimag.v30i2.2240.

Jones, K., Jones, J., & Vermette, P. (2011). Six common lesson planning pitfalls: Recommendations for novice educators. *Education, 131*(4), 845–64.

Kalb, I. (2022). *Object-oriented Python*. No Starch Press.

Kartal, G. (Ed.). (2023). *Transforming the language teaching experience in the age of AI.* IGI Global.

Keerthiwansha, N.W.B.S. (2018). Artificial intelligence education (AIEd) in English as a second language (ESL) classroom in Sri Lanka. *International Journal of Conceptions on Computing and Information Technology, 6*(1), 31–6.

Keiler, L.S. (2018). Teachers' roles and identities in student-centered classrooms. *International Journal of STEM Education, 5*, 1–20. https://doi.org/10.1186/s40594-018-0131-6.

Khalil, M., & Ebner, M. (2016). De-identification in learning analytics. *Journal of Learning Analytics, 3*(1), 129–38. https://doi.org/10.18608/jla.2016.31.8.

Khawaja, S., & Karimi, H. (2024). AI in English higher education: Balancing innovation with equity challenges and opportunities. In *An overview of literature, language and education research* (pp. 55–66). BP International.

Khosravi, H., Shum, S.B., Chen, G., Conati, C., Tsai, Y.-S., Kay, J., Knight, S., Martinez-Maldonado, R., Sadiq, S., & Gašević, D. (2021). Explainable artificial intelligence in education. *Computers and Education: Artificial Intelligence, 3*, 100074. https://doi.org/10.1016/j.caeai.2022.10074.

Kim, D. (2020). Learning language, learning culture: Teaching language to the whole student. *ECNU Review of Education, 3*(3), 519–41. https://doi.org/10.1177/2096531120936693.

Kim, W. (2023). How can artificial intelligence be employed for semantic prosody analysis? *Korean Society for Applied Linguistics, 39*(2), 3–34. https://doi.org/10.17154/kjal.2023.6.39.2.3.

Kingma, D.P., & Welling, M. (2013). Auto-encoding variational Bayes. arXiv 1312. 6114.

Klingbeil, A., Grützner, C., & Schreck, P. (2024). Trust and reliance on AI – An experimental study on the extent and costs of overreliance on AI. *Computers in Human Behavior, 160*, 108352. https://doi.org/10.1016/j.chb.2024.108352.

Knox, J., Williamson, B., & Bayne, S. (2020). Machine behaviourism: Future visions of 'learnification' and 'datafication' across humans and digital technologies. *Learning, Media and Technology, 45*(1), 31–45. https://doi.org/10.1080/17439884.2019.1623251.

Koch, J., & Oulasvirta, A. (2018). Group cognition and collaborative AI. In *Human and machine learning: Visible, explainable, trustworthy and transparent* (pp. 293–312). Springer.

Koedinger, K.R., & Corbett, A.T. (2006). Cognitive tutors: Technology bringing learning science to the classroom. In K. Sawyer (Ed.), *The Cambridge handbook of the learning sciences* (pp. 61–77). Cambridge University Press.

Kohnke, L., Luke Moorhouse, B., & Zou, D. (2023). ChatGPT for language teaching and learning. *RELC Journal*, 1–14. https://doi.org/10.1177/00336882231162868.

Kolb, D.A. (1984). *Experiential learning: Experience as the source of learning and development*. Prentice Hall.

Koltovskaia, S. (2020). Student engagement with automated written corrective feedback (AWCF) provided by Grammarly: A multiple case study. *Assessing Writing, 44*, 100450. https:/doi.org/10.1016/j.asw.2020.100450.

Koltovskaia, S. (2023). Postsecondary L2 writing teachers' use and perceptions of Grammarly as a complement to their feedback. *ReCALL, 35*(3), 290–304. https://doi.org/10.1017/s0958344022000179.

Kong, S.-C., William Cheung, M.-Y., & Tsang, O. (2024). Developing an artificial intelligence literacy framework: Evaluation of a literacy course for senior secondary students using a project-based learning approach. *Computers and Education: Artificial Intelligence, 6*, 100214. https://doi.org/10.1016/j.caeai.2024.100214.

Koraishi, O. (2023). Teaching English in the age of AI: Embracing ChatGPT to optimize EFL materials and assessment. *Language Education & Technology, 3*(1).

Kostka, I., & Toncelli, R. (2023). Exploring applications of ChatGPT to English language teaching: Opportunities, challenges, and recommendations. *TESL-EJ, 27*(3). https://doi.org/10.55593/ej.27107int.

Kramsch, C. (1993). *Context and culture in language teaching*. Oxford University Press.

Kramsch, C. (2014). Language and culture. *AILA Review, 27*(1), 30–55. https://doi.org/10.1075/aila.27.02kra.

Kremling, J., Rothlisberger, C., & Smart, S. (2017). Negative classroom experiences. In *Why students resist learning* (pp. 128–45). Routledge.

Kudritskaya, M., Plastinina, N., Kushnina, L., Plekhanova, Y., Matytcina, M., & Stepanova, M. (2024). Balancing innovation with ethics: AI applications for enhancing language competence in academic writing and reading.

In *2024 4th international conference on technology enhanced learning in higher education (TELE)* (pp. 380–5). IEEE.

Kumar, R., Eaton, S.E., Mindzak, M., & Morrison, R. (2024). Academic integrity and artificial intelligence: An overview. In *Second handbook of academic integrity* (pp. 1583–96). Springer.

Laufer, B., & IS Paul Nation. (2012). Vocabulary. In *The Routledge handbook of second language acquisition* (pp. 163–76). Routledge.

Lee, D. (30 June 2018). At this Chinese school, Big Brother was watching students – and charting every smile or frown. *The Los Angeles Times*. https://latimes.com/world/la-fg-china-face-surveillance-2018-story.html.

Lee, G.-G., & Zhai, X. (forthcoming). Using ChatGPT for science learning: A study on pre-service teachers' lesson planning. arXiv preprint arXiv:2402.01674.

Lee, I. (2008). Student reactions to teacher feedback in two Hong Kong secondary classrooms. *Journal of Second Language Writing, 17*(3), 144–64. https://doi.org/10.1016/j.jslw.2007.12.001.

Lee, S.M. (24 August 2024). AI scientists have a problem: AI bots are reviewing their work. *The Chronicle of Higher Education*. https://chronicle.com/article/ai-scientists-have-a-problem-ai-bots-are-reviewing-their-work?sra=true.

Lee, V.R., Pope, D., Miles, S., & Zarate, R. (2024). Cheating in the age of generative AI: A high school survey study of cheating behaviors before and after the release of ChatGPT. *Computers and Education: Artificial Intelligence, 7*, 100253. https://doi.org/10.1016/j.caeai.2024.100253.

Lee, Y.-W. (2016). Investigating the feasibility of generic scoring models of E-rater for TOEFL iBT independent writing tasks. *English Language Teaching, 28*(1), 100–22. https://doi.org/10.17936/pkelt.2016.28.1.6.

Lee, Y.-W., Gentile, C., & Kantor, R. (2008). *Analytic scoring of TOEFL® CBT essays: Scores from humans and e-rater®. ETS Research Report Series*. Educational Testing Service.

Lenker, J.A., Harris, F., Taugher, M., & Smith, R.O. (2013). Consumer perspectives on assistive technology outcomes. *Disability and Rehabilitation: Assistive Technology, 8*(5), 373–80. https://doi.org/10.3109/17483107.2012.749429.

Lepri, B., Oliver, N., Letouzé, E., Pentland, A., & Vinck, P. (2018). Fair, transparent, and accountable algorithmic decision-making processes: The premise, the proposed solutions, and the open challenges. *Philosophy & Technology, 31*, 611–27. https://doi.org/10.1007/s13347-017-0279-x.

Levy, M., & Stockwell, G. (2013). *CALL dimensions: Options and issues in computer-assisted language learning*. Routledge.

Li, D., He, W., & Guo, Y. (2021). Why AI still doesn't have consciousness? *CAAI Transactions on Intelligence Technology, 6*(2), 175–9. https://doi.org/10.1049/cit2.12035.

Li, F., Huang, W., Luo, M., Zhang, P., & Zha, Y. (2021). A new VAE-GAN model to synthesize arterial spin labeling images from structural MRI. *Displays, 70*, 102079. https://doi.org/10.1016/j.displa.2021.102079.

Li, H. (2023). AI in education: Bridging the divide or widening the gap? Exploring equity, opportunities, and challenges in the digital age. *Advances in Education, Humanities and Social Science Research, 8*(1), 355. https://doi.org/10.56028/aehssr.8.1.355.2023.

Li, K.C., Wong, B.Y.Y., & Chok, E.W.S. (2014). Reconceptualizing analytics in education: A quest for a common ground. In D. Wong, K.C. Li, & K.S. Yuen (Eds.), *Proceedings of the 28th annual conference of the Asian Association of Open Universities* (pp. 589–99). Asian Association of Open Universities.

Li, R. (2023). Still a fallible tool? Revisiting effects of automated writing evaluation from activity theory perspective. *British Journal of Educational Technology, 54*(3), 773–89. https://doi.org/10.1111/bjet.13294.

Liakin, D., Cardoso, W., & Liakina, N. (2015). Learning L2 pronunciation with a mobile speech recognizer: French /y/. *CALICO Journal, 32*(1), 1–25. https://doi.org/10.1558/cj.v32i1.25962.

Liang, W., Yuksekgonul, M., Mao, Y., Wu, E., & Zou, J. (2023). *GPT detectors are biased against non-native English writers*. arXiv preprint arXiv:2304.02819.

Litzler, E., & Young, J. (2012). Understanding the risk of attrition in undergraduate engineering: Results from the project to assess climate in engineering. *Journal of Engineering Education, 101*(2), 319–45. https://doi.org/10.1002/j.2168-9830.2012.tb00052.x.

Liu, B. (2020). *Sentiment analysis: Mining opinions, sentiments, and emotions* (2nd ed.). Cambridge University Press.

Liu, Y., & Quan, Q. (2022). AI recognition method of pronunciation errors in oral English speech with the help of big data for personalized learning. *Journal of Information & Knowledge Management, 21*(Supp02), 2240028. https://doi.org/10.1142/S0219649222400287.

Lock, S. (5 December 2022). What is AI chatbot phenomenon ChatGPT and could it replace humans? *The Guardian*. https://theguardian.com/technology/2022/dec/05/what-is-ai-chatbot-phenomenon-chatgpt-and-could-it-replace-humans.

Lopez, N. (26 July 2016). Microsoft is using AI to give Office spell-check on steroids and more. *The Next Web*. https://thenextweb.com/news/microsoft-using-ai-give-office-spell-check-steroids-much.

Loy, M., Niemeyer, P., & Leuck, D. (2020). *Learning Java: An introduction to real-world programming with Java*. O'Reilly.

Lu, X., & Bluemel, B. (2023). Automated assessment of language. In *The Cambridge introduction to applied linguistics* (pp. 86–98). Cambridge University Press.

Lu, X., Wang, W., Motz, B.A., Ye, W., & Heffernan, N.T. (2023). Immediate text-based feedback timing on foreign language online assignments: How immediate should immediate feedback be? *Computers and Education Open, 5*, 100148. https://doi.org/10.1016/j.caeo.2023.100148.

Lupo, D., & Elrich, Z. (2001). Computer literacy and applications via distance e-learning. *Computers & Education, 36*(4), 333–45. https://doi.org/10.1016/S0360-1315(01)00022-7.

Luxton, D.D. (2014). Artificial intelligence in psychological practice: Current and future applications and implications. *Professional Psychology: Research and Practice, 45*(5), 332–9. https://doi.org/10.1037/a0034559.

Lyster, R., & Ranta, L. (1997). Corrective feedback and learner uptake: Negotiation of form in communicative classrooms. *Studies in Second Language Acquisition, 19*(1), 37–66. https://doi.org/10.1017/S0272263197001034.

Lytvyn, M. (9 November 2022). A history of innovation at Grammarly. *Grammarly Blog*. https://grammarly.com/blog/grammarly-12-year-history/.

Malec, W. (2020). Computer-based testing: A necessary evil or a sensible choice? *The Modern Higher Education Review, 5*, 100–13. https://doi.org/10.28925/2518-7635.2020.5.10.

Manovich, L. (2017). Automating aesthetics: Artificial intelligence and image culture. *Flash Art International, 316*, 1–10.

Marachi, R., & Quill, L. (2020). The case of Canvas: Longitudinal datafication through learning management systems. *Teaching in Higher Education: Critical Perspectives, 25*(4), 418–34. https://doi.org/10.1080/13562517.2020.1739641.

Matheis, P., & John, J.J. (2024). Reframing assessments: Designing authentic assessments in the age of generative AI. In *Academic integrity in the age of artificial intelligence* (pp. 139–61). IGI Global.

McCarthy, J., Minksy, M.L., Rochester, N., & Shannon, C.E. (1955/2006). A proposal for the Dartmouth Summer Research Project on artificial intelligence. *AI Magazine, 27*(4), 12–14. https://doi.org/10.1609/aimag.v27i4.1904.

McFarland, T.D., & Parker, R. (1990). *Expert systems in education and training*. Educational Technology Publications.

McGuire, A. (2023). Leveraging ChatGPT for rethinking plagiarism, digital literacy, and the ethics of co-authorship in higher education: A position paper and comparative critical reflection of composing processes. *Irish*

Journal of Technology Enhanced Learning, 7(2), 21–31. https://doi.org/10.22554/ijtel.v7i2.131.

McKinsey & Company. (2023). *The economic potential of generative AI: The next productivity frontier* [white paper]. McKinsey.

Meniado, J.C. (2023). The impact of ChatGPT on English language teaching, learning, and assessment: A rapid review of literature. *Arab World English Journal, 14*(4), 3–18. https://doi.org/10.24093/awej/vol14no4.1.

Microsoft. (n.d.). Microsoft Editor checks grammar and more in documents, mail, and the web. *Microsoft Support*. https://support.microsoft.com/en-us/office/microsoft-editor-checks-grammar-and-more-in-documents-mail-and-the-web-91ecbe1b-d021-4e9e-a82e-abc4cd7163d7.

Microsoft Translator. (n.d.). *Microsoft Translator for education*. https://translator.microsoft.com/help/education/.

Millman, E. (16 March 2023). A bunch of top music advocates want to ensure AI doesn't replace your favorite artist. *Rolling Stone*. https://rollingstone.com/music/music-news/music-groups-campaign-ai-replacing-artists-1234697985/.

Mitchell, M. (2019). *Artificial intelligence: A guide for thinking humans*. Pelican Books.

MLA-CCCC. (2023). *MLA-CCCC Joint Task Force on Writing and AI Working Paper: Overview of the issues, statement of principles, and recommendations* [working paper]. The Modern Language Association.

Mnih, V., Kavukcuoglu, K., Silver, D., Rusu, A.A., Veness, J., Bellemare, M.G., Graves, A., Riedmiller, M., Fidjeland, A.K., Ostrovski, G., Petersen, S., Beattie, C., Sadik, A., Antonoglou, I., King, H., Kumaran, D., Wierstra, D., Legg, S., & Hassabis, D. (2015). Human-level control through deep reinforcement learning. *Nature, 518*(7540), 529–33. https://doi.org/10.1038/nature14236.

Moorhouse, B.L., Alina Yeo, M., & Wan, Y. (2023). Generative AI tools and assessment: Guidelines of the world's top-ranking universities. *Computers and Education Open, 5*, 100151. https://doi.org/10.1016/j.caeo.2023.100151.

Moqbel, M.S.S., & Talib Al-Kadi, A.M. (2023). Foreign language learning assessment in the age of ChatGPT: A theoretical account. *Journal of English Studies in Arabia Felix, 2*(1), 71–84. https://doi.org/10.56540/jesaf.v2i1.62.

Mueller, D.N. (2009). Digital underlife in the networked writing classroom. *Computers and Composition, 26*(4), 240–50. https://doi.org/10.1016/j.compcom.2009.08.001.

Myers, A. (15 May 2023). AI-detectors biased against non-native English writers. *Stanford University Human-Centered Artificial Intelligence*. https://hai.stanford.edu/news/ai-detectors-biased-against-non-native-english-writers.

Nadeem, M., Farag, W.A., & Helal, M. (2024). Rethinking assessment methodologies in the era of artificial intelligence: Expanding beyond ChatGPT's scope. In *Mediterranean smart cities conference*. IEEE.

Natale, S. (2019). If software is narrative: Joseph Weizenbaum, artificial intelligence, and the biographies of ELIZA. *New Media & Society, 21*(3), 712–28. https://doi.org/10.1177/1461444818804980.

Nicol, D.J., & Macfarlane-Dick, D. (2006). Formative assessment and self-regulated learning: A model and seven principles of good feedback practice. *Studies in Higher Education, 31*(2), 199–218. https://doi.org/10.1080/03075070600572090.

Norton, B., & Toohey, K. (Eds.). (2004). *Critical pedagogies and language learning*. Cambridge University Press.

Novawan, A., Walker, S.A., & Ikeda, O. (2024). The new face of technology-enhanced language learning (TELL) with artificial intelligence (AI): Teacher perspectives, practices, and challenges. *Journal of English in Academic and Professional Communication, 10*(1), 1–18.

Office of Educational Technology. (2023). *Artificial intelligence and the future of teaching and learning: Insights and recommendations* [government report]. U.S. Department of Education.

Oliver, R.M., Wehby, J.H., & Reschly, D.J. (2011). Teacher classroom management practices: Effects on disruptive or aggressive student behavior. *Campbell Systematic Reviews, 7*(1), 1–55. https://doi.org/10.4073/csr.2011.4.

O'Neil, C. (2016). *Weapons of math destruction: How big data increases inequality and threatens democracy*. Crown.

O'Neill, R., & Russell, A.M.T. (2019). Stop! Grammar time: University students' perceptions of the automated feedback program Grammarly. *Australasian Journal of Educational Technology, 35*(1), 42–56. https://doi.org/10.14742/ajet.3795.

OpenAI. (29 May 2023a). ChatGPT – Release notes. *OpenAI Help*. https://help.openai.com/en/articles/6825453-chatgpt-release-notes.

OpenAI. (16 June 2023b). DALL-E 2 – Release notes. *OpenAI Help*. https://help.openai.com/en/articles/6825694-dalle2-release-notes.

OpenAI. (15 June 2023c). Jukebox. *OpenAI Research*. https://openai.com/research/jukebox.

OpenAI. (15 June 2023d). MuseNet. *OpenAI Research*. https://openai.com/research/musenet.

OpenAI. (15 July 2024). Khan Academy GPT-4o math tutor demo – How to. *OpenAI API Documentation*. https://community.openai.com/t/khan-academy-gpt-4o-math-tutor-demo-how-to/746530.

Opps, Z. (2024). *Artificial intelligence and machine learning: Unpacking high school CS teachers' perspectives and pedagogical approaches* [Doctoral dissertation, Michigan State University].

Orsini-Jones, M., Cerveró-Carrascosa, A., & Finardi, K. (2021). Digital critical literacy development and intercultural awareness raising 'in' action, 'on' action, and 'for' action in ELT. In *Teaching culturally and linguistically diverse international students in open and/or online learning environments: A research symposium*. University of Windsor.

Ortega, L. (2008). *Understanding second language acquisition*. Routledge.

Pack, A., & Maloney, J. (2023). Potential affordances of generative AI in language education: Demonstrations and an evaluative framework. *Teaching English with Technology, 23*(2), 4–24.

Paez, D. (15 June 2019). 'This person does not exist' creator reveals his site's creepy origin story. *Inverse*. https://inverse.com/article/53414-this-person-does-not-exist-creator-interview.

Paganini, P. (19 July 2024). Hackers stole OpenAI secrets in a 2023 security breach. *Security Affairs*. https://securityaffairs.com/165349/data-breach/openai-2023-security-breach.html.

Paiz, J.M. (2020). *Queering English language teaching: A practical guide for teachers*. Equinox UK.

Paiz, J.M. (2023). *AI assistance: EAP pedagogy and policy during seismic shifts*. Workshop Presentation, Meeting of the English for Academic Purposes Faculty of George Washington University, Washington, DC.

Paiz, J.M. (2024a). *Teaching in the age of AI: Implications for teaching and learning*. Bahrain Ministry of Education AI Teacher Training Seminars, Manama, Bahrain.

Paiz, J.M. (2024b). *Artificial intelligence and teacher education: An AI handbook for Bahrain Teachers College*. University of Bahrain.

Paiz, J.M., & Kostka, I. (2023). Decipher AI speak: A primer for educators. *TESOL Connections*. Back-to-School Issue. http://newsmanager.commpartners.com/tesolc/issues/2023-08-01/2.html.

Paiz, J.M., Toncelli, R., & Kostka, I. (2025). *Artificial intelligence, real teaching: A guide to AI in ELT*. University of Michigan Press.

Paiz, J.M., & Yamazaki, K. (2023). Toward collaborative AI: AI meets language pedagogy. In *Technology enhanced language learning 2023 conference*, Permian Basin, TX.

Pangrazio, L., & Selwyn, N. (2019). Personal data literacies: A critical literacies approach to enhancing understandings of personal digital data. *New Media & Society, 21*(2), 419–37. https://doi.org/10.1177/1461444818799523.

Pardo, A., & Siemens, G. (2014). Ethical and privacy principles for learning analytics. *British Journal of Educational Technology, 45*(3), 438–50. https://doi.org/10.1111/bjet.12152.

Pasquale, F. (2020). *The new laws of robotics: Defending human expertise in the age of AI.* The Belknap Press of Harvard University Press.

Payne, A., Bauler, C.V., Austin, T., & Clemons, A.M. (2023). Real-time accent-altering technology: The message is clear, and it is dehumanizing. *PsyArXiv.* https://doi.org/10.31234/osf.io/u4p2j.

Pearson. (2018). AI-based tutoring: A new kind of personalized learning. *Pearson Blog.* www.pearson.com/ped-blogs/blogs/2018/11/ai-based-tutoring-new-kind-personalized-learning.html.

Pecorari, D. (2013). *Teaching to avoid plagiarism: How to promote good source use.* McGraw-Hill Education.

Pelton, G., & Speech, C. (2012). Improving intelligent tutoring of pronunciation consonant cluster problems. In Galaczi (convenors), *Cambridge English Centenary Symposium on Speaking Assessment.* Cambridge English.

Pennington, D. (2019). Grammarly is destroying your ability to write. *Medium.* Retrieved 8 January 2024, from https://dtpennington.medium.com/grammarly-is-destroying-your-ability-to-write-6bef0a3056ae.

Pennycook, A. (2021). *Critical applied linguistics: A critical re-introduction* (2nd ed.). Routledge.

Pokrivcakova, S. (2019). Preparing teachers for the application of AI-powered technologies in foreign language education. *Journal of Language and Cultural Education, 7*(3), 135–53. https://doi.org/10.2478/jolace-2019-0025.

Popel, M., Tomkova, M., Tomek, J., Kaiser, Ł., Uszkoreit, J., Bojar, O., & Žabokrtský, Z. (2020). Transforming machine translation: A deep learning system reaches news translation quality comparable to human professionals. *Nature Communications, 11*(1), 1–15. https://doi.org/10.1038/s41467-020-18073-9.

Powers, D.E., Burstein, J.C., Chodorow, M., Fowles, M.E., & Kukich, K. (2001). *Stumping E-rater: Challenging the validity of automated essay scoring* (ETS Research Report Series). Educational Testing Service.

Powerschool. (2022). *Reducing student suspensions with unified classroom behavior support and culture coaching [White paper].* Powerschool.

Prinsloo, P., & Slade, S. (2015). Student privacy self-management: Implications for learning analytics. In *Proceedings of the fifth international conference on learning analytics and knowledge* (pp. 83–92).

Prinsloo, P., & Slade, S. (2016). Student vulnerability, agency, and learning analytics: An exploration. *Journal of Learning Analytics, 3*(1), 159–82. https://doi.org/10.18608/jla.2016.31.10.

Qadhi, S.M., Alduais, A., Chaaban, Y., & Khraisheh, M. (2024). Generative AI, research ethics, and higher education research: Insights from a scientometric analysis. *Information, 15*(6), 325. https://doi.org/10.3390/info15060325.

Quirk, M., & Chumley, H. (2018). The adaptive medical curriculum: A model for continuous improvement. *Medical Teacher, 40*(8), 786–90. https://doi.org/10.1080/0142159x.2018.1484896.

Raheja, V., & Kumar, D. (2024). Learning where to edit: Introducing DELIteraTeR, a delineate-and-edit approach to iterative text revision. *Grammarly Engineering*. Retrieved 8 January 2024, from www.grammarly.com/blog/engineering/learning-where-to-edit/.

Rajapakse, S., Polwattage, D., Guruge, U., Jayathilaka, I., Edirisinghe, T., & Thelijjagoda, S. (2018). ALEXZA: A mobile application for dyslexics utilizing artificial intelligence and machine learning concepts. In *Proceedings of the 2018 3rd International Conference on Information Technology Research (ICITR)* (pp. 1–6). IEEE.

Regan, P.M., & Jesse, J. (2019). Ethical challenges of edtech, big data, and personalized learning: Twenty-first century study sorting and tracking. *Ethics and Information Technology, 21*, 167–79. https://doi.org/10.1007/s10676-018-9492-2.

Reich, J., & Ito, M. (2017). *From good intentions to real outcomes: Equity by design in learning technologies*. Digital Media and Learning Research Hub.

Reidenberg, J.R., & Schaub, F. (2018). Achieving big data privacy in education. *Theory and Research in Education, 16*(3), 263–79. https://doi.org/10.1177/1477878518805308.

Resta, P., & Laferrière, T. (2015). Digital equity and intercultural education. *Education and Information Technologies, 20*(4), 743–56. https://doi.org/10.1007/s10639-015-9419-z.

Reuters. (2024). Samsung to embed Google's generative AI tech in S24 smartphone series. *Reuters*. Retrieved 1 March 2024, from www.reuters.com/technology/samsung-embed-googles-generative-ai-tech-s24-smartphone-series-2024-01-17/.

Reyes, R., Garza, D., Garrido, L., De la Cueva, V., & Ramirez, J. (2019). Methodology for the implementation of virtual assistants for education using Google dialog flow. In *Advances in soft computing: 18th Mexican international conference on artificial intelligence, MICAI 2019, Xalapa, Mexico, October 27–November 2, 2019, Proceedings 18* (pp. 440–51). Springer International.

Richardson, M. (2022). *Rebuilding public confidence in educational assessment*. UCL Press.

Richardson, M., & Clesham, R. (2021). Rise of the machines? The evolving role of artificial intelligence (AI) technologies in high stakes assessment. *London Review of Education*, *19*(1), 1–13. https://doi.org/10.14324/LRE.19.1.09.

Rienties, B., Lewis, T., McFarlane, R., Nguyen, Q., & Toetenel, L. (2017). Analytics in online and offline language learning environments: The role of learning design to understand student online engagement. *Computer Assisted Language Learning*, *31*(3), 279–93. https://doi.org/10.1080/09588221.2018.1401548.

Riyadini, M. V., & Triastuti, A. (2023). Teachers' perspectives on ChatGPT as a language teaching resource: Benefits, challenges, and pedagogical considerations. *Proceedings of the 2023 Conference on English Language Teaching*, 1105-1115. State Islamic University of Prof. K.H. Saifuddin Zuhri Purwokerto.

Rodríguez-Triana, M.J., Martínez-Monés, A., & Villagrá-Sobrino, S. (2016). Learning analytics in small-scale teacher-led innovations: Ethical and data privacy issues. *Journal of Learning Analytics*, *3*(1), 43–65.

Roitblot, H.L. (2020). *Algorithms are not enough: Creating general artificial intelligence*. The MIT Press.

Roll, I., & Wylie, R. (2016). Evolution and revolution in artificial intelligence in education. *International Journal of Artificial Intelligence in Education*, *26*(2), 582–99. https://doi.org/10.1007/s40593-016-0110-3.

Roose, K. (2022). Don't ban ChatGPT in schools. Teach with it. *The New York Times*. Retrieved 12 January 2023, from www.nytimes.com/2023/01/12/technology/chatgpt-schools-teachers.html.

Rosehart, P., Hill, C., Sivia, A., Sadhra, S., & St. Helene, J. (2022). Seeking serendipity: Teacher educators as adaptive experts during COVID. *Journal of Education for Teaching*, *48*(4), 475–89. https://doi.org/10.1080/02607476.2022.2082275.

Rubel, A., & Jones, K.M.L. (2016). Student privacy in learning analytics: An information ethics perspective. *The Information Society*, *32*(2), 143–59. https://doi.org/10.1080/01972243.2016.1130502.

Rudolph, J., Tan, S., & Tan, S. (2023). ChatGPT: Bullshit spewer or the end of traditional assessments in higher education? *Journal of Applied Learning and Teaching*, *6*(1), 1–22. https://doi.org/10.37074/jalt.2023.6.1.9.

Sadasivan, V.S., Kumar, A., Balasubramanian, S., Wang, W., & Feizi, S. (2023). *Can AI-generated text be reliably detected?* arXiv preprint arXiv:2303.11156.

Saffiotti, A., Fogel, P., Knudsen, P., de Miranda, L., & Thörn, O. (2020). On human-AI collaboration in artistic performance. In *First international workshop on New Foundations for Human-Centered AI (NeHuAI) co-located with 24th European Conference on Artificial Intelligence (ECAI 2020)*, Santiago de Compostela, 4 September (pp. 38–43). CEUR-WS.

Sajid, H. (2023). AI bias & cultural stereotypes: Effects, limitations, and mitigation. *Unite.AI*. Retrieved 15 February 2024, from www.unite.ai/ai-bias-cultural-stereotypes-effects-limitations-mitigation/.

Savignon, S.J. (1987). Communicative language teaching. *Theory into Practice, 26*(4), 235–42.

Sawyer, A.G., & Myers, J. (2018). Seeking comfort: How and why preservice teachers use internet resources for lesson planning. *Journal of Early Childhood Teacher Education, 39*(1), 16–31. https://doi.org/10.1080/10901027.2017.1387625.

Sclater, N. (2016). Developing a code of practice for learning analytics. *Journal of Learning Analytics, 3*(1), 16–42. https://doi.org/10.18608/jla.2016.31.3.

Searson, M., Langran, E., & Trumble, J. (Eds.). (2024). *Exploring new horizons: Generative artificial intelligence and teacher education*. Association for the Advancement of Computing in Education.

Selwyn, N. (2020). Online learning: Rethinking teachers' digital competence in light of COVID-19. *Lens, Monash University*. Retrieved 30 April 2020, from https://lens.monash.edu/@education/2020/04/30/1380217/online-learning-rethinking-teachers-digital-competence-in-light-of-covid-19.

Sennrich, R. (2016). How grammatical is character-level neural machine translation? Assessing MT quality with contrastive translation pairs. arXiv preprint arXiv:1612.04629.

Settles, B., Brust, C., Gustafson, E., Hagiwara, M., & Madnani, N. (2018). Second language acquisition modeling. In *Proceedings of the Thirteenth Workshop on Innovative Use of NLP for Building Educational Applications* (pp. 56–65). Association for Computation Linguistics.

Shadiev, R., Hwang, W.-Y., & Huang, Y.-M. (2017). Review of research on mobile language learning in authentic environments. *Computer Assisted Language Learning, 30*(3–4), 284–303. https://doi.org/10.1080/09588221.2017.1308383.

Shalev-Shwartz, S., & Ben-David, S. (2014). *Understanding machine learning: From theory to algorithms*. Cambridge University Press.

Shannon, S., & Chapelle, C. (Eds.). (2017). *The handbook of technology and second language teaching and learning*. Wiley.

Shi, J. (2022). Artificial intelligence, algorithms, and sentencing in Chinese criminal justice: Problems and solutions. *Criminal Law Forum, 33*(2), 121–48. https://doi.org/10.1007/s10609-022-09437-5.

Shum, S., Buckingham, J., & Luckin, R. (2019). Learning analytics and AI: Politics, pedagogy and practices. *British Journal of Educational Technology, 50*(6), 2785–93. https://doi.org/10.1111/bjet.12880.

Shute, V.J., & Rahimi, S. (2017). Review of computer-based assessment for learning in elementary and secondary education. *Journal of Computer Assisted Learning, 33*(1), 1–19. https://doi.org/10.1111/jcal.12172.

Siemens, G., & Baker, R.S. (2012). Learning analytics and educational data mining: Towards communication and collaboration. In *Proceedings of the 2nd International Conference on Learning Analytics and Knowledge* (pp. 252–4). https://doi.org/10.1145/2330601.2330661.

Skrebeca, J., Kalniete, P., Goldbergs, J., Pitkevica, L., Tihomirova, D., & Romanovs, A. (2021). Modern development trends of chatbots using artificial intelligence (AI). In *Proceedings of the 2021 62nd international scientific conference on information technology and management science of Riga Technical University (ITMS)* (pp. 1–6). IEEE.

Slade, S., & Prinsloo, P. (2013). Learning analytics: Ethical issues and dilemmas. *American Behavioral Scientist, 57*(10), 1510–29. https://doi.org/10.1177/0002764213479366.

Slade, S., Prinsloo, P., & Khalil, M. (2019). Learning analytics at the intersections of student trust, disclosure, and benefit. In *Proceedings of the 9th International Conference on Learning Analytics & Knowledge* (pp. 235–44). ACM.

Smolansky, A., Cram, A., Raduescu, C., Zeivots, S., Huber, E., & Kizilcec, R.F. (2023). Educator and student perspectives on the impact of generative AI on assessments in higher education. In *Proceedings of the Tenth ACM Conference on Learning@ Scale* (pp. 378–82). Association for Computing Machinery.

Socher, R. (2019). Introducing a conditional transformer language model for controllable generation. *Salesforce Blog*. Retrieved 16 June 2023, from https://blog.salesforceairesearch.com/introducing-a-conditional-transformer-language-model-for-controllable-generation/.

Soloway, E., Bachant, J., & Jensen, K. (1987). Assessing the maintainability of XCON-in-RIME: Coping with the problems of a very large rule-base. In *Proceedings of the Sixth National Conference on Artificial Intelligence* (pp. 824–9). AAAI Press.

Song, G. (2019). Reform and exploration of accounting professional practice teaching under the background of artificial intelligence. *Materials Science and Engineering, 563*, 052005. https://doi.org/10.1088/1757-899X/563/5/052005.

Sony. (2023). Flow machines: Augmenting creativity with AI. *Sony Design*. Retrieved 15 June 2023, from www.sony.com/en/SonyInfo/design/stories/flow-machines/.

Stronge, J.H. (2018). *Qualities of effective teachers*. ASCD.

Supiano, B. (2023). Will ChatGPT change how professors assess learning? *Chronicle of Higher Education*. Retrieved 10 July 2024, from www.chronicle.com/article/will-chatgpt-change-how-professors-assess-learning.

Susnjak, T., & McIntosh, T.R. (2024). ChatGPT: The end of online exam integrity? *Education Sciences, 14*(6), 656. https://doi.org/10.3390/educsci14060656.

Swiecki, Z., Khosravi, H., Chen, G., Martinez-Maldonado, R., Lodge, J.M., Milligan, S., Selwyn, N., & Gašević, D. (2022). Assessment in the age of artificial intelligence. *Computers and Education: Artificial Intelligence, 3*, 100075. https://doi.org/10.1016/j.caeai.2022.100075.

Switzky, L. (2020). ELIZA effects: Pygmalion and the early developments of artificial intelligence. *Shaw: The Journal of Bernard Shaw Studies, 40*(1), 50–68. https://doi.org/10.5325/shaw.40.1.0050.

Synthesis AI. (2023). Synthesis humans. *Synthesis AI*. Retrieved 9 September 2023, from https://synthesis.ai/synthesis-humans/.

Talkpal. (2023). TalkPal learning: The premium AI-powered tutoring experience. *TalkPal Blog*. Retrieved 15 January 2024, from https://talkpal.ai/press-releases/talkpal-premium-introduction/.

Tan, D., Deng, L., Zheng, N., Yueng, Y. T., Jiang, X., Chen, X., & Lee, T. (2022). *CorrectSpeech: A fully automated system for speech correction and accent reduction*. ArXiv 2204. 05460v2. 1–5.

Taskıran, A., & Goksel, N. (2022). Automated feedback and teacher feedback: Writing achievement in learning English as a foreign language at a distance. *Turkish Online Journal of Distance Education, 23*(2), 120–39.

Toncic, J. (2020). Teachers, AI grammar checkers, and the newest literacies: Emending writing pedagogy and assessment. *Digital Culture & Education, 12*(1), 26–51.

Tondeur, J., Van Braak, J., Ertmer, P.A., & Ottenbreit-Leftwich, A. (2017). Understanding the relationship between teachers' pedagogical beliefs and technology use in education: A systematic review of qualitative evidence. *Educational Technology Research and Development, 65*, 555–75. https://doi.org/10.1007/s11423-016-9481-2.

Tsai, Y.-S., Muñoz-Merino, P.J., Jivet, I., Scheffel, M., Drachsler, H., Tammets, K., & Kloos, C.D. (2020). Learning analytics in European higher education – Trends and barriers. *Computers & Education, 155*, 103933. https://doi.org/10.1016/j.compedu.2020.103933.

van Lier, L. (Ed.). (2004). *The ecology and semiotics of language learning: A sociocultural perspective*. Springer Netherlands.

van den Berg, G., & du Plessis, E. (2023). ChatGPT and generative AI: Possibilities for its contribution to lesson planning, critical thinking, and openness in teacher education. *Education Sciences, 13*(10), 998. https://doi.org/10.3390/educsci13100998.

VanLehn, K. (2006). The behavior of tutoring systems. *International Journal of Artificial Intelligence in Education, 16*(3), 227–65.

Vardi, M.Y. (2016). The moral imperative of artificial intelligence. *Communications of the ACM, 59*(5), 5. https://doi.org/10.1145/2903530.

Vaswani, A., Shazeer, N., Parmar, N., Uszkoreit, J., Jones, L., Gomez, A.N., Kaiser, L., & Polosukhin, I. (2017). *Attention is all you need*. ArXiv. Retrieved 21 May 2023, from https://arxiv.org/abs/1706.03762.

Villasenor, J., & Foggo, V. (2020). Artificial intelligence, due process, and criminal sentencing. *Michigan State Law Review, 2020*, 295–353.

Voigt, P., & von dem Bussche, A. (2017). *The EU General Data Protection Regulation (GDPR): A practical guide*. Springer International Publishing.

Walker Rettberg, J. (2022). ChatGPT is multilingual but monocultural, and it is learning your values. *jill/txt*. Retrieved 6 December 2022, from https://jilltxt.net/right-now-chatgpt-is-multlingual-but-monocultural-but-its-learning-your-values/.

Wallach, W. (2018). *Moral machines: Teaching robots right from wrong*. Oxford University Press.

Wang, H., & Ní Chiaráin, N. (2019). Towards the design of iCALL tools for beginner mandarin Chinese learners in Ireland. *CALL and Complexity*, 385.

Wang, L., Hu, L., Gu, J., Wu, Y., Hu, Z., He, K., & Hopcroft, J. (2018). Towards understanding learning representations: To what extent do different neural networks learn the same representation. In *Proceedings of the 32nd conference on neural information processing systems*, Montreal, CA.

Wang, N., Wang, X., & Su, Y.-S. (2024). Critical analysis of the technological affordances, challenges and future directions of generative AI in education: A systematic review. *Asia Pacific Journal of Education*, *44*(1), 139–55. https://doi.org/10.1080/02188791.2024.2305156.

Wang, Y., Liu, C., & Tu, Y.-F. (2021). Factors affecting the adoption of AI-based applications in higher education. *Educational Technology & Society*, 24(3), 116–29.

Ware, J. (2017). *The effect of whole-language ICALL programs on student achievement scores* [PhD dissertation, Northern Illinois University].

Warschauer, M., & Matuchniak, T. (2010). New technology and digital worlds: Analyzing evidence of equity in access, use, and outcomes. *Review of Research in Education*, *34*(1), 179–225. https://doi.org/10.3102/0091732X09349791.

Weatherbed, J. (2023). Adobe is adding AI image generator Firefly to Photoshop. *The Verge*. Retrieved 23 May 2023, from www.theverge.com/2023/5/23/23734027/adobe-photoshop-generative-fill-ai-image-generator-firefly.

Weinberg, L. (2020). Feminist research ethics and student privacy in the age of AI. *Catalyst: Feminism, Theory, Technoscience*, *6*(2). https://doi.org/10.28968/cftt.v6i2.32943.

Weizenbaum, J. (1966). ELIZA – A computer program for the study of natural language communication between man and machine. *Communications of the ACM*, *9*(1), 36–45.

Weizenbaum, J. (1976). *Computer power and human reason: From judgment to calculation*. W. H. Freeman and Company.

Wenden, A.L. (1998). Metacognitive knowledge and language learning. *Applied Linguistics, 19*(4), 515–37. https://doi.org/10.1093/applin/19.4.515.

Wenger, E. (1987). *Artificial intelligence and tutoring systems: Computational and cognitive approaches to the communication of knowledge*. Morgan Kaufmann Publishers Inc.

Widayanti, R., & Mariyanti, T. (2023). AI dialog: Utilization, challenges, and ethics in the age of artificial intelligence. *International Transactions on Artificial Intelligence*, 2(1), 40–8. https://doi.org/10.33050/italic.v2i1.401.

Williamson, B. (2017). *Big data in education: The digital future of learning, policy and practice*. SAGE.

Wilson, J. (2013). Teaching with Ignatius: Justice in pedagogical practice. *Jesuit Higher Education: A Journal*, 2(1), 99–111.

Wolff, A., Zdráhal, Z., Nikolov, A., & Pantucek, M. (2013). Improving retention: Predicting at-risk students by analysing clicking behavior in a virtual learning environment. In *Proceedings of the 3rd International Conference on Learning Analytics and Knowledge* (pp. 145–9). https://doi.org/10.1145/2460296.2460324.

Woolf, B.P. (1991). AI in education. In S.C. Shapiro (Ed.), *Encyclopedia of artificial intelligence* (pp. 431–9). John Wiley & Sons.

Woolf, B.P. (2009). *Building intelligent interactive tutors: Student-centered strategies for revolutionizing e-learning*. Morgan Kaufmann.

Woolf, B.P., Lane, H.C., Chaudhri, V.K., & Kolodner, J.L. (2013). AI grand challenges for education. *AI Magazine, 34*(4), 66–84. https://doi.org/10.1609/aimag.v34i4.2490.

Woolridge, M. (2021). *A brief history of artificial intelligence: What it is, where we are, and where we are going*. Flat Iron Books.

Yadav, D.K., Mookherji, S., Gomes, J., & Patil, S. (2020). Intelligent navigation system for the visually impaired – A deep learning approach. In *Proceedings of the fourth international conference on computing methodologies and communication* (pp. 652–9). https://doi.org/10.1109/ICCMC48092.2020.ICCMC-000121.

Yan, L., Sha, L., Zhao, L., Li, Y., Martinez-Maldonado, R., Chen, G., Li, X., Jin, Y., & Gašević, D. (2024). Practical and ethical challenges of large language models in education: A systematic scoping review. *British Journal of Educational Technology, 55*(1), 90–112. https://doi.org/10.1111/bjet.13370.

Yu, S. (2021). Feedback-giving practice for L2 writing teachers: Friend or foe? *Journal of Second Language Writing, 52*, 100798. https://doi.org/10.1016/j.jslw.2021.100798.

Zan, G.K., & Yiğitoğlu, N. (2018). Exploring novice and experienced teachers' beliefs and practices of written feedback. *İnönü Üniversitesi Eğitim Fakültesi Dergisi, 19*(2), 355–69. https://doi.org/10.17679/inuefd.335443.

Zanzotto, F.M. (2019). Human-in-the-loop artificial intelligence. *Journal of Artificial Intelligence Research, 64*, 243–52. https://doi.org/10.1613/jair.1.11345.

Zawacki-Richter, O., Marín, V.I., Bond, M., & Gouverneur, F. (2019). Systematic review of research on artificial intelligence applications in higher education – where are the educators? *International Journal of Educational Technology in Higher Education, 16*(1), 1–27. https://doi.org/10.1186/s41239-019-0171-0.

Zechner, K., & Evanini, K. (Eds.). (2019). *Automated speaking assessment: Using language technologies to score spontaneous speech*. Routledge.

Zhai, C., Wibowo, S., & Li, L.D. (2024). The effects of over-reliance on AI dialogue systems on students' cognitive abilities: A systematic review. *Smart Learning Environments, 11*(1), 28. https://doi.org/10.1186/s40561-024-00316-7.

Zhai, X., Chu, X., Chai, C.S., Yung Jong, M.S., Istenic, A., Spector, M., Liu, J.-B., Yuan, J., & Li, Y. (2021). A review of artificial intelligence (AI) in education from 2010 to 2020. *Complexity*, 8812542. https://doi.org/10.1155/2021/8812542.

Zhang, J.Q. (2020). The secrets of consciousness and AI. *iSTEAM Communications, 1*(1), 1–12. https://doi.org/10.37906/isteamc.2020.3.

Zhao, W.X., Zhou, K., Li, J., Tang, T., Wang, X., Hou, Y., Min, Y., Zhang, B., Zhang, J., Dong, Z., Du, Y., Yang, C., Cheng, Y., Chen, Z., Jiang, J., Ren, R., Li, Y., Tang, X., Liu, Z., Liu, P.,..Wen, J. (2023). *A survey of large language models*. arXiv preprint arXiv:2303.18223.

Zhou, J., Zhang, Y., Luo, Q., Parker, A.G., & De Choudhury, M. (2023). Synthetic lies: Understanding AI-generated misinformation and evaluating algorithmic and human solutions. In *Proceedings of the ACM CHI conference on human factors in computer systems*. Association for Computing Machinery.

Zhu, M., & Wang, C. (in press). A systematic review of artificial intelligence in language education from 2013 to 2023: Current status and future implications. *SSRN*. https://doi.org/10.2139/ssrn.4684304.

Zou, B., Liviero, S., Wei, K., Sun, L., Qi, Y., Yang, X., & Fu, J. (2021). Case study 11, Mainland China: The impact of pronunciation and accents in artificial intelligence speech evaluation systems. In *Language Learning with Technology: Perspectives from Asia* (pp. 223–35). Springer Nature.

Index

About the Author

Joshua M. Paiz, PhD, AWS-SAA, Security+ is a scholar-administrator whose work sits at the intersection of applied linguistics, artificial intelligence (AI), and inclusive pedagogy. He currently serves as the assistant dean for technology, trades, business, and hospitality at Frederick Community College, where he oversees programs in computer science, cybersecurity, engineering, business, and math. Previously, he was a classroom educator for 15 years, teaching EAP, professional communication, technical writing, and information technology courses.

With a PhD in applied linguistics from Purdue University and a forthcoming MS in applied computer sciences from GWU, Dr. Paiz's interdisciplinary expertise drives his research agenda. His scholarship explores the transformative potential of AI – particularly natural language processing and machine learning – in English language teaching (ELT), teacher education, and writing center pedagogy. He is the lead author of *Artificial Intelligence, Real Teaching: A Guide to AI in ELT* (2025, University of Michigan Press) and the sole author of *Queering the English Language Classroom: A Practical Guide for Teachers* (2020, Equinox UK).

Beyond AI, Dr. Paiz is internationally recognized for his work in queer applied linguistics. His book *Queering the English Language Classroom* has been widely cited for its actionable framework for fostering LGBTQ+-inclusive learning environments. His academic writing also appears in *TESOL Journal*, *RELC Journal*, *Journal of Language, Identity, and Education*, and *TESOL Connections*, among others.

A firm believer in scholarship for social good, Dr. Paiz combines research with service. He contributes to organizations such as the Montgomery Coalition for Adult English Literacy (MCAEL), where he advocates for equitable hiring and inclusive language education. As a US State Department English language specialist, he recently supported teacher education in Bahrain with a focus on AI in pedagogy.

At heart, Dr. Paiz is a mentor, innovator, and inclusion advocate. He is committed to preparing educators and students alike for a future shaped by intelligent technologies, while never losing sight of the deeply human – and humane – dimensions of learning.